THE GUINNESS BOOK OF

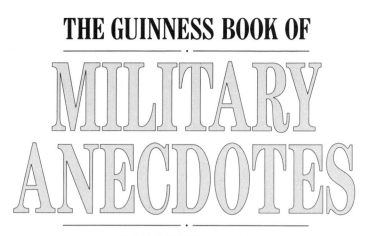

MILITARY ANECDOTES

GEOFFREY REGAN

CANOPY BOOKS
A division of Abbeville Press, Inc.
NEW YORK

To Gill, with all my love.

First published in the United States of America in 1992 by Canopy Books, a division of Abbeville Press, Inc., 488 Madison Avenue, New York, NY 10022.

First published in Great Britain in 1992 by Guinness Publishing Ltd. 33 London Road, Enfield, Middlesex.

'GUINNESS' is a registered trademark of Guinness Publishing Ltd.

ISBN 1-55859-441-8

Designed by Cathy Shilling

Acknowledgments

The author and publishers gratefully acknowledge permission to reproduce copyright material in this book.

The extracts from the Authorized Version of the Bible (the King James Bible), the rights in which are vested in the Crown, are reproduced by permission of the Crown's patentee, Cambridge University Press.

We would also like to thank: Oxford University Press for permission to quote from Rev. Andrew Clark, *Echoes of the Great War*, edited by James Munson, Oxford University Press, 1985; Souvenir Press Ltd for permission to quote from Neville Cardus, *A Cardus for all Seasons*, Souvenir Press, 1985; Faber and Faber Ltd for permission to quote from Ian Morrison, *Malayan Postscript*, Faber and Faber, 1942; Leo Cooper for permission to quote from Anthony Babington, *For the Sake of Example*, Leo Cooper/Secker & Warburg, 1983; HarperCollins Publishers Ltd for permission to quote from Arthur Bryant, *The Turn of the Tide*, Collins, 1957; Michael Joseph Ltd for permission to quote from Lyn Macdonald, *Voices and Images of the Great War*, Michael Joseph, 1988.

The publishers also wish to thank the following for permission to reproduce pictures in this book: Archiv für Kunst und Geschichte; Collection Viollet; Image Select; The Hulton Picture Company; Mary Evans Picture Library; Peter Newark's Historical Pictures.

CONTENTS

THE WHIMS OF WAR

1 NEGOTIATING WITH THE ZULUS

At the end of the Zulu War in 1879 it became necessary for the British authorities to negotiate with a beaten Zulu army. It was a dangerous job.

Some negotiations had now to be undertaken with the Zulu nation, and General Sir Evelyn Wood was entrusted with them . . .

Our destination was Conference Hill, which we reached after a ten days' march. Here we found the Zulu army, or nation, formed up in a huge crescent, their chiefs at their head, ready for the palaver. A ragged tent was pitched, and in front of this we took up our station, with the assembled Zulus facing us. They were strangely apathetic at first, and remained squatting on the ground in their crescent formation, while Sir Evelyn Wood and his staff dismounted and entered the tent. For some time we sat at attention on our horses. Presently the general came out and ordered the band to play 'God save the Queen' and the men to give a cheer. As we did this, the Zulus half rose in an almost threatening way, but their head men remaining seated, they squatted down again. There seemed to be some hitch in the negotiations, for the chiefs remained very grave and quiet. At last an order came to the bandmaster to strike up something lively, and he, being an Irishman, treated them to 'Patrick's Day in the Morning'.

Never have I seen any tune produce such a magical effect as this one did. First a few of the Zulus rose, then a few more, and then the whole lot, as if the Pied Piper of Hamelin was after them, and they could not help themselves. In less than five minutes the whole of that dusky host was swaying and dancing to the music. When it was over they swarmed around us, patting our horses, laughing and talking, all in the best of humours. Above all things, they admired the big drummer, who could sit on his horse, and whack out such a fine tune. In the end the negotiations were successfully completed, and the Zulu army escorted us during the first day of our return march, and then left us with every token of amity.

Source: Sergeant-Major E. Mole, *A King's Hussar* (collected and condensed by Herbert Compton, 1893)

2 AULD LANG SYNE

During the 17th and 18th centuries many Scotsmen found employment on the continent of Europe. Some rose to prominence in the Austrian and Russian service.

In 1739, the Russians and Turks, who had been at war, met to conclude terms of peace. The commissioners were Marshal Keith for the Russians and the Grand Vizier for the Turks. These two personages met and carried on their negotiations by means of interpreters. When all was concluded they rose to separate, but just before leaving the Grand Vizier suddenly went to Marshal Keith, and, taking him cordially by the hand, declared in the broadest Scotch dialect that it made him 'unco' happy to meet a countryman in his exalted station. As might be expected, Keith, who himself was a Scotsman in the service of Russia, stared with astonishment, and was eager for an explanation of the mystery. 'Dinna be surprised,' the Grand Vizier exclaimed; 'I'm o' the same country wi' yoursell, mon! I mind weel seein' you and your brother, when boys, passin' by to the school at Kirkcaldy; my father, sir, was bellman o' Kirkcaldy.'

Source: James Settle, *Anecdotes of Soldiers in War and Peace* (1905)

3 WORTH PURSUING

The career of the German cruiser Emden *in 1914 was so successful that she became a household name in Britain and throughout the Empire. Her many successes were even exploited by advertisers, as in the case of the merchant vessel* Indus, *which had been carrying 150 cases of soap when stopped by the German raider. An Indian newspaper ran the following curious advertisement:*

There is no doubt that the German cruiser *Emden* had knowledge that the *Indus* was carrying 150 cases of North-West Soap Company's celebrated ELYSIUM Soap, and hence the pursuit. The men on the *Emden* and their clothes are now clean and sweet, thanks to ELYSIUM Soap. Try it!

4 A RIPPING YARN

In 1882, during the British campaign in Egypt against Arabi Pasha, Colonel Evelyn Wood witnessed the following incident.

James Keith (1696–1758). Like many exiled Jacobites, Keith embarked on a distinguished military career in Europe. It was while serving the Russians that he came across a fellow Scot in extraordinary circumstances (see number 2). He later entered the Prussian service and was made a field marshal by Frederick the Great, fighting in the Seven Years War and dying at the battle of Hochkirch.

A shell fell sixty yards to my left and apparently struck down a soldier of the 1st Berkshire Regiment. I saw the flash immediately in front of his feet and the man fell headlong. One or two men near him wavered but on my speaking to them they resumed their places and moved steadily on. When retiring an hour or so later we repassed opposite the spot. I was then riding on the bank of the Mahmoudieh Canal and said to Captain Hemphill, the Adjutant, send a stretcher and four men to bring in your man's body. He replied, 'The man is in the ranks. He was not much hurt.' 'But I saw him struck by a shell. He was killed.' 'No, he's in the ranks.' 'I should like to see him.' 'Well, you must look at him only in front, sir.' When I overtook the company to which the man belonged I asked for him and a titter went round as the man, halting, faced me. He had all his clothes on in front but the shell had burst immediately at his feet and the flash of the explosion had burnt off the back of his socks, the whole of the back of his trousers and the skirt of his serge up to the waistbelt, so that from heels to belt he was absolutely naked. He was bleeding from burns to the more protuberant parts up to the waist but was not permanently injured.

Source: Sir Evelyn Wood, *From Midshipman to Field Marshal* (1906)

5 FORTIFIED WITH LEARNING

During the defence of the Lucknow Residency in the Indian Mutiny of 1857 all kinds of unusual items were used to construct barricades.

Some works of great literature, complete with leather bindings, served to hold the Sepoys at bay. On one occasion just one hundred pages of a copy of Lardner's *Encyclopaedia* stopped a musket ball, while Byron's *Complete Poems*, although suffering complete destruction in the process, stopped a cannonball. Apparently, so impressive were the defensive qualities of such heavy reading that Financial Commissioner Martin Gubbins wished that every door could be protected by books. On the other hand, unbound oriental manuscripts, at the house of the French merchant Depratt, proved incapable of stopping musket shots and were consumed by fire.

6 WHEELS IN MOTION

Looting can open the eyes to what one is missing. . . .

In 1899, during the Second Boer War, the British evacuated the town of Dundee in Natal and the Boers immediately occupied and looted it. One Boer was seen riding away from the town with a bicycle strapped to his horse.

7 A LIFE SAVER

During the Second Boer War one British company, J.S. Fry and Sons of Bristol, sent a tinned box of chocolate from Queen Victoria herself to each of her 'dear, brave, soldiers', each carrying the Queen's portrait and bound with red, white and blue ribbon.

On one occasion, Private James Humphrey, of the 2nd Royal Lancaster Regiment, credited the Queen's chocolate tin with saving his life and asked that it be sent to the Queen. This was done, a doctor testifying that, 'Had the bullet not been stopped by the chocolate it would undoubtedly have passed through this structure into the abdomen and have caused a fatal wound.' Sir Arthur Bigge, the Principal Medical Officer, sent the tin of chocolate with the bullet still in it to the Queen with a note saying, 'Your Majesty would doubtless wish another box to be sent to Private Humphrey.'

8 REMNANTS I

Medieval battles, involving so much hand-to-hand fighting with cutting and crushing weapons, must have left behind sights more typical of a slaughter house. And when, in the 16th century, firearms and cannon were added to the close-quarter fighting, the results were truly horrific. The age of chivalry was ended and mercenary troops such as the German and Swiss pikemen made the most of their opportunities.

After the battle of Pavia in 1525 the victorious German landsknechts set about exploiting their victory. They set up a battlefield shop at which grieving relatives, valets or squires could buy the corpses of their masters, to give them proper burial. The body of Guillaume Bonnivet, Admiral of France, was sold at bargain price, while the gruesome remnants of La Trémoille fetched three times as much. The Spaniards hung up La Palisse, the Marshal of France, on a meat hook and concluded a private deal with his family, of which the details are not recorded. When the body of de Saint-Mesmes proved too expensive for his secretary the vendor refused to lower the price and had the

German landsknechts (mercenaries) in the early 16th century were the terror of Europe, fighting in Switzerland, Bavaria, the Netherlands, and most notably against the French in the Italian Wars. Many tales are told of their ruthless and business-like approach to their profession (see number 8, and also numbers 319, 327, 328 and 434).

body thrown in the River Ticino. However, the secretary waited until nightfall and dredged the body out, so gaining his lord for nothing.

9 INTEGRITY

The battle of Waterloo in 1815 was a battle of many tragedies, some national, some merely personal.

Sergeant Weir, of the Scots Greys, was pay sergeant to his troop, and as such might have excused himself from serving in action; but on such a day as the battle of Waterloo, he disdained to avail himself of his privilege, and requested to be allowed to join his regiment in the mortal fray. In one of the charges, he fell mortally wounded, and was left on the field. Corporal Scot, of the same regiment, who lost a leg, asserts that when the field was searched for the wounded and slain, the body of Sergeant Weir was found *with his name written on his forehead with his own hand, dipped in his own blood!* This his comrade said he was supposed to have done, that his body might be found and recognised, and that it might not be imagined that he disappeared with the money of his troop.

Source: *The Percy Anecdotes* (Ed. S. & R. Percy 1823)

10 CLASSICS

British officers of the 19th century had in almost every case enjoyed – or endured – a public-school education, in which classical studies had played a dominant part. This may explain two famous signals by officers serving in India.

When Sir Charles Napier had conquered Sind province in 1843 he signalled his success with the single word *'Peccavi'* ('I have sinned'). Not to be outdone, one of Sir Colin Campbell's ADCs, a man with a knowledge of history to match his command of Latin, signalled the relief of Lucknow in 1857 with the words *'Nunc fortunatus sum'* – 'I am in luck now.'

11 CRAN – GUTS!

At the battle of Waterloo in 1815 the spirit of the French soldiers was not broken by defeat.

One soldier in the French ranks was seen, when his arm was shattered by a cannon ball, to wrench it off with the other; and throwing it up in the air, he exclaimed to his comrades, *'Vive l'Empereur jusqu'à la mort!'*

12 EXECUTING FELONS

During the advance of the Polish and Lithuanian armies into Masovia in 1410, prior to the great battle of Tannenburg, the Grand Duke Witold of Lithuania imposed severe penalties on any of his men who molested the local inhabitants.

Duke Witold sentenced two Lithuanian soldiers to death for despoiling a church. It was the Lithuanian custom for felons to build their own gallows and hang themselves, and so great was the duke's authority that the two men were heard to hurry each other up to avoid causing Witold any further offence.

13 RAMRODS

Training new recruits in the use of the musket was always an important part of soldiering, though rarely can it have been as dangerous as it was for General Jean Malher of Napoleon's Grand Armée at Valladolid in 1808.

Putting the raw recruits through their paces General Malher ordered them to load and fire their blanks. Unfortunately he got in the way of the volley and was transfixed by a ramrod, one of eighteen that the soldiers had failed to remove from the barrels before firing. On another occasion during manoeuvres at Leghorn in 1804 a French soldier fired his ramrod, which accidentally killed a civilian spectator. Luckily for the soldier the victim turned out to be a brigand wanted by the police.

14 THE TRAGIC MESSENGERS

The Dutch War of Independence from Spain lasted for some eighty years, between 1567 and 1648. In its early days it was marked by a series of disasters for the Dutch, none more severe than at the battle of Jemmingen.

After the Dutch defeat at the battle of Jemmingen in 1568 many Dutch soldiers drowned in trying to cross the river Scheldt. It is said that news of the disaster was carried on the tide to the burghers of Emden at the mouth of the river, when thousands of broad-brimmed felt hats, the normal headgear of the Dutch infantry, were seen floating by like some stricken armada.

15 A NOVEL DEFENCE

Some British officers have held the view that their role in wartime was to lead their men by example, rather than indulge in the business of killing. As a result, some have gone into battle armed with a weird variety of implements, from umbrellas to cricket bats. This has not prevented them from deterring the enemy when the need arose.

During the British campaign against the French in Egypt in 1801, the first British officer ashore was Colonel Brent Spencer, who prepared to engage the French defenders on the beach armed only with a walking stick. When one Frenchman levelled his gun and took careful aim at the colonel, Brent Spencer had to think quickly. Shouting at the top of his voice, 'Get away, you scoundrel!' he shook his cane so vigorously at his assailant that the Frenchman thought better of it and ran away.

16 BEATING THE GENERAL

The symbols left behind by great leaders can sometimes be as effective in inspiring future generations as the leaders were themselves in their own lifetime. Few generals, however, went as far in bequeathing a legacy to their people as Jan Zizka (1360–1424).

The Bohemian general, Jan Zizka, who successfully led the Hussite revolt. Having lost both eyes during the course of his career, he lost his skin after his death (see number 16).

During the Hussite Wars of the 15th century the blind general Zizka successfully defended his native Bohemia against overwhelming odds. On his deathbed he ordered that his skin be used to cover a drum so that it could sound defiance to his enemies. The drum in question survived for several centuries and was beaten on the outbreak of the Thirty Years War in 1618.

17 THE HONOURABLE LIMB

During Paraguay's wars against her neighbours in the 1860s the courage of the Paraguayan soldiers became legendary. Nor were their leaders far behind in their dedication to their leader, Francisco Solano López.

On one occasion in 1867 General José Diaz decided to display his absolute contempt for his enemies. Taking with him just two aides-de-camp the general paddled out in a canoe and sat fishing in full view of the Brazilian ironclad warships. For a while all went well until one of the warships opened fire on him and a shell exploded overhead, severely injuring one of his legs. Diaz managed to reach the shore, bleeding profusely, and an English surgeon was obliged to amputate the leg. Following the example of the Mexican President Santa Anna, who had his amputated leg buried with full military honours in

1838, Paraguay's President López presented his wounded general with the amputated leg in its own coffin.

Alas, the story had no happy ending as both Diaz and his leg were soon reunited – underground.

18 THE FRUITS OF DEFEAT

The great battle of Lepanto in 1571 was one of history's decisive battles, ending Turkish power in the Mediterranean and contributing to the rise of Spain. But even such a battle can have its lighter moments.

It is doubtful if battles can ever be fun. Yet when the Turks ran out of ammunition at the battle of Lepanto in 1571, Janissaries were seen to pelt their opponents with oranges and lemons, many of them laughing as they did so.

19 A WISE NEUTRALITY

During the English Civil War, 1642–8, some parts of England had been hardly touched by the fighting between Parliament and the King even as late as 1644.

Just prior to the great battle of Marston Moor a Parliamentary officer reported meeting a labourer who, when questioned whether he was for King or Parliament, replied, 'Be them two fall'n out then?'

20 FOLLOWING ORDERS

During the French siege of Prague in 1741 Marshal Saxe instructed his men to mount a surprise attack using the bayonet rather than muskets, so as not to alert the defenders.

Colonel de Chevert, commanding the French grenadiers, instructed the leading man in the following way:
   'Do you see that sentry over there?'
   'Yes, Colonel.'
   'He will shout out "Who goes there?" You will say nothing in reply, but just keep on going.'
   'Yes, Colonel.'
   'He will fire at you and he will miss.'
   'Yes, Colonel.'
   'You will then cut his throat. I shall be there to back you up. That's all.'

21 GAMESMANSHIP

Aircraft were still a rarity in 1914. When one appeared in the sky, the soldiers on the ground would have a go at shooting it down with their rifles. Most such attempts were in vain . . .

In August 1914, a column of the British Expeditionary Force was marching from Mauberge to Mons when a German plane flew over them. Immediately everyone began firing into the air. After a few moments puffs of smoke were seen coming from the plane and it was brought crashing to the ground. The British soldiers cheered and broad smiles broke out on the faces of their officers. While the British were celebrating their success, an old man in the tattered uniform of a French territorial soldier emerged from behind a hedge, wiping his rifle in a business-like fashion. As he passed by smiling, a British officer heard him mutter, 'Not a bad shot, eh?'

22 KEEPING A WATCH

General Haig's memories of Landrecies, during the British retreat from Mons in 1914, could not have been happy ones. Confident that the British had come to stay, Haig had entrusted a local watchmaker with the task of putting a new glass in his wristwatch. However, the fierceness of the German advance and the speed of the British retreat meant that he had had to leave without it.

Four years later, on 10 November 1918, Haig found himself in Landrecies again. He soon located the watchmaker and demanded the return of his watch. The man said that he remembered the incident well but that he had given the watch to one of Haig's officers and asked him to pass it on. Baffled – and unconvinced – Haig was left to reflect on Belgian honour.

23 WAR MINIATURES

The great castle of Colditz was used by the Germans during the Second World War to hold the most determined of escapees. While the British spent their time trying to escape the French had other ideas.

Prisoners of war in Colditz often occupied their time in bizarre ways. The French, for example, built mouse tanks. The tanks were toy-sized, made of wood and operated from the inside by a mouse running round a wheel. It was even possible to stage mouse battles.

24 UNGRACIOUS VICTORS

The great Indian war leader, Tecumseh, had been a thorn in the side of the Americans for a generation. His death in battle at the hands of Colonel Richard Johnson was a national event.

After the battle of the Thames in 1813, at which the Indian chief Tecumseh was defeated by General William Henry Harrison, vengeful frontiersmen skinned the body of the Indian chief. With typical entrepreneurial spirit they soon found a use for the chief's skin, and 'Tecumseh razor strops' became extremely fashionable for a while afterwards.

25 LIBERTY, EQUALITY, FRATERNITY

The clash of philosophies involved in the French Revolutionary Wars was marked. To the other peoples of Europe the new French ideas of equality and brotherhood were difficult to grasp.

During the French Revolutionary Wars the King of Prussia once noted a grenadier of a French volunteer battalion who, though wounded and left alone, still stuck to the defence of a bridge. By the king's orders the man was taken prisoner and brought to him.

The Shawnee chief Tecumseh dies at the battle of the Thames. His slayers soon found a gruesome use for his body (see number 24).

When the king said, 'Frenchman, you are a brave fellow. What a pity you are not fighting for a better cause,' the volunteer was equal to the occasion. 'Citizen William,' said he, 'we shall not agree on that point. Let us talk of something else.' The phrase pleased the Prussian army and the king when passing along the tents of his men often heard himself called 'Citizen William'.

26 FACING UP TO THE ENEMY

In 1939 the 'Phoney War' was a time for self-confessed experts.

During the Phoney War a former First World War pilot warned that people should on no account look up at the sky when enemy aircraft were overhead. He said the white blobs of numerous upturned faces can be seen from an aeroplane at a considerable height and form a good and tempting target. Those unable to control their curiosity were advised to shade their faces with their hats.

27 THE WRONG TYPE

During the War of 1812 the British troops burned Washington. Admiral Cochrane had a particular score to settle with the Washington press, which had vilified him in print.

As well as burning the White House, the British troops also burned the Library of Congress and the offices of the *National Intelligencer* newspaper. Admiral Cochrane lent his

During the siege of Delhi (1857) incoming shot was assiduously collected (see number 28).

own hands to the work of arson and ordered his men to scatter the printing type, shouting gleefully, 'Be sure that all the Cs are destroyed so that the rascals cannot any longer abuse my name.'

28 TOO HOT TO HANDLE

During the siege of Delhi in 1857 ammunition shortages were a constant problem for the British artillery. The field guns were so short of shot that a reward of half a rupee was offered for every one of the enemy's shot brought into the British camp. A British general recorded this curious incident.

On one occasion I saw a party of native servants, carrying on their heads provisions for the men on the picket, wend their way up the slope from the camp. Two round-shots fired by the enemy struck the top of the Ridge and rolled down the declivity. Here was a prize worth contending for, and the cooks, depositing the dishes on the ground, ran in all haste to seize the treasures. I watched the race with some interest, and anticipated some fun, knowing that in their eagerness they would forget that the shots had not had time to cool. Two men in advance of the rest picked up the balls, and, uttering a cry, dropped them quickly, rubbing and blowing their hands. The remainder stood patiently waiting, and then, after a time, spent evidently in deliberation, two men placed the shot on their heads, and all in a body moved off towards the Commissariat quarters to receive and divide the reward.

Source: C.J. Griffiths, *The Narrative of the Siege of Delhi* (1857)

29 THE SWEET EARTH

During the Second World War, the siege of Leningrad by the Germans was one of the most severe in history.

During the siege of Leningrad in 1941 German bombing had set fire to huge sugar warehouses in the city. The sugar had melted and soaked through the floors into the earth below to a depth of ten feet. After the fire had died down hungry Leningraders went into the ruins and began digging up the frozen soil in an attempt to extract the sugar. Glasses of this earth, known as 'Badayev Earth', were on sale in the Haymarket, with high prices being charged for earth cut from within three feet of the surface. Housewives tried to melt the earth in a pan to separate the sugar, while others simply mixed the earth with flour or paste, calling the substance 'candy' or 'custard'.

30 MATT'S MOUTH

At the battle of Chancellorsville in 1863 Stonewall Jackson's flank attack broke the back of Union General Sickles' Third Corps, sending many Federal soldiers fleeing in confusion. One company had an extraordinary encounter.

There were six of us; and Matt Jenkins, a little corporal with a big voice, was the ranking man of the squad. We had lost the points of the compass as completely as if there were none, though there was no mistaking where the fight was. We were cautiously groping through the brushwood, where the occasional flash of musketry only made us all the blinder, when a blaze and the roar of a volley on our front showed us that we had encountered an enemy. Their shot, however, had pattered all around without injuring any of us.

Our little corporal, with his big voice, which sounded for all the world like a major-general's, shouted out: 'Reserve your fire, men!' and then gave orders to Captain *this* and Major *that* and Colonel *someone else*, as if he was in command of a brigade.

'Thunder!' said someone in the party we had encountered. 'You needn't make all that fuss. We'll surrender!'

'And then, about twenty of *our own company*, including the Captain, came in and surrendered to Matt Jenkins!'

Source: Warren Lee Goss, *Recollections of a Private* (1888)

31 THE TAXICABS OF PARIS

In the early stages of the decisive battle of the Marne in 1914 General Gallieni used an unusual form of transport to take his men to the battlefront.

Another car followed in its wake, then others and still others, in endless, silent succession. The moon had risen and its rays shone reflected on the shiny peaks of taxi drivers' caps. Inside the cabs, one could make out the bent heads of sleeping soldiers. Someone

The Gneisenau *being battered by* Invincible *and* Inflexible *at the battle of the Falkland Islands (1914). One of the* Gneisenau's *officers was to experience an intriguing coincidence after his ship sank (see number 32).*

asked, 'Wounded?' and a passing voice replied, 'No, seventh division from Paris. Going into the line. . .'

Source: Paul Lintier, *My Seventy-Five: Journal of a French Gunner* (1929)

32 STRANGE ENCOUNTER I

At the battle of the Falkland Islands in 1914 Admiral Sturdee, with the battle cruisers Invincible *and* Inflexible, *destroyed the German Far Eastern Squadron of Admiral Graf von Spee.*

At 4.16 the *Scharnhorst* sank, fighting magnificently to the end against overwhelming firepower. The British ships continued firing at the *Gneisenau* and at about a quarter to six one of *Gneisenau*'s funnels went and she took on a heavy list to starboard. One by one her guns were destroyed but she kept firing to the last and went down at 6.02 blazing. A thick cloud of smoke hung over the place where she sank. The British immediately lowered rescue boats into the rough and icy sea, but it was an hour before they could reach the survivors, of whom a mere hundred and fifty were saved. All the *Scharnhorst*'s crew died in the water or went down with their ship. One of the *Gneisenau*'s officers, who was pulled out of the water, turned out to be a first cousin of the British commander. He had an extraordinary escape. Half the *Gneisenau*'s men had been killed by shellfire alone. He was in an 8.2 turret as second torpedo officer but the turret was knocked out and he was the sole survivor. He then went to a casemate gun, which was also knocked out and practically all the crew killed. He next tried a third gun which was also knocked out and he was again practically the sole survivor. He went to another gun and the ship then went down around him. He remained in icy water for nearly one and a quarter hours and was picked up by a British cutter. He was rather dazed but cool and collected in the boat. After lying shivering in the bottom of a cutter for half an hour he was hauled up by a bowline. When he got on board the *Carnarvon* he said, 'I believe I have a first cousin in one of your ships. His name is Stoddart.' Then to find him as admiral in the ship that picked him up! He went into the admiral's quarters and was apparently none the worse for his experiences.

33 PRIORITIES

Napoleon once said – rightly – that an army marches on its stomach.

At the battle of Chancellorsville in 1863 a Confederate soldier, while in the act of 'drawing a bead' on a Yank, was distracted by a wild turkey that landed in a tree in front of him. Forgetting the Yank, the Reb instantly shot the turkey and ran to collect the valuable addition to his rations.

34 NO RESTING PLACE

In 1882 James Wickenden was with the British forces in Egypt.

I was groom to Lieutenant Sir Godfrey Thomas, and, in addition to my own work, had to do little jobs for him; but I was not overworked, for the officers had to rough it quite as much as the men, with the exception of a few more luxuries to eat and drink.

One evening he said to me, 'I think I'll sleep here tonight, Wickenden; down by this gun.' I answered, 'Very good, sir'; and scraped a hole in the sand and laid his blanket in it. As a rule we could always sleep directly we lay down, but in a few moments he said, 'I can't sleep here, Wickenden.' 'Can't you, sir?' I asked. 'What's wrong, sir?' 'Why, there's such an abominable smell just here.' 'Oh, that comes from over the hill yonder, sir, where there are a few dead horses,' I replied. However, I scraped a hole for him somewhere else, and while I was moving the blanket I discovered the body of a black, buried just below the surface, which my master had exposed by twisting and turning about in his restlessness. It gave me a bit of a shock, but I called out to one of my comrades to come and look, and we had a good laugh about it.

Source: Driver James Wickenden, *Told from the Ranks* (1897)

35 AN UNCOMFORTABLE FLIGHT

The dangers of operating field guns has always been severe. A lack of concentration can have alarming results.

One occurrence I witnessed here was almost incredible: a Portuguese governor touched at Colombo early in the year 1811. On the firing of the salute Gunner Richard Clark was blown from the mouth of his gun right into the air and alighted upon a rock at a considerable distance in the harbour . . . he was but an awkward soldier at the best; the gun of which he was number one went off by accident but not just at the time of loading otherwise the left arm or perhaps both arms of number two had been blown off as number two loads and rams home, along with number one. The gun was just loaded when she went off through the negligence of Clark in not spunging properly. He was not at his proper distance like the other man nor yet near enough to receive the whole flash. To the astonishment of everyone he was seen in the air, the spunge staff grasped in his right hand, the rammer head downwards which first struck the rock as he alighted on his breech. The rock was very thickly covered with seaweed. A Party was sent down to bring up the body as all concluded him killed upon the spot; he was brought up only stunned and slightly singed and was at his duty again in a few days . . .

Source: Alexander Alexander, *Life of Alexander Alexander* (Ed. John Howell 1830)

36 **USEFUL SIGNALS**

During the relief of Chitral in 1895 George Pridmore of the Bedfordshire Regiment recorded a remarkable instance of marksmanship.

We noticed a man standing on a high peak with a signalling-flag. He had evidently belonged to some of our native troops, for he was an expert signaller, and as he watched our operations with the batteries – which were now aimed at the sangars – he signalled the result of each shot for the benefit of his comrades. Thus we saw him making the usual signals for 'too high', 'too low', 'on the right', and so on, as the case might be. Of course that sort of thing was not convenient, so we sent a shell where we thought it would do most good and blew the signaller all to pieces. The moment he was hit, another native sprang to the spot, caught up the flag, and signalled a bull's eye!

Source: Private George Pridmore, *Told from the Ranks* (1897)

37 **THE SURVIVORS**

Napoleon's retreat from Moscow in 1812 was one of the greatest of all military disasters. The losses suffered by the Grand Armée were astonishing, as Sergeant Bourgoyne illustrates in this episode.

A large sledge, pulled by two strong horses, passed us by. It was going so fast that we could not make out to what regiment the men in it belonged. In about half an hour we came in sight of a posting-station and also an inn. There were several soldiers of the Guard at the door, setting out on sledges that had been provided for them.

We dismounted and went in, asking for wine, as we had been just told that there was plenty of it and that it was very good. The men who told us seemed to have drunk a lot themselves and were in a state of wild gaiety. This happened to almost all those who, like ourselves, had been through so much hardship and privation. The smallest amount of drink went straight to our heads. One of the men asked us if we had met the regiment of Dutch Grenadiers who had been part of the Imperial Guard.

'No,' we said.

'It passed you just a moment ago,' said the Velite, 'and yet you didn't see it? That big sledge that overtook you contained the entire Dutch regiment! There were seven of them!'

Source: Sergeant Bourgoyne, *Memoirs* (19th century)

38 SKULLS

Herodotus describes the battlefield at Pelusium, many years after the battle which took place in 525 BC.

On the field where this battle was fought I saw a very strange thing which the natives pointed out to me. The bones of the slain lie scattered on the field in two lots, those of the Persians in one place by themselves, as the bodies lay at the first – those of the Egyptians in another place, apart from them: if, then, you strike the Persian skulls, even with a pebble they are so weak, that you break a hole in them; but the Egyptian skulls are so strong, that you may strike them with a rock and you will scarcely break them in.

Source: Herodotus, *Histories* (5th century BC)

39 THE GORDIAN KNOT

Alexander the Great had a way with knots, as Arrian describes.

The following report was current concerning the wagon, that whoever could loosen the cord with which the yoke of the wagon was tied, was destined to be the ruler of Asia. The cord was made of cornel bark, and neither the start nor the end to it could be seen. It is said by some that when Alexander could find out no way to loosen the cord and yet was unwilling to allow it to remain unloosed, lest it should exercise some disturbing influence on the multitude, he struck the cord with his sword and cut it through, saying he had untied it. But Aristobulus says that he pulled out the pin of the wagonpole, which was a wooden peg driven right through it, holding the cord together. Having done this he drew out the yoke from the wagonpole.

Source: Arrian, *The Life of Alexander the Great* (2nd century AD)

40 SAVAGE CUTS

At the battle of Talavera between the British and the French in 1809 at least one British cavalryman revealed the effectiveness of the cavalry sabre.

I saw [Harry Wilson] engaged hand-to-hand with a French dragoon; I saw him – for I was by this time disabled by a severe wound and stretched at length beside others of my suffering comrades – give and receive more than one pass, with equal skill and courage. Just then a French officer delivered a thrust at poor Harry Wilson's body and delivered it effectually. I firmly believe that Wilson died on the instant; yet, though he felt the sword in its progress, he, with characteristic self-command, kept his eye still on the enemy in his front, and raising himself in his stirrups let fall on the Frenchman's helmet such a blow, that the brass and skull parted before it, and the man's head was cloven asunder to the chin. It was the most tremendous blow I ever saw struck; and both he who gave, and his opponent who received it, dropped dead together. The brass helmet was afterwards examined by order of an officer, who, as well as myself, was astonished at the exploit; and the cut was found to be as clean as if the sword had gone through a turnip, not so much as a dent being left on either side of it.

Source: J.H. Stocqueler, *The British Soldier* (1857)

41 HEDGING YOUR BETS

During the Peninsular War foreign armies, both British and French, marched and counter-marched through the Spanish countryside, making it difficult for the local population to know which army was occupying them at any one moment.

On the 11th we marched through a small market town, the inhabitants of which lined the streets and windows, and shouted 'Viva los Ingleses!' until some of them were quite exhausted. One poor woman came out of her house in a great hurry, and began to shout 'Viva los Franceses' or 'Long live the French'. From this it appears that the Spaniards used to cheer the French army, as well as ours; but the woman had forgotten which army it was, and perhaps to her it was of little importance.

Source: John Green, *A Soldier's Life: 1806–1815* (1827)

42 AN OUTSIZE PROBLEM

So great was the expansion of the British military establishment in 1914 that many recruits found that their requirements could not be fulfilled within the normal channels of the service.

In 1914 Private Beale presented the Army with a particular problem – namely the size of his feet. Unable to equip him with the size-14 boots he needed for the front line, the authorities were forced to send him to work in the artillery, where marching would not be such an important feature of his service.

43 AN OLD COWHERD

In 1914, some men with special skills found that they were too useful to be risked in the front line.

Private Williams of the King's Liverpool Regiment had been a farm labourer in civilian life and in view of this he was selected to act as the Colonel's personal 'cowman'. This had the effect of keeping him out of the front line and, even during the worst of the Somme campaign in 1916, Williams got no closer to the enemy than the cow barn.

44 UNITED WE FALL

During the Dutch War of Independence (1567–1648) two brothers discovered each other, if only for a moment.

Two Spaniards, brothers, who although they had for a long series of years always sought each other, were never able to meet, at last accidentally came in contact at the siege of Bommel, then the seat of war, where they served in two different companies. Being unknown to each other at first some little explanation made their relationship known, when they fell on each other's neck. While they were thus locked in an affectionate embrace, a cannon ball took off both their heads, without separating their bodies, which fell clasped together into the arms of Death, who thus summoned them away in the happiest moment of their lives.

Source: *The Percy Anecdotes* (Ed. S. & R. Percy 1823)

45 FLUSHED OUT

During 1940 the British public were encouraged to be on the look-out for German spies. This had the effect of making everyone paranoid, particularly when dealing with strangers.

One British officer, billeted on a Winchester clergyman, fell foul of his daughter's spy mania. She reported him to the police as a suspect on the grounds that he had failed to pull the chain after visiting the lavatory.

46 MIXED FORTUNES

During 1941 the fighting in the Western Desert became very confused at times . . .

One British officer, looking for shelter, noticed an apparently unoccupied Italian truck. Cautiously opening the door he jumped in only to find the other seat occupied by a slumbering Italian driver. Pulling out a revolver he jabbed it in the man's chest and muttered *'Alto in mano'*, which was the best Italian he could manage at short notice. The startled Italian woke up, sized up the situation and put his hands in the air. Then he gently corrected the officer's grammar, *'Mani in alto.'*

On another occasion General Rommel himself was to lose his way, with consequences that were nearly very embarrassing (see illustration).

47 DECLINE AND FALL

During the period known to historians as 'The Dark Ages', the Arab raids on the Christian lands of the Mediterranean were very destructive. In recounting them the great 18th-century historian, Edward Gibbon, could not always resist his taste for irony.

It was the amusement of the Saracens to profane, as well as to pillage, the monasteries and churches. At the siege of Salerno a mussulman chief spread his couch on the communion table, and on that altar sacrificed each night the virginity of a Christian nun. As he wrestled with a reluctant maid, a beam in the roof was accidentally or dexterously thrown down on his head; and the death of the lustful emir was imputed to the wrath of Christ, which was at length awakened to the defence of his faithful spouse.

Source: Edward Gibbon, *History of the Decline and Fall of the Roman Empire* (1776–1788)

48 CANNY

Of the many British soldiers who escaped from occupied France in 1940 few can have had such a close encounter with the enemy as this.

Two Scots taken prisoner when France fell escaped and made their way towards the Spanish border. They were about to row across a river when two Germans stopped them. They thought their number was up but stalled in broken French and finally found that the Germans only wanted to cross too. 'So we paddled them across,' said one of the Scots later, 'and charged them five francs each.'

Source: John T. Whittacker, *We Cannot Escape History* (1943)

49 THE COUGHING PICKET

During the jungle fighting against the Japanese in the Second World War a single sound could often prove fatal.

To avoid giving away artillery positions, one British officer in Burma in 1943 placed anyone prone to coughing in the early morning on 'coughing picket' 500 yards away from the main position. Knowing that the Japanese would open fire at the first sound, he noted that the coughing picket was remarkably effective in curing the Indian troops of their tendency to cough on awakening from sleep.

50 WAR BABIES

War can become a way of life, even among children.

A recent survey of London schoolchildren shows that youngsters between the ages of

Even the Desert Fox himself was to find the topography of the Western Desert confusing (see number 46). On one occasion, losing his way along the wire, Rommel had to spend the night out in the open. Only when dawn came did he discover that he had spent the night in the company of the 4th Indian Division – undetected. With a sigh of relief he slipped away.

five and seven have forgotten, or have never known, many of the attributes of peacetime living. When questioned about such things as streetlights and bananas they stared suspiciously and indicated plainly that they did not believe that such things existed . . .

When one teacher brought a seashell to school and asked her pupils to name it none of them could do it. 'It's a shell,' she explained finally. 'That's no shell,' a little boy replied heatedly, 'shells come out of guns.'

Source: Tania Long, *New York Times*, 1942

51 SOUVENIRS

During the First World War soldiers of many nations were brought together for the first time. Their customs were often markedly different.

Thursday 21 Jan, 1915. Many of the Indian troops are fine, tall, well-built men and physically command great respect from the English soldier, but their tastes have too much of savagery about them to win favour. A Territorial was very proud of the piece of shell which had burst near him, and of the spike and badge from a German helmet. A Pathan listened gravely while these were being shown. 'Souvenir!' he said scornfully, 'No good. Here right souvenir.' He put his hand into the voluminous folds of the shawl wrapped round his breast and produced a cord on which he had strung the ears of all the Germans he counted himself to have slain. These he was keeping carefully to take back to India to his wife.

Source: Rev. Andrew Clark, *Echoes of the Great War* (1985)

52 THE PRICE OF BLOOD

It was rare to find a philosopher in the ranks of an 18th-century army.

The Duke of Marlborough, who was always remarkable for his humanity, observing a soldier leaning thoughtfully on the butt of his firelock, just after victory had signally crowned the British arms at the battle of Blenheim, accosted him thus:- 'Why so sad, my friend, after so glorious a victory?' 'It may be glorious, my lord,' replied the fellow, 'but I am thinking how much blood I have spilled this day for fourpence.' (A private soldier's daily pay at that time.)

Source: Lord de Ros, *The Young Officer's Companion* (1868)

53 EXCHANGING COMPLIMENTS

During the 18th century the military code of honour was of prime importance to any officer.

General Oglethorpe, when a very young officer, was invited to a military dinner at which the Prince of Wurtemberg was the guest. The prince took up a glass of wine; and, by a fillip, made some of it fly in Oglethorpe's face. Here was an awkward dilemma. To have challenged him outright might have fixed a quarrelsome character upon the young soldier; to have taken no notice of it would have been considered as cowardice.

Oglethorpe, therefore, keeping his eye upon the prince, and smiling all the time, as if he took in jest what His Highness had done said: 'Prince, that's a good joke; but we do it much better in England;' and threw a whole glass of wine in the prince's face. An old general who sat by said: 'He is in the right, prince; you began it!' The prince at once saw his error and the justice of this reproof of the old officer, and shaking young Oglethorpe by the hand, the whole ended in good humour.

Source: Lord de Ros, *The Young Officer's Companion* (1868)

54 SON OF A GUN

The American Civil War (1861–5) was full of remarkable incidents, though it is doubtful if any of them were more remarkable than this one.

During a skirmish outside a small settlement, a young Federal soldier was hit by a shot that carried his genitals away, wounding him so severely he was left for dead on the battlefield. But the bullet, like an arrow fired by Cupid, seemed to have a mind of its own. Having hit the young soldier it passed through the wooden walls of a small log cabin and hit a pretty 17-year-old girl who was sheltering from the fighting. The bullet lodged in her groin and though painful it was later removed by the doctor. To everyone's astonishment the girl proved to be pregnant three months later, even though she was still a virgin. The unlikely solution to what otherwise appeared as a miracle was supplied by the doctor, who had also treated the young soldier wounded no more than a hundred yards from the girl's house. In view of the nature of the young man's wounds and the otherwise miraculous conception by the young girl, the doctor was able to reconstruct a picture of what exactly had happened. The young man was eventually restored to health, and the story was rounded off with a happy ending when the two young people were brought together in marriage not long after the birth of their first, and, necessarily, only child.

WARS OF WORDS

55 THE COST OF LIVING

The Victorian Army was very cost conscious.

At the battle of Abu Klea in the Sudan in 1885, the Dervishes broke through into a British square and a gunner was forced to use a rammer from his artillery piece to defend himself against a Dervish who was about to spear him. The next day he was called to account by one of his officers and hastily apologized: 'Please, sir, I'm sorry I broke the rammer, but I never thought the nigger's head could be so hard.'

56 BITING THE HAND . . .

Casualties were high among senior officers in the battles of the 18th century.

During the early encounters at Hochkirk in 1758 a group of Austrian generals came under fire from Prussian infantry. As the bullets buzzed past them, General Serbelloni laughed, 'They're only flies.' A moment later a bullet shattered his hand. Marshal Daun turned to him, 'Yes, but they seem to bite.'

57 OFFICIAL SECRETS

Frederick the Great was notably secretive about his military planning, not even taking his most senior officers into his confidence. Thus when his old tutor, Christoph von Kalckstein, tried to prise some information from him the following conversation ensued:

Kalckstein: Your Majesty, am I right in thinking there is going to be a war?
Frederick: Who can tell?
Kalckstein: The movement seems to be directed on Silesia.
Frederick: Can you keep a secret?
Kalckstein: Oh yes, Your Majesty.
Frederick: Well, so can I.

58 UNGENTLEMANLY CONDUCT

At the battle of New Orleans in 1815 Lieutenant-Colonel Francis Brooke of the British Army was severely wounded and captured by a rough band of Kentucky backwoodsmen.

'Are there no regular officers in your army?' Brooke demanded, horrified at the scruffy appearance of his captors. 'I would like to be attended by gentlemen.'
    'Let's leave the conceited bastard to wallow in his own blood,' suggested one of the Kentuckians in disgust.
    'No,' said their leader, Lieutenant Wickliffe, 'Don't mind his impudent tongue. His wound makes a gentleman of him. Nothing else could.'

59 SIR 'REVERSE' BULLER

Sir Redvers Buller had been an excellent junior officer, but he was promoted beyond his capacity and his reputation suffered badly during the Second Boer War (1899–1902), for part of which he was commander of British forces in South Africa.

On one of the occasions that Sir Redvers Buller was forced to retreat during the Second Boer War, he told his superiors in London that he had accomplished the task without losing a man, a flag or a cannon. On hearing of the story Whistler acidly added, 'or a minute'.

60 WAIT AND SEE

After Frederick the Great's disastrous defeat at Kunersdorf it seemed that Prussia must

The aftermath of the battle of New Orleans (1815). One snobbish British officer was to receive a vigorously democratic response from his American captors (see number 58).

inevitably be overcome by her Russian, Austrian and French opponents.

Many Prussian soldiers deserted in despair. One such man was recaptured and brought before the king, who asked him why he had left the colours. 'Because things were going so badly for Your Majesty,' the man replied. Frederick thought for a moment and then with a confidential wink told the deserter, 'I suggest you wait a week. Then if things are no better, we'll both desert together.'

61 WAR AIMS I

In 1914 Britain had rather vague war aims – for example, 'the defence of civilization against the beastly Hun'.

During the First World War a distinguished classical scholar was accosted in a London street by a lady who tried to hand him a white feather as he was not in uniform. 'I am surprised that you are not fighting to defend civilization,' she added. 'Madam,' replied the scholar, 'I am the civilization they are fighting to defend.'

62 REPUTATIONS

The Union general Ulysses S. Grant was surprisingly ignorant of military affairs.

Introduced, on one occasion, to the second Duke of Wellington, Grant innocently commented, 'They tell me that your father was also a military man.'

Frederick the Great on the field of Zorndorf (1758) – a battle that even he found perplexing (see number 63).

63 A GENERAL VIEW

It is sometimes supposed that battles operate entirely according to the plans of the generals. This conversation between Frederick the Great and his friend Catt after the battle of Zorndorf may suggest otherwise.

Frederick: That was a diabolical day. Did you understand what was going on?
Catt: Your Majesty, I had a good grasp of the preliminary march, and the final arrangements for the battle. But all the rest escaped me. I could make no sense of the various movements.
Frederick: You were not the only one, my dear friend. Console yourself, you weren't the only one!

64 TONE DEAF I

Union general Ulysses S. Grant had no appreciation of music and tried his hardest to avoid concerts.

On one occasion, asked if he had enjoyed some music, he replied, 'I know only two tunes; one of them is "Yankee Doodle" and the other one isn't.'

65 AMBITION

General, later Field Marshal, Montgomery's autocratic behaviour often made his superiors as uneasy as the men who served under him.

In 1944 the Chief of the Imperial General Staff, Sir Alan Brooke, commented to King George VI at a social function that the problem with Monty was that 'every time I meet him I think he's after my job'. 'You should worry,' replied the king, 'When I meet him I always think he's after mine.' Two years later, Montgomery got Brooke's job – although he never quite made king.

66 A SPANISH OLIVER

During the Spanish Civil War the Republican defenders of the Alcazar were reduced to virtual starvation by the Nationalist troops.

An officer, well-known as a grumbler, came to the commander and asked that he be served more than the daily allowance of food. The commander heard the request in silence, then, pulling a 50-peseta note from his pocket, handed it to the grumbler. 'Take this,' he said, 'and go outside and buy something. It's the best I can do for you at the moment.'

67 THE RESERVES

During his battles Napoleon paid little attention to casualties.

After the battle of Eylau, a Pyrrhic victory for the French, Napoleon walked across the battlefield, turning over with his foot the corpses of French soldiers, saying 'Small change, small change. One Parisian night will soon replace these losses.'

68 PUT IN HIS PLACE

During the disastrous campaign of 1812 Napoleon, fearing for his position at home, abandoned his army in Russia and hurried back to France.

Reaching the River Neman Napoleon asked the ferryman there whether many French deserters had passed that way. 'No,' replied the man, 'you are the first.'

69 THE ART OF WAR

During the Second World War the great painter Picasso lived in Nazi-occupied Paris, where he was subject to harassment by the Gestapo.

One German officer, during a search of his apartment, saw a photograph of the painting entitled *Guernica*. 'Did you do that?' the German asked Picasso. 'No,' he replied, 'You did.'

70 THE GENOCIDAL GENERAL

At a conference held with Indian chiefs at Fort Cobb in 1869, the Commanche chief Toch-a-way introduced himself to American general Philip Sheridan.

'Me Toch-a-way,' said the chief, 'Me good Indian.' 'The only good Indians I ever saw were dead,' replied Sheridan.

71 WAR AIMS II

At the end of the Mexican War in 1848 William Tecumseh Sherman, later to be a Union general in the Civil War, was sent to survey the lands of New Mexico and Arizona, recently won from the Mexicans.

On his return President Taylor asked Sherman what he thought of the lands. Had they been worth fighting for? Recalling the arid lands from which he had just returned Sherman replied, 'Between you and me, sir, I feel that we'll have to go to war again.' Taylor was horrified. 'What for?' he exclaimed. 'To make them take the darn country back again,' said Sherman.

72 TONE DEAF II

The Duke of Wellington shared with the great American general, Ulysses Grant, a dislike of music.

At the Congress of Vienna in 1815 the Duke of Wellington was forced to sit through a performance of Beethoven's *Battle of Vittoria*, or *Wellington's Victory*. Afterwards, a Russian envoy asked him if the music had been anything like the real thing. 'By God, no, sir,' replied the Duke. 'If it had been that bad I would have run away myself.'

73 WITH GOD ON THEIR SIDE

In the colonial wars between Britain and France for control of North America the Indians proved a vital source of manpower for both sides. Neither side was particularly scrupulous about what it told the Indians to win their support.

Three Indians captured by the British in 1692 revealed that they were Christians and had been told by Jesuit missionaries that the Virgin Mary was a French lady whose son Jesus had been murdered by the English. Jesus had apparently risen to heaven and had told his followers that they must avenge his death by killing the English.

74 EARTHY ENCOURAGEMENT

In selecting his generals Napoleon paid no attention to a man's social background. It was said of the French soldier that every one of them carried a marshal's baton in his knapsack.

General Louis Friant, for all his ability, was certainly not prone to over-refinement. At the battle of Austerlitz in 1805 he saw his soldiers lowering their heads to avoid the barrage of shot and bullets. Furiously he called out to them 'What are you scared of? It's only cannonballs that are flying around not pieces of shit!'

75 AN UNDERRATED OFFICER

During the Seven Years War the Hon. George Townshend had a reputation for coolness under fire.

On one occasion a German officer, standing next to him, had his head blown to pieces by an exploding shell. Townshend was splattered with gore. However, he merely took out his handkerchief and started wiping his uniform, muttering as he did so, 'I never suspected that Scheiger had so many brains.'

76 A FRENCH REVERSE

The Duke of Wellington possessed diplomatic skills to match his military ones.

When some French officers, angered by France's defeat, turned their backs on Wellington at the Congress of Vienna in 1815, a sympathetic onlooker tried to apologize for their rudeness. But Wellington simply smiled, adding 'I've seen their backs before, madam.'

77 POETIC LICENCE

Great general that he was, James Wolfe was undoubtedly an eccentric man.

Before the attack on Quebec, General James Wolfe stood mutely in one of the foremost boats. Suddenly the general began to speak in a low voice. He was reciting Gray's 'Elegy

James Wolfe before Quebec. His enthusiasm for poetry of a melancholy bent was to prove rather an embarrassment on the eve of battle (see number 77) – but perhaps at Quebec he had some premonition of the fate that was shortly to befall him.

in a Country Churchyard', which he had only just memorized. His aides listened quietly. Wolfe finished and said softly, 'Gentlemen, I would rather have written those lines than take Quebec.' An embarrassed silence followed. No one believed him.

78 CUSTOM AND PRACTICE

After the battle of Kambula in 1879, Colonel Evelyn Wood interrogated some Zulu prisoners.

When I had obtained all the information I required I said, 'Before Isandwhlana we treated all your wounded men in our Hospital. But when you attacked our camp your brethren, our black patients, rose and helped to kill those who had been attending on them. Can any of you advance any reason why I should not kill you?' One of the younger men, with an intelligent face, asked, 'May I speak?' 'Yes.' 'There is a very good reason why you should not kill us. We kill you because it is the custom of the black men. But it isn't the white man's custom.'

Wood had no answer to this and had the men placed under guard before eventually freeing them.

Source: Sir Evelyn Wood, *From Midshipman to Field Marshal* (1906)

79 AN OFFICER'S RESOURCES

In the absence of Lord Roberts, General Kitchener sometimes took command during the Second Boer War.

At the battle of Paardeburg in 1900 Major-General Horace Smith-Dorrien, commanding the 19th Brigade, was told by one of General Kitchener's staff officers to take his men and establish a position across the Modder river. Smith-Dorrien asked where he should make his crossing and was casually informed, 'The river is in flood and as far as I have heard Paardeburg drift is the only one available and is unfordable. But Lord Kitchener, knowing your resourcefulness, is sure you will get across somehow.'

80 OUT ON A LIMB

Among Waterloo stories, this one is only slightly less famous than Lord Uxbridge's leg (see number 98).

When Lord Fitzroy Somerset, later Lord Raglan, had his arm amputated on the evening after the battle of Waterloo he shouted, 'Here, bring that arm back. There's a ring my wife gave me.'

81 A BAD LOOKOUT

To prevent the possibility of American attacks on Japan, Admiral Yamamoto had placed a line of picket boats some 700 miles from Tokyo.

On 18 April 1942 the lookout on one of these boats sighted aeroplanes overhead. He woke his captain with the news but the officer was not interested, asserting that there could be no enemy planes so close to the Japanese mainland. He simply turned over and went back to sleep. An hour passed and this time the lookout sighted two aircraft carriers on the horizon. He reported to the captain, 'Two of our beautiful carriers ahead, sir.' This time the captain came to look for himself and went rigid with horror. 'They are beautiful,' he said, 'but they are not ours.' He went below and shot himself in the head.

82 A NEAR THING

Sang froid was a feature of the British military effort in the Crimea, often as an alternative to common sense and efficiency.

During the battle of Inkermann in 1855, a sergeant of the 7th Foot passed Lord Raglan and, drawing himself up to his full height to salute the commander-in-chief, he had his forage cap knocked off by a cannon ball. Apparently unconcerned, the man simply bent down to pick up his cap and dusted it off before replacing it on his head. He then completed his salute. 'A near thing that, my man,' said Lord Raglan. 'Yes, my Lord,' the sergeant replied, 'but a miss is as good as a mile they say,' and he went on his way.

83 KING'S MOVE

During the 12th century, Louis VI of France, in one of his battles, was in some danger.

An enemy soldier seized his horse's bridle and shouted, 'The King is taken.' Louis called in reply, 'No, sir,' raising his battle-axe and bringing it crashing down on the soldier's head. 'A King is never taken, not even at chess.'

Source: *The Percy Anecdotes* (Ed. S. & R. Percy 1823)

84 ENGLAND'S PRIDE

The arrogance of the English soldier was a feature of military affairs in the 18th century.

Frederick the Great of Prussia asked Sir Robert Sutton at a review of his tall grenadiers if he thought an equal number of Englishmen could beat them. 'Sir,' replied Sir Robert, 'I do not venture to assert that; but I know that half the number would try.'

Source: *Naval and Military Anecdotes* (1824)

85 IF I WERE PARMENIO

After his defeat at the battle of Issus, the Persian king Darius was prepared to negotiate with Alexander the Great.

Darius at that time wrote unto Alexander, and unto certain of his friends also, to pray him to take ten thousand talents for the ransom of all those prisoners he had in his hands, and for all the countries, lands and signories on this side of the river Euphrates, and one of his daughters also in marriage, that from thence forth he might be his kinsman and friend. Alexander imparted this to his council. Amongst them Parmenio said unto him: If I were Alexander, quoth he, surely I would accept this offer. So would I indeed, quoth Alexander again, if I were Parmenio.

Source: Plutarch, *Life of Alexander* (1st century AD; trans. Sir Thomas North, 1579)

86 THIS IS A MAN!

Tecumseh was a highly regarded ally of the British. It was even alleged that he was offered the rank of Brigadier-General in the British Army. General Sir Isaac Brock's biographer tells us of the meeting in 1812 where the British general first met the great Indian and the impression each formed of the other.

The following was related . . . by one who was present when General Brock first met Tecumseh and his Indians. Among other topics touched upon by the general in a brief speech, he observed to Tecumseh: 'I have fought against the enemies of our great father, the king, beyond the great salt lake, and they have never seen my back. I am come here to fight his enemies on this side of the great salt lake, and now desire with my soldiers to take lessons from you and your warriors that we may learn how to make war in these great forests.' After a pause, Tecumseh, who was evidently struck with the commanding figure and fine countenance of the general, turning round to his people, stretched out his hand, and exclaimed with a long ejaculated Ho-o-o-e: 'This is a man!' Brock, when he got to know Tecumseh well, referred to him as 'the Wellington of the Indians'.

Source: Ferdinand Brock Tupper, *The Life and Correspondence of Major-General Sir Isaac Brock, K.B.* (1847)

87 THE PYRRHIC VICTORY

King Pyrrhus defeated the Romans at the battle of Asculum (279 BC). But his losses had been terribly severe.

And some say, that it was at that time Pyrrhus answered one, who rejoiced with him for the victory they had won: If we win another of the price, quoth he, we are utterly undone. For indeed then had he lost the most part of his army he brought with him out of his realm, and all his friends and Captains in manner every one, or at least there lacked little of it: and besides that he had no means to supply them with other from thence, and perceived also that the confederates he had in Italy began to wax cold. Where the Romans to the contrary, did easily renew their army with fresh soldiers.

Source: Plutarch, *Life of Pyrrhus* (1st century AD; trans. Sir Thomas North, 1579)

88 NO BLOT ON HIS RECORD

Napoleon, of course, was a great believer in the career open to talent. Thus many of his senior generals and marshals were promoted from the ranks, as in the case of a certain Sergeant Junot. During the British attack on Toulon in 1793 Junot showed great calmness under fire.

During an artillery exchange between British and French guns at Toulon, the young Bonaparte first met Sergeant Junot, who was to have a glittering career in the future emperor's service. At that time Bonaparte was only looking for a soldier who could write legibly and take dictation. Junot was the man chosen, and while he was writing a

The battle of Asculum – the original Pyrrhic victory (see number 87).

letter under Bonaparte's dictation a British shell exploded nearby, showering the parchment on which he was writing with sand. Junot, completely unruffled, blew the sand from the paper, saying 'Good, we won't need to blot this page.' From that time onwards, Bonaparte appointed Junot to his staff.

89 KEEPING THE BUGS WARM

In the European wars of the 16th and 17th centuries, huge bands of soldiers roved the countryside looking for food and shelter. Many were billeted on the peasantry, while others made do in deserted huts or tents. The bitter weather inflicted many casualties, although the lice seem to have been an ever present problem for soldiers in any age.

A young Welsh soldier in the army of Henry VIII overheard one of his colleagues complaining: 'Ah, sirs, if I'd known at the beginning of the night that there would be as much frost and snow as this I would not have taken so much trouble to search my shirt for lice, but I should have hung it out in the wind and let them die of cold as we shall do if we stay here any longer.'

90 INTO THE WOODS

The annihilation of three Roman legions commanded by Quintilius Varus at the hands of

German tribes in the gloomy region of the Teutoburger Wald in AD 9 was one of the worst disasters suffered by Rome. The Emperor Augustus was deeply shocked by the news.

In all his wars [Augustus] never received any signal or ignominious defeat, except twice in Germany under his lieutenants Lollius and Varus. The former had in it indeed more of dishonour than disaster; but that of Varus threatened the security of the empire itself; three legions, with the commander, his lieutenants and all the auxiliaries, being cut off. Upon receiving intelligence of this disaster, he gave orders for keeping a strict watch over the city, to prevent any public disturbance, and prolonged the appointments of the prefects in the provinces that the allies might be kept in order by the experience of persons to whom they were used. He made a vow to celebrate the great games in honour of Jupiter, Optimus, Maximus, if 'he would be pleased to restore the state to more prosperous circumstances'. This had formerly been resorted to in the Chimbrian and Marsian wars. In short, we are informed that he was in such consternation at this event, that he let the hair of his head and beard grow for several months, and sometimes knocked his head against the doorposts, crying out, 'Oh, Quintilius Varus! Give me back my legions!'

Source: Suetonius, *Lives of the Twelve Caesars* (2nd century)

91 SAVING WIT

Frederick the Great was very slow to forgive generals who had failed him.

On one occasion General von Winterfeldt, who was out of favour, met the king at Potsdam and saluted with great respect. Frederick, however, simply turned his back on him. 'I am glad,' said Winterfeldt, 'that His Majesty is no longer angry with me.'

Verdun, where one American soldier was to leave some poignant graffiti (see number 94).

'How so?' demanded Frederick. 'Because Your Majesty has never in his life turned his back on an enemy,' replied Winterfeldt. Struck by this reply the king was soon reconciled to his general.

92 BACK-DOOR DIPLOMACY

The German decision to attack the Soviet Union in June 1941 came as a shattering blow to the Soviet leadership. In spite of intelligence reports of German military build-up and diplomatic reports from embassies throughout the world, Stalin obstinately refused to accept the inevitable and vainly clung to the defunct Nazi-Soviet Non-Aggression Pact of 1939.

At six o'clock in the morning of 22 June 1941, the German ambassador, Count von Schulenburg, handed Molotov a Note of the German Government declaring war on the Soviet Union.

Both Count von Schulenburg and Molotov were pale with emotion. The Commissar for Foreign Affairs took the Note wordlessly, spat on it and then tore it up. He rang for his secretary Poskrebichev.

'Show this gentleman out through the back door.'

93 LIBERATION

The fighting in Normandy in 1944 between the Anglo-American troops and the Germans was extremely severe, with both sides suffering heavy casualties. The assault on St Lô caused one American soldier to comment:

We sure liberated the hell out of this place.

94 OVER THERE . . .

In 1944 American soldiers came to Europe for the second time in a generation to redress the wrongs of the Old World. The following inscription was observed on a wall at the fortress of Verdun.

Austin White - Chicago, Ill – 1918
Austin White – Chicago, Ill – 1945
This is the last time I want to write my name here.

95 OLD HABITS

When Marshal Blücher was invited to England to commemorate his glorious part in the Allied victory at Waterloo he was astounded at the size and obvious wealth of London and was heard to say:

What a town to loot!

96 I WILL REPAY . . .

Although Poland had been overrun by the Germans in 1939, many Poles escaped to Britain and carried on the fight in all three branches of the British services. Above all they wished for vengeance on the Germans.

During the final stage in the battle against the *Bismarck*, one observer from the decks of the British battleship *Rodney* had particular reason to feel satisfied. Sub-Lieutenant Eryk Sopocko, a young Polish officer who had escaped from his conquered homeland and was serving in the Royal Navy, took especial delight in the terrible punishment administered by the British ships to the shattered hulk of the German battleship. While some felt sympathy for the German sailors, who had fought with great gallantry against overwhelming odds, Sopocko had none, reflecting: 'Justice, you still exist.'

97 RAKING UP THE PAST

During the Second World War Winston Churchill always found Free French leader Charles de Gaulle difficult to deal with.

On one occasion, in 1941, Winston Churchill's meal was interrupted by a phone call from Charles de Gaulle. On returning to the table, some ten minutes later, he told his startled guests that the French leader had had the effrontery to tell him that he was viewed by his people as the reincarnation of Joan of Arc. Churchill chuckled when he recalled that he had replied that the English had had to burn the last one.

98 NO LAUGHING MATTER

Lord Uxbridge's injury at the battle of Waterloo in 1815 provides probably the most famous anecdote in military history.

Lord Uxbridge: By God, sir, I've lost my leg!
Wellington (unperturbed): By God, sir, I believe you have.

99 LIONHEART?

William Marshal, later Earl of Pembroke, was one of the most highly regarded knights of the early Middle Ages. His loyalty was unmatched and it is not surprising to learn that even in spite of the incident recorded here he was able to serve Richard throughout his reign and John afterwards.

In June 1189 Henry II was facing an attack from the French under Philip Augustus in league with Henry's son, Richard, later known as Coeur de Lion. Henry was retreating from Le Mans and Richard was leading the pursuit. But so precipitate was the chase that Richard had neglected to wear his armour and when he caught up with the king's rearguard he found it was commanded by William Marshal. Marshal wheeled back to face Richard and toppled him from his horse. Richard, knowing the reputation of this great knight, pleaded: 'By the legs of God, Marshal, do not kill me! I am not armed.' Marshal looked at him scornfully for a moment and then, instead of striking him, plunged his lance into Richard's horse. 'No, I will not kill you,' said William Marshal, 'but I hope the Devil will.'

Even the fury of the battle of El Teb failed to dull the English penchant for cricketing analogies (see number 100).

100 CAUGHT

In 1883 the Mahdi began a rebellion in the Sudan against Anglo-Egyptian power. For some fifteen years war raged intermittently in the region until the Sudanese were finally defeated by General Kitchener at the battle of Omdurman in 1898.

At the battle of El Teb in February 1884, the Sudanese dervishes attacked a British force commanded by General Graham. The British formed square and held the tribesmen off at the point of their bayonets. When one Sudanese warrior leaped over the front rank of the British he was impaled on a bayonet held by a trooper in the rear rank. The soldier, presumably a sportsman, shouted 'Owzat, sir,' to which his officer replied, 'Well caught!'

101 A KNOCK-ON EFFECT

Early in the American Civil War, Confederate general Ewell had one of his legs amputated and replaced by a wooden one, of which he became very proud. In 1863 at the battle of Gettysburg he was injured again.

As we rode together, a body of Union soldiers, posted behind some fences and buildings on the outskirts of the town, suddenly opened a brisk fire. A number of Confederates were killed and wounded, and I heard the ominous thud of a Minié ball as it struck General Ewell at my side. I quickly asked, 'Are you hurt, sir?' 'No, no,' he replied, 'I am not hurt. But suppose the ball had struck you; we would have had the trouble of carrying you off the field, sir. You see how much better fixed for a fight I am than you are. It don't hurt a bit to be shot in a wooden leg.'

Source: General John B. Gordon, *Reminiscences of the Civil War* (1903)

ALARMS AND DIVERSIONS

102 SANG FROID

The sense of humour of the ordinary British soldier in the First World War mystified the Germans, who never felt that the Tommies took war seriously enough.

During the battle of Passchendaele, in the autumn of 1917, a German field gun had targeted a British tank and was trying to knock it out. On top of the tank an infantryman tired of trudging through the sea of mud had hitched a lift, when suddenly a shell filled with shrapnel exploded above the tank and dozens of steel balls rained down on man and machine.

Some watching British soldiers waited to see the passenger fall dead from his perch. But instead he emerged unhurt from the deadly hail of shrapnel and, cupping his hands to his mouth, yelled to the tank commander inside, 'Hi, conductor! Any room inside? It's raining!'

103 BACK PAY

The Victorian Army was ruled by men with a civil-service mentality.

Colonel Henry Hallam Parr was once asked to provide proof of the existence of one of his officers so that the man could draw his pay. Colonel Parr was only too happy to oblige and wrote out a certificate to the effect that the officer was alive, dated it and returned it to the man. But that was not good enough, the officer explained, as he had already proved that he was alive in the current month. What he needed was proof that he had been alive the previous month. Could the Colonel kindly backdate the certificate?

104 A NATURALIZED BRITON

With the outbreak of war against Germany in 1914 British patriotism took many unusual forms. Anything of German origin immediately became suspect.

In a side street off the Strand yesterday I met a jolly little dachshund – the dachshund might be called the national dog of Germany – walking cheerfully along well-bedecked in red, white and blue ribbons. And round his neck he wore this label, 'I am a naturalized British subject.' And he seemed mighty proud of the fact, too.

Source: *Daily Mirror*, 18 August 1914

105 AN ARMY MEDICAL

In Victorian times the medical examinations for entry to the officer training college at Sandhurst were quite stringent: the eye test was particularly demanding.

One prospective candidate for Sandhurst, aware that his short-sightedness might disqualify him from entry, thought up a cunning solution. Learning from previous candidates that the examiner asked each candidate in turn to look out of the window and describe the most distant object he could see, this resourceful individual hired a man to stop at the end of the road with his cart and feed his horse with an apple. When it was his turn to take the test the candidate told the examiner that the furthest thing that he could see was a horse and cart in the far distance, at the end of the road. And this was not all, for he could see that the man was feeding the horse with an apple. The examiner was astonished and had to use field glasses to check the accuracy of his claim, finally acknowledging that his eyesight was perfect.

106 AN UNUSUAL ESCAPE ROUTE

Allied flyers and escaped POWs followed many unusual paths to safety from occupied Europe in the Second World War.

In Paris one escape network operated through a brothel in Montmartre to which the escapees would be taken and disguised as customers in the event of a raid by the Gestapo. One particular English pilot was so embarrassed at being taken there that word of his odd behaviour reached the ears of an informer. A member of the Gestapo visited the brothel the next day in the guise of an ordinary client, but fortunately the manageress saw through his cover. In the event of a full Gestapo raid she realized that the young pilot would be too embarrassed to play the part of a client with one of her girls and so dressed him as a prostitute instead.

107 A THICK EAR

During the wars of the 18th century the Austrian cavalry had a very low opinion of the Prussian Hussars, considering them a vulgar copy of the real thing, only to be found in the Habsburg ranks.

At the battle of Hohenfriedberg in 1745 the Austrian general Berchingen was furious at being captured by just such a Prussian hussar: 'Do I really have to be taken by a mob like this? I saw the Prussian Hussars at Mollwitz. They're a tatty crowd and they ran for their lives at the sight of the first Hungarians.' He went on in this vein until the hussar lost all patience and silenced him with a punch in the head. The general's hat fell off, then his wig, and finally his whole bulk toppled from the saddle onto the ground.

108 IRISH WIT

An Irish officer in the Austrian service named Butler was invited to dine with the Margravine of Bayreuth, through whose territory the Austrians were marching.

'What do you think of this war?' the Margravine asked. 'And what is going to become of the king of Prussia?' 'Madame,' said Butler, 'I believe he is all fucked up.' 'That would displease me somewhat,' she replied, 'for he's my brother.' 'In that case, madame, I am the one who is all fucked up.'

109 **IRISH LOGIC**

The Irish have made fine soldiers in the armies of numerous states, but they have always possessed an individual view of the world.

At the battle of New Orleans in 1815 between the British and the Americans, the British quartermaster, William Surtees, witnessed a shell land in the British encampment and blow off both legs of an Irish lieutenant named Darcy who was asleep at the time. Rudely awakened to his plight, the Irishman assured Surtees that his sympathy was misplaced. Had he only lost one leg there would have been cause for regret as he would not have been entitled to any financial compensation. But having lost two legs he was entitled to a double pension and would live like a prince.

110 **SPLASH!**

The Greek dictator Metaxas was highly unpopular with his own people, who loved to celebrate his faux pas.

Some very unpleasant creatures crawled in and out of the Union trenches during the siege of Petersburg (see number 111).

General Metaxas, a virtual dictator of Greece in the 1930s, once undertook an inspection of an air base and was invited to try out a new flying boat. He eagerly took the seaplane for a short flight and was coming in to land when the commander of the airbase broke in from the control tower to say, 'Excuse me, general, it would be better to put the aircraft down on the water; remember, it is a flying boat.' Metaxas had clearly forgotten and had been about to land on a runway. Swerving away at the last moment he made another circuit and then landed safely on the water nearby. Switching off the engine Metaxas radioed his thanks to the control tower. 'Thank you, commander, for preventing me from making a complete fool of myself.' He then opened the door and stepped straight out into the sea.

111 ARMY GRUB

Veterans of the American Civil War had no more reason than veterans of other wars of the 19th century to remember their victuals with pleasure.

During the siege of Petersburg in 1864 the Union troops were often issued with wormy hardtack or ship's biscuit. It was almost universally unpopular with the men, who were nauseated by finding live worms when they broke open the biscuit. Most of them simply threw away the biscuits in the trenches where they were doing duty, although they had been ordered to keep the trenches clean, for sanitary purposes. One day a brigadier was passing a group of men and noticed biscuits lying everywhere in the trench. He shouted at the soldiers, 'Throw the hardtack out of the trenches. Don't you know better than to just drop it anywhere?' At which one of the soldiers reasonably replied, 'We've thrown it out two or three times, sir, but it just goes on crawlin' back.'

Source: H. Clay Trumbull, *War Memories of an Army Chaplain* (1898)

112 GOOD MANNERS

Even in wartime the negroes of the Confederacy remembered their place.

During the siege of Vicksburg in 1863 a Catholic nun, Sister Serephena, had a narrow escape. Returning from an errand of mercy amongst the sick and wounded and escorted by a small black boy, she stopped to speak to a Confederate corporal who had recently recovered from his injuries. Suddenly a shell landed at their feet, with its fuse still burning. The three of them were transfixed with horror and the corporal leapt backward and took to his heels ignominiously. As the corporal fled the little black boy picked up the smouldering shell and threw it as far as he could away from them. He was only just in time as the shell exploded in mid-air.

'Why didn't you do that immediately?' asked the trembling nun. 'Your hesitation might have cost us our lives.'

'Lord! Miss Sister Serephena,' said the little boy. 'I got too much respect for white folks to do a thing like that while there was a white gentleman standing there.'

Source: Robert Talley, *The Commercial Appeal* (1940)

113 HOME FROM HOME I

During the evacuation of children from British cities in 1939 there were many awkward moments caused by the enforced proximity of people from very different social backgrounds.

One 13-year-old boy rejected the cereal and milk he was offered for breakfast in one rural village, saying 'I want some bloody beer and some chips.'

Some city children appeared to have had no toilet-training. One Glaswegian mother, evacuated with her son, complained when the boy defecated in the middle of the carpet of the host family. 'You dirty thing,' she said, 'messing up the lady's carpet. Why didn't you do it in the corner like I showed you?'

114 JUST CHECKING

On 4 February 1943 an American military policeman had occasion to stop a car driving at high speed out of Casablanca. The driver was smartly dressed in European clothes and the MP was suspicious.

MP: Pull over to the kerb. OK, what's your name?
Driver: Sidi Mohammed ben Youssef.
MP: And your profession?
Driver: Fonctionnaire.
MP: What function?
Driver: Sultan of Morocco.

115 A LIKELY STORY

During the fighting in Italy in 1943 a British officer with his American driver were travelling towards Naples when they gave a lift to an American GI.

The soldier asked the driver why he was working with the British. The reason, apparently, was that he had been turned down on medical grounds by the Americans. The GI was very interested to hear that but told him that they took anyone nowadays.

'There's a guy goes up for his medical with no arms,' says the GI, 'but they enlist him and post him to a unit. When he gets there the adjutant tells him, "You got no arms. Never mind, son. There's a place for you in this Army. Just go and help those guys over there pumping water into buckets." "But I can't help them," says the recruit, "I've got no arms." "Never mind. Just tell them when to stop," says the adjutant, "They're both blind."'

116 THE ENGLISH ABROAD

The troopers of the British Expeditionary Force were no great linguists, though many of them had served in far-flung parts of the empire before 1914. For many of them foreign tongues were just variations of English, spoken slowly or quaintly accented, as they had been accustomed to do for centuries in Eastern bazaars.

One pair of soldiers were overheard in a shop in Zeebrugge, trying to buy postcards from a pair of baffled shopkeepers.

'How moochee moonee?' asked one Tommy. But the old couple shook their heads in bafflement.

Brandishing the postcards the Tommy repeated his question more loudly and more slowly this time. 'How moo-chee moo-nee?'

Again the old Belgians shook their heads and smiled.

Frustrated, the Tommies gave up and left the shop without their postcards.

'Stupid old buggers,' said one Tommy to the other, 'they don't even understand their own bloody language.'

117 DEMAND AND SUPPLY

During the Second World War, Xiel Federmann, who was to become one of Israel's most skilful agents, had been a prime supplier of equipment to the British Army and the Royal Navy.

On one occasion the Navy had asked him to acquire 100,000 sailor's caps at short notice. Undeterred by the knowledge that nowhere in the whole Middle East could such a consignment be found, Federmann found an old hatmaker in Tel Aviv, who was skilled in making the flat round hat worn by orthodox Polish Jews. Federmann persuaded the old man to call in help from all his friends who had escaped the ghettoes of Poland and soon the navy caps were being made at an astonishing rate.

Federmann produced the consignment of caps and was duly paid. A few months later curiosity brought him to the docks where an official ceremony was taking place aboard the battleship *Warspite*. As he watched it began to rain and from all sides there arose a terrible stench. Federmann immediately recognized the smell. It was his caps – or more precisely the glue he had used, made from crushed cattle bones. As he quietly withdrew from the scene, the stinking paste began to run in little rivulets down the faces of His Majesty's sailors.

118 DOWN TO EARTH

During the Napoleonic Wars, French generals needed luck and a sense of humour.

On 22 December 1793 General Hoche was engaged in fierce fighting against the Austrians. A gunshot brought down a tree whose branches fell on him, bringing him to the ground. Extricating himself from the foliage he remounted his horse only to have it immediately killed under him by another shot, sending him toppling onto his backside. 'These gentlemen want to make me serve in the infantry,' he said, rising from the mud.

119 HOME FROM HOME II

Evacuees often found it difficult to adjust to their surroundings.

Children from one inner-city area told their startled hosts, 'We don't have our milk from a dirty cow; we have it from a clean bottle.' Another city child staggered into his foster-home with an armful of vegetables, saying 'Blimey, I've never seen anything like it. The bloomin' things grow wild about here.'

120 THEATRE OF WAR

During the American War of Independence the British Army did its best to destroy the notion that they were invaders. They tried to portray the Americans as rebels and themselves as the legitimate force of order. They found it helped to maintain as normal a social life as possible, with dinners, balls and theatrical evenings.

Plays were acted twice every week by the officers and some of the Boston ladies. Miss Sally Fletcher acted the part of Zara. She was a very pretty girl and did it very well. A farce called *The Blockade of Boston*, written, I believe, by General Burgoyne, was acted. The enemy knew the night it was to be performed and made an attack on the mill at Charlestown at the very hour that the farce began. I happened to be on duty in the redoubt at Charlestown that night. The enemy came along the mill-dam and surprised a sergeant's guard that was posted at the mill. Some shots were fired and we all immediately turned out and manned the works. A shot was fired by one of the advanced sentries, and instantly the firing commenced in the redoubt, and it was a considerable time before it could be stopped. Not a man of the enemy was within three miles of us, and the party that had come along the mill-dam had effected their object and carried off the sergeant's guard. However, our firing caused a general alarm at Boston and all the troops got under arms.

   An orderly sergeant that was standing outside the playhouse door heard the firing and immediately ran into the playhouse, got up onto the stage and cried, 'Turn out! Turn out! They are hard at it, hammer and tongs.' The whole audience thought that the sergeant was acting a part in the farce, and that he did it so well that there was a general clap and such a noise that he could not be heard for a considerable time. When the clapping was over he again cried, 'What the deuce are you all about? If you won't believe me, by Jasus, you need only go to the door and there you will see and hear both!' If it was the intention of the enemy to put a stop to the farce for that night they certainly succeeded as all the officers immediately left the playhouse and joined their regiments.

Source: Sir Martin Hunter, *The Journal of General Sir Martin Hunter* (Ed. Hunter and Bell 1894)

121 HOSPITALITY

After the Duke of Marlborough's great victory over the French at the battle of Blenheim in 1704, Louis XIV's marshals Marsin and Tallard were taken to England as prisoners.

As their coach was driven through Nottingham a genial butcher called to them, 'Welcome to England, sirs. We hope to see your master here next year.'

122 A KISS

During the successful siege of Delhi in 1857 fierce street fighting took place between the British and the Indian mutineers

One house that was broken into seemed to be entirely full of women. Ensign

The capture of Marshal Tallard at Blenheim. When taken to England he was to receive a cheeky greeting from a Nottingham butcher (see number 121).

Wilberforce ordered his men upstairs, but one refused to leave and instead struck one of the women on the head with his musket. Horrified, Wilberforce asked why he had struck the woman.

'Och, yer honour,' he replied, 'did ye ever see a woman with such a prutty moustache as this?' and he raised from the bed the face of a sepoy.

Wilberforce was impressed and asked the soldier why he had been suspicious. The man explained that Wilberforce had given orders not to hurt the women. Nothing was said about not kissing them . . .

Source: Ensign R.G. Wilberforce, *An Unrecorded Chapter of the Indian Mutiny* (1894)

123 AN EXPLOSIVE INNINGS

During the siege of Ladysmith in 1900 the boredom was reduced by typical British pastimes like cricket.

In spite of the continual bombardment a cricket pitch was set up on the racetrack, in sight of the Boer guns on Bulwana Ridge. On one occasion Colonel Rawlinson witnessed a bizarre incident, which could have been fatal but fortunately had no such ill consequences.

'I spent a few idle moments watching the Imperial Light Horse play cricket. They kept a man to watch Bulwana "Tom" and when he saw the flash he shouted, "Here she comes". The batsman pretended to play the shell when, to his astonishment, it landed on the pitch about three feet from him. The concussion knocked him down but he was not a bit hurt.'

124 THAT'S THE SPIRIT

Many units in both Confederate and Federal armies in 1861 had been set up by individuals, or by club, school or factory groups. This created a camaraderie that was hard to create in any other way.

Our company was made up of young men from the country and was sometimes called, 'Merritt's Sabbath-School Children' on account of their goodness. But at Harper's Ferry, as is often the case, these good men fell. Captain Merritt, as Provost-Marshal, captured six barrels and a ten-gallon keg of whiskey. The keg was lost in transit and could not be accounted for. We were quartered in a deserted house and the captain came to inform me that we were to march to Bolivar Heights to join the regiment. He soon saw that the missing keg must have been found for the men were in every stage of intoxication from the moderate drinker to the gutter drunkard. As we were going through the rooms we met Uncle Ben, perfectly sober. The captain, feeling sad that the company had gone wrong said, 'Ben, I am sorry.' Ben said, 'It is not my fault, Captain. I have been on guard and have not found the stuff. But as soon as I do I will catch up and be just as drunk as the best of them.'

Source: Captain John Adams, *Sunshine and Shadows of Army Life* (1900)

125 A TERRIBLE THIRST

Confederate general Thomas 'Stonewall' Jackson was a legend in his own lifetime and the tales told of him are legion.

On the 8th July 1862 the Army of Northern Virginia began to move back to the vicinity of Richmond. When Jackson's command started he and his staff remained behind until some time after the rest of the party had gone. It was after dark when he started and about midnight when he reached his headquarters. He was riding along at ten or eleven o'clock at night with his drowsy staff, nodding on 'Little Sorrel' as was his custom and trusting to that intelligent beast not to give him a fall. More than once did we see his head nod and drop to his breast and his body sway a little to one side or the other, expecting to see him get a tumble, but he never got it. On this occasion, our sleepy cavalcade at different times passed small squads of soldiers in fence corners before blazing fires, roasting green corn and eating it. Passing one of these our staggering leader was observed by one of those thirsty stragglers who was evidently delighted at the sight of a drunken cavalryman. Perhaps encouraged with the hope of a drink ahead the ragged

Reb jumped up from his fire and brandishing a roasting-ear [of corn] in his hand sprang into the road and to the head of the general's horse with, 'Hello, I say, old fellow. Where the devil did you get your licker?'

The general suddenly woke up and said, 'Doctor McGuire, did you speak to me? Captain Pendleton, did you? Somebody did,' and reined up his horse. The soldier got a look at him and took in the situation. He saw whom he had thus spoken to. 'Good God, it's Old Jack,' he cried, and with several bounds and a flying leap he had cleared the road and was over the fence and had disappeared in the dark.

Source: Major Henry Kyd Douglas, *I Rode with Stonewall* (1940)

126 UNDER FIRE

Humour can have a very beneficial effect in releasing tension in wartime.

In Korea in April 1953, a group of US soldiers were under heavy Chinese fire at Pork Chop Hill. One GI muttered, 'Jesus Christ, this is worse than Custer's last stand.' 'Were you there, too?' inquired an officer.

127 VIVE LA DIFFERENCE!

The arrival of French soldiers under Lafayette to help the Americans in their struggle against Britain produced some amusing misunderstandings, as the Chevalier de Pontgibaud found out.

The Chevalier was astonished to find what strange ideas his hosts the Americans of New England had of the French. One day he dismounted from his horse at the house of a farmer upon whom he had had billeted. No sooner had he entered the good man's house than the farmer said, 'I am very glad to have a Frenchman in the house. You see the barber lives a long way off so you will be able to shave me.' 'But I cannot even shave myself,' de Pontgibaud replied. 'My servant shaves me and he will shave you also if you like.' 'That's very odd,' said the American, 'I was told that all Frenchmen were barbers and fiddlers.' A few minutes later the farmer served him some food, which included some beef. 'You're lucky to be able to come over to America and get good beef to eat,' he added. When the Frenchman tried to assure him that they had beef in France and excellent beef too, the American responded, 'That is impossible, or you wouldn't be so thin.'

128 A CHARACTER REFERENCE

On 9 September 1876 when General Sheridan was in the West he asked to meet Buffalo Bill Cody.

One of Cody's friends decided to impersonate the great man as a joke and told Sheridan that he was Buffalo Bill. Sheridan looked him up and down and said, 'Buffalo Shit, more likely,' and the name stuck.

129 POYNTZ REMEMBERS

During the Thirty Years War, Sydnam Poyntz fought as a mercenary, returning to England later to become a general in the Parliamentary armies. His description of his part in the battle of Lützen in 1632 is particularly down to earth.

At the beginning great store of prisoners were taken on both sides. I myself was taken prisoner three times but twice I was rescued by my fellows; the third time, being taken hold of by my belt, having my sword in my hand, I threw the belt over my ears and rescued myself. I lost three horses that day being shot under me and I was hurt under my right side and in my thigh but I had horses without masters enough to choose and horse myself; all had pistols at their saddle bow but shot off and all that I could do, was with my sword without a scabbard, and a daring pistol but no powder nor shot: my last horse that was shot had almost killed me for being shot in the guts as I think, he mounted on a sudden such a height, yea I think on my conscience two yards and suddenly fell to the ground upon his bum and with his sudden fall thrust my bum a foot into the ground and fell upon me and there lay groveling upon me that he put me out of my senses. I knew not how I was, but at length coming to myself with much ado got up and found two or three brave horses stand fighting together. I took the best but when I came to mount him I was so bruised and with the weight of my heavy armour that I could not get my leg into the saddle that my horse run away with me in that posture, half in my saddle and half out, and so run with me till he met with Picolomini coming running with a troop of horse and my horse ran among them that I escaped very narrowly from being thrown clean off but at length got into my saddle full of pain and could hardly sit, and followed the troop, having nothing but a daring pistol and a naked sword . . .

Source: Sydnam Poyntz, *The Relation of Sydnam Poyntz, 1624-36* (1908)

130 UNPATRIOTIC FEET

Much of Robert E. Lee's success as a commander was due to his skilful use of flank attacks by fast-marching generals like 'Stonewall' Jackson and A.P. Hill. But such marching was exhausting for the men and very hard on their shoes, with the result that there were many stragglers.

General Lee's invasion of Maryland was especially notable for the number of worn soldiers who fell by the wayside when nature could endure no more. Some of the stragglers were returned to their regiments by the strong arm of the military law; others voluntarily returned. In the latter class was a tall, gaunt farmer from the mountains north of Georgia. When asked by his commanding officer to explain his absence from the battle of Antietam, he dryly said: 'I had no shoes. I tried it barefoot, but somehow my feet wouldn't callous. They just kept bleeding. I found it so hard to keep up that though I had the heart of a patriot, I began to feel I didn't have patriotic feet. Of course, I could have crawled on my hands and knees but then my hands would have got so sore I couldn't have fired my rifle.'

Source: Helen Dortch Longstreet, *In the Path of Lee's 'Old War Horse'* (1917)

Frederick William I of Prussia inspecting his giant guards. Like his father, Frederick the Great chose his guards more for their size than their linguistic abilities (see number 131).

131 IN TRANSLATION

It was customary with Frederick the Great of Prussia, whenever a new soldier appeared in his guards, to ask him three questions, viz., 'How old are you? How long have you been in my service? Are you satisfied with your pay and treatment?'

It happened that a young soldier, a native of France, who had served in his own country, desired to enlist in the Prussian service and his figure was such as to cause him to be immediately accepted. He was, however, totally ignorant of the German language, but his captain gave him notice that the king would ask him certain questions in that language the first time he saw him, and therefore instructed him to learn by heart the three answers which he was to make to the king. The soldier learned them by the next day; and as soon as he appeared in the ranks, Frederick came up to interrogate him. His majesty, however, happened to begin with the second question first; and asked him, 'How long have you been in my service?' 'Twenty one years,' answered the soldier. The king struck with his youth, which contradicted his answer said to him, much astonished, 'How old are you?' 'One year an't please your majesty.' Frederick, still more astonished, cried, 'You or I must certainly be bereft of our senses.' The soldier, who took this for the third question, about 'pay and treatment', replied firmly, 'Both an't please your majesty.' 'This is the first time I ever was treated as a madman at the head of my army,' rejoined

Frederick. The soldier, who had exhausted his stock of German, stood silent; and when the king again addressed him, in order to penetrate the mystery, the soldier told him in French that he did not understand a word of German. The king laughed heartily, and, after exhorting him to perform his duty, left him.

Source: *Naval and Military Anecdotes* (1824)

132 THE BEEKEEPER

During the Peninsular War the soldiers of Wellington's army became adept at living off the country.

On one occasion the Iron Duke himself caught a soldier staggering along carrying a stolen beehive.

'Hallo, sir, where did you get that beehive?' asked Wellington.

The soldier obviously did not recognize his commander nor understand his question, for he replied, 'The beehives, sir, are over that hill. But you'd better hurry before they've all been taken.'

133 THE MISSING WIG

At the battle of Vimeiro in Spain, in 1808, Rifleman Harris recorded an incident concerning his commanding officer, Major Travers.

Down galloped the major in front just in the same good spirits he had been all day, plunging along, avoiding with some little difficulty the dead and dying which were strewn about. He was never a very goodlooking man, being hard featured and thin; a hatchet-faced man, as we used to say. But he was a regular good-un, a real English soldier; and that's better than if he had been the handsomest lady's man in the army. The major just now disclosed what none of us, I believe, knew before, namely, that his head was bald as a coot's, and that he had covered the nakedness of his nob up to the present time, by a flowing Caxon, which during the heat of the action, had somehow been dislodged; yet was the major riding hither and thither, digging his spurs into his horse's flanks, and just as busy as before the firing had ceased. 'A guinea,' he kept crying as he rode, 'to any man who will find my wig!' The men, I remember, notwithstanding the sight of the wounded and dead around them, burst into shouts of laughter at him as he went and 'A guinea to any man who will find my wig,' was the saying amongst us long after that affair.

Source: Rifleman Harris, *Recollections of Rifleman Harris* (Ed. Capt H. Curling 1848)

134 THINKING POSITIVELY

During Napoleon's campaign in Russia in 1812 one French officer was able to look on the bright side of losing a leg.

In the campaign of 1812 a distinguished general officer of the French army was severely wounded in the leg. The surgeons, on consulting, declared that amputation was indispensable. The general received the intelligence with much composure. Among the persons who surrounded him, he observed his valet-de-chambre, who shewed by his profound grief the deep share which he took in the melancholy accident. 'Why dost thou weep, Germain?' said his master smilingly, to him. 'It is a fortunate thing for thee, you will have only one boot to clean in future.'

Source: *Naval and Military Anecdotes* (1824)

135 A JOKER IN THE PACK

During the 18th century the punishment of flogging was so common in the British Army that it scarcely raised a stir. It could be imposed for the most absurd of reasons.

On one occasion a company major was giving a reading at church parade. His broad Yorkshire dialect amused some of the men and when he read the words, 'suffered under Pontius Pilate,' one of the men, a known wag, muttered, 'What's Ponchews Peelatt?' The officer heard the comment, stopped reading and turned to look at the culprit. 'Up to your old tricks again, are you Jock?' The major summoned Jock to a drumhead court-martial at which he was sentenced to one hundred lashes, which were carried out immediately at the church parade, and to which Jock submitted without a murmur. Once the flogging was completed, the major returned to his text, 'Now where was I? Oh, that's right . . . suffered under Pontius Pilate.'

136 STRANGE ENCOUNTER II

William Grattan records the experiences of an English officer wounded on 7 April 1812 at Badajoz, during the Peninsular War.

The two faithful soldiers, Bray and Mcgowan, that conducted me there, on entering, found my truss of straw or bed . . . occupied by Mrs. Nelly Carsons, the wife of my batman, who, I suppose, by the way of banishing care, had taken to drinking divers potations of rum to such an excess that she lay down in my bed, thinking perhaps that I was not likely again to be its occupant or more probably not giving it a thought at all. Mcgowan attempted to wake her, but in vain – a battery of a dozen guns might have been fired close to her ear without danger of disturbing her repose! 'Why then, sir,' said he, 'sure the bed's big enough for yees both and she'll keep you nate and warm, for be the powers your kilt with the cold and the loss ov blood.' I was in no mood to stand on ceremony or, indeed to stand at all. I allowed myself to be placed beside my partner without any further persuasion; and the two soldiers left us to ourselves and returned to the town. Weakness from loss of blood soon caused me to fall asleep but it was a sleep of short duration. I awoke unable to move and in fact lay like an infant. A fire of small arms, the screams of the soldiers' wives and the universal buzz throughout the camp acted powerfully upon my nervous and worn-out frame; but Somnus conquered Mars, for I soon fell into another doze in which I might have remained very comfortable had not my companion awoke sooner than I wished; discharging a huge grunt and putting her hand upon my leg she exclaimed, 'Arrah! Dan, jewel, what makes you so stiff this morning?'

Source: William Grattan, *Adventures with the Connaught Rangers, 1808–14* (Ed. Sir C. Oman 1902)

137 THE SECOND COMING

Both sides during the American Civil War had their fair share of devout Christians.

In March 1863, one of our captains was a quaint, impulsive, energetic officer, and a good disciplinarian. A private named Hackett in Company E, 11th Vermont Volunteers, was the most ungainly soldier in the regiment; he could not keep step with one marching by his side or in front of him, and never learned the manual of arms. He should have remained at home and become a minister of the gospel. He was eccentric and had formerly been a Biblical student. He could recite Scripture from Genesis to Exodus.

The guard-house was located just inside the Fort entrance and a bridge spanned the moat to the entrance. Once, when Captain R was Officer of the Day, it was his duty to inspect the guard at least once after midnight. Hackett was at Post Number One, near the gateway of the Fort. It was a dark, rainy night when Hackett heard Captain R approach, and called out, 'Who comes there?'

Captain R, being on one side of the bridge, stumbled and fell headlong into the moat; as he fell he exclaimed in a loud voice, 'Jesus Christ!'

Hackett faced about and called out promptly, 'Turn out the Apostles. Jesus Christ is coming.' Then the guard helped the captain out of the moat.

Source: Brevet Major Charles H. Anson, *Reminiscences of an Enlisted Man* (1914)

138 TEA UP

In 1914, many of the British soldiers from farming areas billeted in the towns had little experience of urban life.

So many young men from farming communities had difficulty adjusting to the refuse system used in British towns and cities. Accustomed to a rubbish pit as a suitable place for household waste, they were at a loss to understand the function of the urban dustbin. Assuming that a container of that size must be intended for a week's supply, many of them brewed up dustbins full of tea, while continuing to throw their rubbish into the gardens of their irate landlords.

139 ROUND THE BEND

The problems experienced by the rural recruits in 1914 were not confined to dustbins.
Accustomed to washing under an outside pump, and using earth closets as lavatories, some of the men found the inside water closet baffling.

A soldier, returning from a lengthy route march, decided to wash his socks in the toilet. Having started the task he found that he needed more water and so he asked one of his colleagues, who replied, 'Pull the chain.'

The soldier duly obliged only to see his socks disappear in a swirling rush of water. His explanation, the following day, was accepted by a weary officer, who by that stage had seen and heard just about everything.

140 ONCE A COSSACK . . .

The Soviet advance into Germany in 1945 was accompanied by terrible scenes of pillaging and rape. Many Germans fled westwards in an attempt to reach the American and British armies moving eastwards. But even amidst all this horror there was a lighter side.

Almost all the women had fled, horrified by the stories of rape which had spread like wildfire over East Prussia, through which three motorized divisions of Cossacks had passed. It was not difficult to protect the few who were left. It was more difficult to prevent sudden 'visitations' in private houses. Cossacks had been waging war for generations, and the customs and habits of their profession are very well established. On one occasion I had to arrest a Cossack captain who had allowed his men to disobey orders.

'According to our custom when a town is taken by storm the men have the right to do their own individual commandeering,' the arrested *Sotnik* explained to me patiently. He was a good fellow, and he had been twice decorated. 'Long established custom allows a Cossack to carry off as much as he can load on his horse. But you see, my men are motorized, and they interpret the custom in their own way, by loading up their lorries.'

Source: Ivan Krylov, *Soviet Staff Officer* (1951)

141 OUCH!

When war between Britain and Germany became an actuality in 1939, the Germans became very concerned with the neutral position adopted by Franco's Spain.

In October 1940 Hitler met the Spanish dictator, Francisco Franco, in a compartment of the Führer's personal train. For hours Hitler tried to persuade the Spanish leader to occupy Gibraltar, a strategic British base, but without effect. Apparently the experience was so draining for Hitler that he said, rather than go through it again, he would prefer 'to have three or four teeth taken out'.

142 THE COLONEL SINGS

On the long marches of the First World War, singing by the soldiers helped to relieve the boredom. Some of the songs contained words or themes that would not have graced the parlours of the men's civilian homes in Blighty. The Commander-in-Chief, Sir Douglas Haig, was known to have very strict views on the immoral tone of many soldiers' songs.

During the battle of the Somme in 1916 a battalion of British troops was marching through a small village at precisely the time that General Haig was visiting an ordnance officer there. The troops were lustily singing a bawdy song as they marched past the house where Haig was. Haig was incensed and, sending for his horse, he set out to put a stop to such nonsense. But the battalion stretched down the road for almost a mile and it took the general some while to reach the head of the column. As he did so the men he passed stopped singing but those ahead continued to give full voice to the words that had so irritated him. At last Haig could detect just one strong voice, supported by a few ranks of men. It was the colonel, riding at the head of his troops, and giving forth in a manly bass voice,

> *Can you sling them on your shoulder*
> *Like a lousy fucking soldier?*
> *Do your balls hang low?*

By this stage all the men had stopped, leaving the colonel to hammer home the final refrain.

Suddenly the shadow of the commander-in-chief passed across the colonel and he jerked to attention, trying to button up his tunic and remove a knotted handkerchief from his head, which he wore on that sweltering summer's day in place of his regulation headgear. Haig bent low and whispered in the colonel's ear, that he liked the tune but found the words quite unacceptable. The Colonel gulped, saluted and struggled to put on his hat. Haig turned his horse and rode away. Silence followed. All that could be heard was the rhythmic pounding of the men's boots. Suddenly a small voice was heard, somewhere far back in the column, singing

> *After the ball was over . . .*

The whole battalion burst out laughing, none more so than the colonel, and the singing returned to relieve the boredom of the march.

Field Marshal Haig congratulating officers and men of a Canadian battalion on the Western Front. His callousness as regards high losses was matched by his lack of sympathy for the culture of the common soldier (see number 142).

143 WAR RATIONS

Bronislaw Malinowski, the famous anthropologist, found it difficult to explain to the so-called 'savages' of the South Seas the 'civilization' of the advanced nations at war with each other in 1914.

I once talked to an old cannibal who, hearing of the Great War raging in Europe, was most curious to know how we Europeans managed to eat such huge quantities of human flesh. When I told him the Europeans did not eat their slain foes he looked at me with shocked horror and asked what sort of barbarians we were, to kill without any real object.

Source: Bronislaw Malinowski, *Reader's Digest*, March 1938

144 THE INVITATION

Not all American soldiers were 'over-sexed, overpaid and over here'.

Something awfully funny happened to me. A young American soldier was looking at the outside of the Houses of Parliament. I said to him, 'Would you like to go in?' He told me, 'You are the sort of woman my mother told me to avoid.'

Source: Lady Astor, quoted in Christopher Sykes, *Nancy, the Life of Lady Astor* (1972)

145 PATTON'S PRIDE

American general Patton was a great soldier with a rough tongue.

General Patton received a message from headquarters ordering him to by-pass Trier [in western Germany] as it would take four divisions to capture the city. But when the message arrived the city had already fallen. Patton replied, 'Have taken Trier with two divisions. Do you want me to give it back?'

Source: Brooks B. Mills, *Reader's Digest*, August 1945

146 MISTAKEN IDENTITY

During the Second World War the fear of German invasion reached extraordinary levels.

During the war my father was a meter reader. The odd thing about him was that he looked like Hitler – the same lock of hair, the same little moustache. When he was reading a meter one day the woman in the house pushed him in a cupboard and locked the door, then rang up the police and said she'd captured Hitler.

Source: Eileen Atkins, quoted in the *Sunday Times*, 15 March 1970

THE GENTLE SEX?

147 A NURSE'S STORY

Nursing in wartime has its heartbreaking moments. This example is from the American Civil War.

Following the nurse to his bed, and turning down the covering, a small jet of blood spurted up. The sharp edge of the splintered bone must have severed an artery. I instantly put my finger on the little orifice and awaited the surgeon. He soon came – took a long look and shook his head. The explanation was easy; the artery was imbedded in the fleshy part of the thigh and could not be taken up. No earthly power could save him.

There was no object in detaining Doctor ——. He required his time and strength, and long I sat by the boy, unconscious himself that any serious trouble was apprehended.

Wounded soldiers being nursed and comforted during the American Civil War. The reality was usually much grimmer than this sentimental depiction suggests (see number 147).

The hardest trial of my duty was laid upon me; the necessity of telling a man in the prime of his life, and fullness of strength, that there was no hope for him.

It was done at last, and the verdict received patiently and courageously, some directions given by which his mother would be informed of his death, and then he turned his questioning eyes upon my face. 'How long can I live?' 'Only as long as I keep my finger upon this artery.' A pause ensued. God alone knew what thoughts hurried through that heart and brain, called so unexpectedly from all earthly hopes and ties. He broke the silence at last, 'You can let go –' But I could not. Not if my own life had trembled in the balance. Hot tears rushed to my eyes, a surging sound to my ears and a deathly coldness to my lips. The pang of obeying him was spared me, and for the first and last time during the trials that surrounded me for four years, I fainted away.

Source: Phoebe Yates Pember, *A Southern Woman's Story* (1879)

148 AN OLD FLAME

It was common knowledge among the troops of both sides during the American Civil War that Union general George B. McClellan and Confederate general A.P. Hill had been rivals for the hand of the beautiful Miss Nellie Marcy, daughter of General Randolph B. Marcy, while they had been at West Point. Nellie had been undecided for some while and had flirted with both men before eventually marrying McClellan.

It was noticeable that during McClellan's campaigns around Richmond in 1862 Hill was always in the forefront of Confederate attacks. Union soldiers got so tired of being hit in flank or rear by Hill's men that they attributed the Confederate general's actions to a personal vendetta.

On one occasion, before the sun had even come up, Hill's men began an attack on the Union lines. Forced to roll out of their beds and stand to arms the Union troopers began to grumble, one veteran crying out in disgust, 'My God, Nellie, why didn't you marry him!'

Source: Major Henry Kyd Douglas, *I Rode with Stonewall* (1940)

149 FEATHER-BRAINED

During the First World War the bellicosity of some women was almost as terrible to the young man who had no stomach for fighting as an enemy with banners and guns.

Karl Wehner, a young German internee, was accosted by a woman in a London park. She said, 'Young man, why aren't you in the army?' 'Because I am a German,' replied Wehner. Even this did not deter her and she handed him a white feather all the same.

150 THE PILOT IN PASTEL SHADES

At the height of the fighting on the Eastern Front in the Second World War the Soviet authorities took the revolutionary step of calling up women to train as pilots. No concessions were to be made to their femininity and the recruits were told that they would soon come to grips with the enemies of their country.

The women were only too happy to fight, but they defied regulations about short hair and no make-up, dyeing their silk under-helmets pastel shades and wearing lipstick and eye shadow. The cockpits of the planes had to be adjusted, with seat cushions raised and blocks placed under foot pedals. So old and heavy were some of the bombers the girls learned to fly that it was sometimes necessary for both pilot and co-pilot to pull the take-off control stick together. Nevertheless, some of these women pilots were soon to silence the male chauvinists who doubted that they would ever be able to fly. One female pilot, Olga Yemshokova, flying at ten thousand feet, was horrified to find a mouse in the cockpit, placed there as a prank by her male aircrew. Forgetting the fear of facing German fighters, Olga could think of nothing but her terror of the mouse. Eventually, she managed to catch it and throw it out of her cockpit.

The most famous of these women pilots was Lily Litvak, a beautiful blonde who became the scourge of German fighter pilots during 1943. The death in action of her lover, the flying ace Alexi Salomaten, only made Lily more determined to kill Germans. Her greatest achievement was in shooting down a renowned German ace who survived the action and was introduced to his conqueror but refused to believe he had been shot down by a woman. Only when Lily had gone through every manoeuvre of the dog-fight in detail with him would the German accept the truth. After a total of twelve victories Lily's fighter, decorated with white rose emblems, became a target for German pilots. On her last mission Lily was overwhelmed by Messerschmitt 109s, shot down in flames and killed.

151 NAKED DEFIANCE

During a civil war in Aztec Mexico in the late 15th century Great Speaker Axayácatl led his Aztec warriors to victory over Moquihuix of Tlatelolco.

Besieged in their own city the Tlatelolcans adopted the unusual ruse of sending naked women against their enemies. The women squeezed milk from their bare breasts and sprinkled it on the Aztec warriors, unnerving them because they felt it unmanly to slay women. But the Great Speaker was unimpressed and sacked the city, killing Moquihuix and his warriors and taking many prisoners as sacrifices. Some Tlatelolcan women were so terrified that they took refuge in the lagoon, standing with the water right up to their necks. The Aztec soldiers pretended to be confused and forced them to make the sounds of ducks and other water fowl to explain why they were in the water. Eventually tiring of the game they allowed the women to return to their homes.

152 A NAPOLEONIC ROMANCE

During the reign of Napoleon, a young French soldier named Giraud was on garrison duty at Wissembourg and became friendly with some civilians, including the daughter of a local book dealer with whom he soon fell in love.

When she invited him to a ball he asked permission of his officer to attend but was refused. Nevertheless he was determined to attend and so, with the help of some of his colleagues, he slipped out of camp unobserved. Knowing that some of the regiment's officers would be at the ball his resourceful sweetheart dressed Giraud up in one of her dresses. Unfortunately Giraud's disguise was too good and he was immediately asked to dance by a number of officers, including the regimental major, who had clearly taken a fancy to him.

When he returned to barracks he found that his absence had been discovered and he was due to report the next morning to the regimental major for punishment. The next day dawned and Giraud was paraded before the hung-over and rather grumpy major, who sentenced him to 25 lashes. When his captain interceded with the major on account of Giraud's previous good record, the major asked him where he had been anyway.

'At the ball, sir.'

'I don't believe it.'

'You should, sir. I was the young lady you danced with so often, plied with refreshments, tried to . . .'

'Case dismissed.'

153 CHASTE SUZANNE

There were always a number of women fighting in the ranks of Napoleon's Grand Armée.

One, known as 'chaste Suzanne of Calais' enlisted at 14 as a drummer, without even having to disguise herself. When in 1798 her regiment was sent to Egypt she found that some of her colleagues began to press their attentions more than they had while in France. Suzanne's solution to an over-insistent colleague was to challenge him to a duel. She served throughout the Napoleonic Wars and was badly wounded at Waterloo.

154 A PRICE ON THEIR HEADS

Frontier wives had to be as tough as their husbands during the colonial wars of the 17th century. They never knew when they might have to fight to protect their own and their children's lives.

In 1697 a war band of Abenakis attacked a settlement at Haverhill in Massachusetts. Mrs Hannah Dustin, only recently delivered of her eighth child, was being helped around the house by Mary Neff, while her husband and the seven children were outside in the fields. When the Indians struck, Mr Dustin tried to hold them off while the children ran to a fortified house nearby. However, the Indians broke into his own house and carried off his wife and baby, as well as Mary Neff.

As the war band made off into the forest Hannah's baby began to cry, whereupon an Indian seized it by the feet and smashed its head against a tree. The distraught women were dragged on until in a clearing several bands of Indians met together. There were many captives and some of them were killed. Afterwards they were divided up between the warriors. Hannah, Mary and a young boy were taken by a pair of Indians and their squaws, being made to carry heavy loads. The Indians, converts to Christianity, apparently prayed at night with their rosaries. Hannah and Mary were treated harshly, being told that when they reached the Indian village they would be stripped and made to run the gauntlet until they died. At this Hannah decided it was time to escape. After six weeks of travelling, she managed to catch the Indians off guard. The braves, their wives and children to the number of a dozen were asleep around the fire, while Hannah and her companions shivered. Hannah crept up to the sleeping braves and took their tomahawks. Then she and Mary proceeded to kill the braves and all of the other sleeping Indians except an old woman and a child who ran screaming into the trees. Not satisfied with this Hannah now scalped each one of them and returned to Haverhill with her trophies of war. She was reunited with her husband and children and received, moreover, a sum of £50 for the ten Indian scalps.

155 FLOWERS FOR THE EMPRESS

During the Napoleonic Wars it would appear that chivalry was not entirely dead.

On learning that the Empress Josephine was developing a garden of exotic blooms at her palace of Malmaison, their lordships of the Admiralty ordered British sea captains to ensure that any plants and seed collections addressed to Her Imperial Highness found aboard captured vessels were to be forwarded to her with all despatch.

156 A NEW JUDITH

During the English siege of Leith in Scotland in 1560, the French garrison showed great ingenuity in defending the port.

On one occasion a group of French soldiers disguised as women emerged from a side gate and so infatuated one of the English scouts that he abandoned his post and went over to join the 'young ladies'. The unfortunate scout found to his cost that these ladies demanded a high price for their favours. No sooner was he ensconced with them than one had cut off his head and carried it back within the walls, later prominently displaying it on one of the town spires.

157 MOLLY PITCHER MANS THE GUN AT MONMOUTH

Molly Pitcher was a famous heroine of the American struggle against British tyranny.

A woman whose husband belonged to the artillery and who was then attached to a piece in the engagements stayed with her husband by the gun the whole time. While in the act of reaching a cartridge and having one of her feet as far before the other as she could step, a cannon shot from the enemy passed directly between her legs without doing any other damage than carrying away all the lower part of her petticoat. Looking at it with apparent unconcern she observed that it was lucky it did not pass a little higher for in that case it might have carried away something else, and continued her occupation.

Source: Joseph P. Martin, *A Narrative of Some of the Adventures, Dangers and Sufferings of a Revolutionary Soldier* (1830)

Molly Pitcher in action at the battle of Monmouth (1778) – her petticoat still intact (see number 157).

158 GOODBYE DOLLY

In the War of 1812 between Britain and the United States, British troops occupied Washington and burned the White House. President Madison was condemned by many Americans for bringing down a disastrous war on the country, and his wife, the famous Dolly Madison, bore the brunt of his unpopularity.

As the British troops occupied Washington, Dolly Madison fled from the White House, hoping to meet her husband 16 miles up the Potomac. En route she stopped off at what appeared to be a friendly farmhouse. She went upstairs while her attendants announced her presence to the housewife. However, news of Dolly's arrival so enraged the woman that she ran up the stairs and shouted, 'Mrs Madison, if that is you, come down and get out. Your husband has got mine out fighting and damn you you shan't stay in my house. So get out!'

Dolly went, her humiliation symbolizing the lowest state into which the American presidency had fallen. In the distance her home, the White House, was burning.

159 FOR SERVICES RENDERED

In wartime the British honour their nurses, the French their whores.

Two prostitutes were awarded the Croix de Guerre during the French wars in Indo-

China for making a 30-mile march in 48 hours through enemy territory to 'relieve' a distant outpost. They even survived an ambush on their return journey.

160 SERGEANT IN PETTICOATS

Annie Etheridge joined the Union army in 1861 as laundress to the 3rd Michigan Regiment. She later became officers' mess cook to Phil Kearney's division, and eventually earned three stripes on her black riding habit, drawing a sergeant's pay.

In May 1863 at the battle of Chancellorsville Annie rallied a Union artillery unit, shouting 'That's right, boys, now you've got good range. Keep it up and you'll soon silence those guns.'

The men could not have fought any better, one admitted, for any officer in the army than for 'the brave little sergeant in petticoats'.

161 CORDIAL RELATIONS

In 1741, during the siege of the French-held town of Pondicherry by the Maratha general Raghuji Bhonsla, the French governor Dumas sent a present of ten bottles of liqueurs to the enemy commander.

Raghuji Bhonsla was not to be bought so easily and he gave them to his wife. However, the lady was so impressed by the cordials, as she called them, that she insisted that her husband acquire more, whatever the cost. This placed Raghuji on the horns of a dilemma. He was most unwilling to reduce his demands on Pondicherry yet the Nantes cordials had given the French a lever to use against him. More cordials would have to be gained otherwise his wife might prove impossible to live with. The surest way of gaining the liqueurs was by friendly relations with the French, and so he agreed to begin negotiations. At least thirty of the cordials were used by the French as bargaining counters, serving as they did to sweeten Raghuji's temper. He soon saw that in attacking Pondicherry he had more to lose than to gain, and so he withdrew his troops and left the French in peace, laden with a suitable supply of liqueurs . . .

162 APPLES FOR ALL

There were some neutrals in the American Civil War.

At the battle of Wilson's Creek in 1861 both Confederate and Union armies suffered heavy casualties. When the fighting had died down a farmer's wife emerged from a cellar under her farmhouse, which was situated near one of the Confederate batteries, in time to find a group of soldiers scrumping apples from her trees. When one of their officers told the men to stop at once she told him that she did not mind as everyone had had a bad morning and they must be tired after the fight. In any case, she added, 'Are you Abe Lincoln's folk, or Jeff Davis's folk?' They told her they were Confederates. 'Don't much matter,' she concluded, 'there's plenty of apples to go round.'

163 COSY TOES

During the German siege of Leningrad (1941–44) conditions were so bad that a million people died of starvation or the cold. With public services at a minimum it became almost impossible to keep warm.

Nevertheless, the musicians and dancers of the Musical Comedy Theatre tried to continue their performances to help keep up morale. The theatre's most famous ballerina, Nina Peltser, faced the continual danger of frozen feet. Aware that her most valuable asset could be lost in a single bitter Leningrad night, she visited the chief of the Leningrad Bus Company with the appeal, 'For the people of Leningrad, save my feet.' The chief was a ballet fan and supplied her with a pair of enormously thick and heavy conductor's felt boots, each big enough for both of her feet at the same time. Nina wore the boots constantly, even climbing into them between acts at the chilly theatre. Her feet were saved and the people of Leningrad never forgot the beauty of her performances as the bombs and shells fell outside.

164 NURSING A GRIEVANCE

During the early months of the First World War atrocity stories were widely circulated to win the support of neutral opinion against the Germans.

In World War I, reports of outrageous behaviour by German troops against British nurses were widespread. Some, like the story of Edith Cavell, were true, while others, like that of Grace Hume (see number 164), were completely fabricated.

The *Dumfries Standard* of 16 September 1914 carried the story of a 23-year-old nurse, Grace Hume, who was serving in the hospital at Vilvorde in Belgium. The paper claimed that the Germans had attacked the hospital, ruthlessly killing the patients and mutilating Miss Hume by cutting off her right breast and leaving her to die. Apparently a scribbled note from the dying Grace found its way to her sister Kate. In it Grace revealed the horrors of the German attack including the taking away of her breast. Versions of the story swept the national press of Britain and France, under the headline 'Dumfries Girl Victim of Shocking Barbarity'. Another letter, this time from a Nurse Mullard, who had been with Grace when she died, gave further details of the atrocities at Vilvorde, revealing that the heroic young woman had shot a German soldier who was attacking one of her patients and had paid for this action when the Germans cut off her left breast as well.

On 18 September *The Times* led with a report on the enquiry into the Grace Hume affair, revealing that far from being mutilated and dying in Belgium, Grace Hume was in fact in Huddersfield, had never been to Belgium and had no knowledge of anyone named Mullard. In fact, Kate in Dumfries, Grace's 17-year-old sister, had invented the whole story. There was no happy ending: Kate was later tried and convicted of forgery.

165 DIVINE HEALING

As Lee surrendered at Appomattox, some of his wounded soldiers were receiving treatment at Petersburg from volunteer nurses.

A beautiful Southern girl on her daily mission of love and mercy asked a badly wounded soldier boy what she could do for him. He replied, 'I am greatly obliged to you but it is too late for you to do anything for me . . . I can't live long.'

'Will you not let me pray for you? I hope that I am one of the Lord's daughters and I would like to ask him to help you.'

Looking intently into her bewitching face he replied, 'Yes, pray at once, and ask the Lord to let me be his son-in-law.'

Source: General John B. Gordon, *Reminiscences of the Civil War* (1903)

166 GENERAL BARKSDALE HAS A VISITOR

In the early stages of the battle of Fredericksburg in 1863 the town came under heavy bombardment from Union batteries. Adjutant Robert Stiles of the Richmond Howitzers records an unusual incident he experienced at this time.

I saw walking quietly and unconcernedly along the same street I was on, and approaching General Barksdale's headquarters from the opposite direction, a lone woman. She apparently found the projectiles which were screaming and exploding in the air, and striking and crashing through the houses, and tearing up the streets, very interesting – stepping a little aside to inspect a great gaping hole one had just gouged in the sidewalk, then turning her head to note a fearful explosion in the air. I felt as if it really would not do to avoid a fire which was merely interesting . . . to a woman; so I stiffened my spinal column as well as I could and rode straight down the street towards headquarters and the self-possessed lady; and having reached the house I rode around back of it to put my horse where he would at least be safer than in front. As I returned on foot to the front, the lady had gone up on the porch and was knocking at the door. One of the staff came to hearken, and on seeing a lady, held up his hands, exclaiming in amazement, 'What on earth, Madam, are you doing here? Do go to some safe place, if you can find one!'

She smiled and said, with some little tartness, 'Young gentleman, you seem to be a little excited. Won't you please say to General Barksdale that a lady at the door wishes to see him?'

The young man assured her that General Barksdale could not possibly see her just now; but she persisted. 'General Barksdale is a southern gentleman, sir, and will not refuse to see a lady who has called upon him.'

Seeing that he could not otherwise get rid of her, the general did come to the door, but actually ringing his hands in excitement and annoyance.

'For God's sake, Madam, go and seek some place of safety. I'll send a member of my staff to help you find one.'

She again smiled gently – while old Barksdale fumed and almost swore – and then she said quietly, 'General Barksdale, my cow has just been killed in my stable by a shell. She is very fat, and I don't want the Yankees to get her. If you will send someone down to butcher her, you are welcome to the meat.'

Source: Adjutant Robert Stiles, *Four Years under Marse Robert* (1910)

167 CIVVY STREET

During the First World War, the 'white feather' campaign pursued by many women caused great bitterness to men.

On one occasion I had changed into my civvy clothes and was going to visit my parents. On the tram it is crowded with girls going to munition work. I hear giggling behind me and one says, 'Go on, give it to him.' A girl sitting behind me touches my shoulder and hands me a white feather. I get up and, taking out my pay book, smack it across her face and say, 'Certainly I'll take your feather back to the boys at Passchendaele. I'm in civvies because people think my uniform might be lousy, but if I had it on I wouldn't be half as lousy as you.'

Source: Private Ernest Atkins (1917)

168 THE CURTAIN FALLS

The end of the fighting in 1918 came as an anti-climax for many of the young British women who had worked as VADs – nurses working for the Voluntary Aid Detachment.

I was sitting alone in the driver's seat and at eleven o'clock these sirens went off and they went on and on. Then the men up at the Bull Ring started to blow the reveille, and we heard the bugles and we knew that it was all over.

I didn't feel a bit elated. The men who were shovelling coal were quite depressed and one of them said, 'So that's it, then. The bloody war's over.' It wasn't an exciting time at all . . . It wasn't very easy to feel jubilant when we seemed to be surrounded by rows and rows of white crosses and acres and acres of hospitals with beds full of wounded men. We just thought, 'Thank God it's over. Let's go home.'

Source: Lorna Neill, Motor Ambulance Convoy, remembering Etaples, 11 November 1918

169 MOTHER ROSS

The famous female warrior – Mother Ross – was wounded at the battle of Ramillies in 1706 and her sex was at last discovered.

I escaped unhurt though in the hottest of the battle till the French were entirely defeated; when an unlucky shell from a steeple on which before the battle they had planted some mortars and cannon which played all the time of the engagement struck the back part of my head and fractured my skull. I was carried to Meldre or Meldert, a small town in the quarter of Louvain, two leagues southeast from that university and five leagues northwest from Ramillies, upon a small brook which washes Tirlemont. I was here trepanned and great care taken of me but I did not recover in less than ten weeks. Though I suffered great torture by this wound yet the discovery it caused of my sex in the fixing of my dressing by which the surgeons saw my breasts and by the largeness of my nipples concluded that I had given suck was a greater grief to me. No sooner had

'*Miss Wheeler Defending Herself Against the Sepoys at Cawnpore*' – *just one of the many tales of female martial prowess to have emerged from the 1857 Indian Mutiny.*

they made this discovery but they acquainted Brigadier Preston that his pretty dragoon (so I was always called) was in fact a woman. He was very loath to believe it and did me the honour to say he had always looked upon me as the prettiest fellow and the best man he had. His incredulity made him send for my brother, whom he now imagined to be my husband; when he came the brigadier said to him, 'Dick, I am surprised at a piece of news these gentlemen tell me; they say your brother is in reality a woman.' 'Sir,' said he, 'since she is discovered I cannot deny it; she is my wife and I have had three children by her.' The news of this discovery spread far and near and, reaching among others, my Lord John Hay's ear, he came to see me as did all my former comrades. My Lord would neither ask me nor suffer anyone else any questions, but called for my husband though first for my comrade who had been long my bedfellow and examined him closely. The fellow protested as it was truth that he never knew I was a woman or even suspected it. 'It is well known,' continued he, 'that she had a child lain to her and took care of it.' My Lord then calling in my husband desired him to tell the meaning of my disguise. He gave him a full and satisfactory account of our first acquaintance, marriage and situation, with the manner of his having entered into the service and my resolution to go in search of him; adding the particulars of our meeting and my obstinate refusal of bedding with him. My Lord seemed very well entertained with my history and ordered that I should want for nothing and that my pay should be continued while under care.

Source: Daniel Defoe, *The Life and Adventures of Mrs. Christian Davies, commonly called Mother Ross* (18th century)

170 ON THE REBOUND

Wives in the Victorian Army lived an insecure life. Many married and re-married a number of times as their husbands succumbed to the many dangers of army life, notably disease.

In India burials followed death very rapidly, and in one instance at all events, a widow's re-engagement was equally hasty. She attended her husband's funeral the day after he died, and on the same day the Colour Sergeant of the company proposed to her. She burst into tears and the NCO, thinking perhaps that he had been too hasty, said he would come again in two or three days. 'Oh, it isn't that,' said the bereaved one, 'but on the way back from the cemetery I accepted the corporal of the firing party.'

Source: General Sir Neville Lyttelton, *Eighty Years Soldiering* (1927)

171 FOR BETTER FOR WORSE

In the past, soldiers' marriages were rarely secure. Death in battle, disease or even an overseas posting of long duration could divide a soldier's wife from her man, and she was often not slow in finding another.

Although in wartime the number of wives allowed to travel with the troops was limited to six per company, in peacetime no such limitation was imposed. The result was that the 54th Foot Regiment, en route to Egypt in 1800, was found on reaching Malta to be carrying too many wives, and General Abercrombie decreed that those women not required for hospital work should be sent back to England. Two ships were filled with the excess women but these fell foul of the French who, showing typical Gallic gallantry, returned the captive wives to the British base at Minorca. Here the stranded women fell in with an Irish regiment, then part of the garrison. But fate was playing her tricks. News reached Minorca that Abercrombie's expedition had suffered a disaster and that most of the men of the 54th were lost. The 'widows', seeking consolation, now married men of the Irish garrison and settled down for a new life. However, fate had not finished with them yet. The Irish soldiers were soon sent to Egypt themselves, where they discovered that Abercrombie's expedition had not foundered, nor had the 54th ceased to exist. Soon the erstwhile 'widows' found themselves with two husbands and a difficult choice ahead of them. In the end just one of the previous husbands took back his wife.

172 REWARD ENOUGH

Women faced many dangers following the British army in the Peninsular War.

One evening the 66th Regiment was advancing towards the river Adour when a cannon shot flattened a soldier's wife, leaving her apparently dead. Surgeon Henry, hurrying towards the victim, found to his surprise that she was only shocked and bruised. When he had assured her that she was not injured and would live, she was so delighted she decided to reward him, pulling out from one of her voluminous pockets a fowl, and half a yard of black pudding from the other. The surgeon tried to assure her that payment was not necessary – the story itself was reward enough.

173 A WOMAN'S WRATH

Alexander the Great was capable of magnanimity towards the conquered.

Now amongst the other miseries and calamities of the poor city of Thebes, there were certain Thracian soldiers, who having spoiled and defaced the house of Timoclea, a virtuous lady and of noble parentage, they divided her goods among them; and their captain having ravished her by force, asked her, whether she had anywhere hidden any gold or silver. The lady told him she had. Then leading him into her garden, she brought him unto a well: where she said she had cast all her jewels and precious things, when she heard the city was taken. The barbarous Thracian stooped to look into the well: she standing behind him, thrust him in, and then threw stones enough on him, and so killed him. The soldiers when they knew it, took and bound her, and so carried her unto Alexander. When Alexander saw her countenance, and marked her gait: he supposed her at the first to be some great lady, she followed the soldiers with such a majesty and boldness. Alexander then asking her what she was: she answered, that she was the sister of Theagenes, who fought a battle with king Philip before the city of Chaeronea, where being general he was slain, valiantly fighting for the defence of the liberty of Greece. Alexander wondering at her noble answer and courageous deed, commanded no man should touch her nor her children, and so freely let her go whether she would.

Source: Plutarch, *Life of Alexander* (1st century AD; trans. Sir Thomas North 1579)

174 A SOLDIER'S WIFE

The harsh climate of many foreign stations lowered the life expectancy of European troops posted abroad. Some married local women not for love but as a way of obtaining an unpaid servant. An example of this comes from Alexander Alexander, who was posted to India in the early 19th century.

I then began to look for a wife, or rather a nurse – love was out of the question. My affections were elsewhere all engrossed; but I must either take a wife or die.

My choice fell upon a Cingalese; she was of a clear bronze colour, smooth-skinned, healthy and very cleanly in her person and manner of cooking, which was her chief recommendation. Puncheh was of a good or bad temper just as she had any object to gain, for ever crying out poverty, and always in want of money or clothes. She imagined every person better off than herself; often pretended to be under the necessity to pawn her necklace and other ornaments, and boasted how much she was reduced since she came to live with me. Then she would pretend to be sick, and lie in bed for twenty-four hours together; and neither speak, nor take food or medicine, but lie and sulk. I was completely sick of her at times, for she would not leave me, neither would she stay.

When these sullen fits came on, I in vain endeavoured to sooth or flatter her; I had not money to satisfy her extravagance, my victuals remained uncooked, and the hut in confusion. There was no alternative but to follow the example of the others. I applied the strap of my great coat, which never failed to effect a cure, and all went on well for a time. She bore me a son, a fine little boy, who died young. Often have I sat and looked with delight upon his infant gambols. As is the custom here, he smoked cigars as soon as he could walk about. It was strange to see the infant puffing the smoke into the air, and forming circles with it, until weary, then running and placing his head upon his mother's bosom, to quench his thirst from her breast, before finishing his cigar.

Source: Alexander Alexander, *The Life of Alexander Alexander* (Ed. J. Howell 1830)

175 THE PRESIDENT PAYS A VISIT

The war between the states, like any civil war, set brother against brother, and broke old friendships. But President Lincoln looked further than most, beyond the bitterness of war itself to a period of reconstruction, when the country would be reunited and broken friendships renewed. Confederate general George Pickett, whose wife recounts the following incident, was famous for leading the disastrous charge up Cemetery Ridge at the battle of Gettysburg in 1863.

I was in Richmond when my Soldier fought the awful battle of Five Forks, April 1st 1865. Richmond surrendered, and the surging sea of fire swept the city. News of the fate of Five Forks had reached us, and the city was full of rumours that General Pickett was killed. I did not believe them. I knew he would come back; he had told me so. But they were very anxious hours. The day after the fire, there was a sharp rap at the door. The servants had all run away. The city was full of Yankees, and my environment had not taught me to love them. The fate of other cities had awakened my fears for Richmond. With my baby on my arm I opened the door and looked up at a tall, gaunt sad-faced man, in ill-fitting clothes. He asked, 'Is this George Pickett's home?'

With all the courage and dignity I could muster, I replied: 'Yes, and I am his wife and this is his baby.'

'I am Abraham Lincoln.'

'The President!' I gasped. I had never seen him, but I knew the intense love and reverence with which my Soldier always spoke of him. The stranger shook his head and replied; 'No; Abraham Lincoln, George's old friend.'

The baby pushed away from me and reached out his hands to Mr. Lincoln, who took him in his arms. As he did so an expression of rapt, almost divine tenderness and love lighted up the sad face. It was a look that I have never seen on any other face. The baby opened his mouth wide and insisted upon giving his father's friend a dewy, infantile kiss. As Mr. Lincoln gave the little one back to me, he said: 'Tell your father, the rascal, that I forgive him for the sake of your bright eyes.'

Source: LaSalle Corbell Pickett, 'My Soldier', in *McClure's Magazine* (1908)

176 DEFENDING THEIR INTERESTS

During the siege of Leith in 1560 the besiegers suffered at the hands of the 'trollops' of the town.

Unwilling to see the French garrison driven out, with the subsequent loss of business, these Scottish prostitutes inflicted as heavy losses on the English attackers as the French soldiers. They threw down stones and rocks, timber and heavy objects, as well as 'chimneys of burning fire'.

But the English were to have their revenge. When it was suggested that the women and children should be allowed to leave Leith because of a shortage of food, the English commander, the Duke of Norfolk, absolutely refused to allow it. Claiming that these women had done 'much woe' to his men, he said that they should stay within the city and help to eat up the town's fast-diminishing food supply.

177 A LADY TO COUNT ON

During the early period of the Hundred Years War the fate of Brittany became a major issue between England and France. The Earl of Montfort, who held the duchy, was captured by Charles of Blois, but his wife – the Countess – continued the struggle to free her husband with English help. She was besieged in the castle of Hennebon and sent for help to the king of England. Edward III ordered Sir Walter Manny to take troops to rescue her. In the event the lady proved more than capable of looking after herself.

For several days Lord Charles and his men had been encamped before the place, and were unable to make any effect upon it; the barriers resisted their utmost efforts. On every attack the Countess, who had clothed herself in armour, and was mounted on a war horse, galloped up and down the streets entreating and encouraging the inhabitants to make a brave resistance; at her orders the ladies and other women carried the paving stones of the streets to the ramparts, and threw them at the enemy, she also had pots of quicklime brought to her for the same purpose.

During the siege the Countess performed a very gallant action; she had ascended a high tower to see how her people behaved, and having observed that all the lords and others of the enemy had quitted their tents, and were come to the assault, she immediately descended, mounted her horse, and having collected 300 horsemen about her, sallied out of Hennebon by a gate which was not attacked, and, galloping up to the tents, cut them down and set them on fire without any loss to her own party. As soon as the French saw their camp on fire they left off assaulting the town, and hastened thither; but the Countess and her little company made good their escape to Brest.

Source: Sir John Froissart, *Chronicles* (Trans. T. Johnes 1839)

178 CHANGING HER MIND

During a battle in India in 1795 between the Nizam of Hyderabad and the Mahrattas, each employing European mercenary troops and commanders, the influence of one lady, the Nizam's new wife or 'Begum', was to have the most unexpected results. To please her Nizam Ali Khan had allowed her to travel with his army, under the protection of the dashing French mercenary François Raymond, to witness his expected victory over the Mahrattas. Unfortunately, not everything went to plan.

The Begum had insisted on being by her new husband's side, in his command post, but when the Mahrattas opened fire with their cannon, the lady was terrified and wanted to be taken away immediately. The sight of so many men killing or trying to kill each other was not at all what she had expected. When the Nizam Ali Khan ordered her to be taken home the Begum refused to go unless her husband accompanied her. The poor man tried to explain that he was the army commander and that his retreat would be a signal for his whole army to flee. Then, remembering his glamorous French cavalry officer, and how the Begum's eyes had lighted up at the mention of his name, he decided to order the Frenchman to bring his troops and completely surround the Begum so that she would feel safe. However, at that moment, Raymond was having his work cut out holding back the enemy left wing, commanded by his countryman Perron. When he received orders to come to the aid of the Begum he could hardly believe what he was reading. While he was considering an appropriate response, orders came direct from the Nizam's command post ordering his men to fall back. As Raymond's troops began to retreat in confusion, Perron struck and swept his enemy away in confused flight. Pursuing his enemy relentlessly, Perron eventually cornered the Nizam and the Begum in a tiny fortress, where they were quick to surrender. Only after he had promised to pay reparations in money and land was the Nizam allowed to return home with his foolish young wife.

179 AN UNWISE REFUGE

In the biblical struggle between the Syrians under Sisera and the Israelites led by Barak, Sisera is defeated and forced to flee the field on foot. He hopes to find sanctuary with Jael, wife of Heber the Kenite.

And the Lord discomfited Sisera and all his chariots and all his host, with the edge of the sword before Barak; so that Sisera lighted down off his chariot, and fled away on his feet.

But Barak pursued after the chariots, and after the host, unto Harosheth of the Gentiles: and all the host of Sisera fell upon the edge of the sword; and there was not a man left.

Howbeit Sisera fled away on his feet to the tent of Jael, the wife of Heber, the Kenite: for there was peace between Jabin the king of Hazor and the house of Heber the Kenite.

And Jael went out to meet Sisera, and said unto him, Turn in, my lord, turn in to me; fear not. And when he had turned in unto her into the tent she covered him with a mantle.

And he said unto her, Give me I pray thee, a little water to drink; for I am thirsty. And she opened a bottle of milk, and gave him drink and covered him.

Again he said unto her, Stand in the door of the tent, and it shall be when any man doth come and inquire of thee, and say, Is there any man here? that thou shalt say No.

Then Jael, Heber's wife, took a nail of the tent, and took an hammer in her hand, and went softly unto him, and smote the nail into his temples, and fastened it into the ground: for he was fast asleep and weary, so he died.

During the Second World War the Soviets often used women in combat units. This photograph is of Ludmilla Pavlichenko, a former history student turned sniper who was credited with killing 309 Germans.

And behold, as Barak pursued Sisera, Jael came out to meet him and said unto him, Come, and I will shew thee the man whom thou seekest.

Source: Judges 4:15–22

180 COLONEL MRS SUMMERS

Indian rulers of the 18th century employed European mercenary soldiers to stiffen their native levies. In time these men became almost the equivalent of the Italian Condottieri of the Renaissance period, and as such something of a law unto themselves.

At the time of his death in 1778, mercenary leader Walter Rheinhardt commanded a brigade for the Mogul emperor Ali Johur Shah Alam II. On his death his wife, an attractive but diminutive ex-dancing girl, whose father was an Arab trader and whose mother was a Sikh, and who was variously known as Mrs Summers or the Begum Somru, pleaded with the emperor to be allowed to take on her husband's mantle and command the brigade. Surprisingly permission was granted, but the Begum found that she had taken on a difficult job. The mercenary troops her husband had employed had an established lifestyle which they had no intention of surrendering on the orders of a woman. They had had a gentleman's agreement with her husband about such things as discipline and fighting; basically this consisted of a moratorium on such activities. Wining, dining and socializing, on the other hand, had been recognized as prerequisites for European soldiers in India. The little Begum found it impossible to order, cajole or persuade such men to do anything.

But a rescuer was at hand, in the shape of a British soldier named George Thomas who, in the next twenty years, was to become the most famous European mercenary in India. During the siege of Gokalgarh in 1788, in a dispute between two Mogul warlords, the Begum's brigade had been called out to protect the person of the emperor. One of the warlords, Ismael Beg, held the old emperor at that time and had summoned the Begum to his aid. The battle was being conducted in a desultory fashion, with neither side committing themselves wholeheartedly – at least until Ismael Beg's opponent learned that many of the imperial troops had been indulging themselves with opium and were quite unfit for action. Galvanized by such news he ordered a massed attack, which overran Ismael Beg's army and sent it reeling back in confusion. Watching all this from some distance was the Begum's brigade, adopting its normal approach of only joining in when it saw which side was winning. Deaf to the Begum's pleas to go to the aid of the emperor, the mercenaries looked on disinterestedly. Then, like a sudden storm, George Thomas appeared on the scene with a hundred volunteers and a single cannon. He soon animated the slothful brigade and, with the Begum personally leading the attack from her palanquin, screeching abuse at her enemies, the emperor's reluctant mercenaries charged into battle, routing the rebels and shaming Ismael Beg's troops, who were, with difficulty, being separated from their hookahs. It was a triumph for the Begum – for Colonel Mrs Summers – and she never looked back after that. And it was the first step for George Thomas on a ladder that was to earn him a fame that, in India at least, almost rivalled that of Clive and Wellesley.

The Begum died in 1836, immensely rich and fêted by the British, who believed her to be of pure Mogul blood and descended from the Prophet.

181 A NEW LUCRETIA

Behind every great man . . .

In 1675 the Turks, having made themselves masters of Sbarras, laid siege to Trembaula. The Polish nobility residing in the environs, who had taken refuge in the fortress, seeing the imminence of the danger, and despairing of succour, communicated their fears to the garrison and determined to deliver up the place. The wife of the governor, having heard the resolution they had taken, flew to the breach to inform her husband of what had passed. Chrosonowski instantly repaired to the council. 'It is yet uncertain,' said he, 'whether the enemy will master us: but this is certain, that, if you persist in your dastardly resolution, I will burn every one of you alive in this hall. The soldiers are at this moment at the doors, and the torches lighted, ready to execute my orders.' This firmness had the desired effect, and they at once abandoned their cowardly design. Chrosonowski himself showed signs of anxiety, when his wife, mistaking this disquietude for weakness, presented to him two poniards: 'If thou surrenderest,' said she to him fiercely, 'one of these shall be against thy life, and the other against my own.' Happily at that instant the advanced guard of the Polish army arrived in view, and compelled the Turks to raise the siege.

Source: Lord de Ros, *The Young Officer's Companion* (1868)

THE CRUELTY OF WAR

182 POSTSCRIPT

The Prussian army of Frederick the Great was noted for its severe discipline, and the king himself set the harshest standards of all.

During a campaign in Silesia Frederick ordered all fires and lights in the camp to be extinguished by a certain time. To enforce the order he decided to go the rounds himself. Passing the tent of a certain Captain Zietern he detected the glimmer of a candle and entering found the officer completing a letter to his wife. Unable to justify his disobedience the officer simply grovelled at Frederick's feet begging for mercy. Coldly Frederick told him to unseal his letter to his wife and add a postscript which Frederick would dictate. Zietern duly began to write down Frederick's words: 'Tomorrow I shall die on the scaffold.'

183 BASIL THE BULGAR SLAYER

The Byzantine Emperor Basil II pursued a relentless thirty-year war against the Bulgars until in 1014 he inflicted a decisive defeat on their forces. Although Tsar Samuel escaped Basil's clutches the bulk of his army fell into the hands of the Byzantines.

Faced with the problem of dealing with over 14,000 prisoners the Emperor came up with a solution that was both militarily effective and politically decisive. By character a severe rather than a cruel man, Basil decided to put an end to Bulgar resistance once and for all: he would burden the Bulgar state with a host of helpless men. The Emperor ordered that the prisoners should be divided into groups of a hundred and that ninety-nine of them should be blinded forthwith, while the fortunate hundredth was to lose just one eye so that he could lead the others home.

The grisly process completed, the columns of men set off through the mountains, each man holding on to the belt of the man in front. How many were lost on the return journey we do not know, but what is certain is that when the mutilated survivors reached the Bulgar capital, Tsar Samuel fell down in a fit at the sight and died within two days. So famous – or infamous – did Basil's action become that his name became synonymous with terror far beyond his own lands and he earned the sobriquet, 'The Bulgar Slayer'.

184 A STRANGE CATCH

In 1807 the French under Napoleon were campaigning in Germany, against the Prussians and Russians.

While fishing in a lake near Peterswald, East Prussia, a French soldier hooked something heavy and brought a corpse to the surface. Further investigation produced the naked bodies of thirty-seven French soldiers and one woman, all obviously killed in their sleep by hatchet blows. They had been reported missing and were thought to be prisoners of war. Peterswald was surrounded and searched; their uniforms and weapons were found. Thirty-eight villagers were shot and the village burned.

185 THE WORST OF FRIENDS

British soldiers in the Peninsular War often despised their Spanish allies for their ferocity and ungentlemanly ways, and preferred their fellow professionals in the French army.

After the battle of Salamanca men of the 34th Foot had to fight the Spaniards to retrieve the body of a French general, which their 'brave allies' had dug up and were mutilating. The British rescued the body and it was reburied with due military honours.

186 A FOREST OF CORPSES

Vlad Dracul was a Transylvanian prince who lived in the 15th century. He fought an almost genocidal war against the Turkish invaders of his country. Some of his methods, though not unusual by the standards of his day, served to earn him a reputation for bloodthirstiness and fuelled speculation that he was a vampire.

Vlad Dracul, aka Vlad the Impaler, happily overseeing the butchery of some twenty thousand Turkish prisoners (see number 186). In his figure of Count Dracula, Bram Stoker combined the aristocratic cruelty of Vlad with the quite separate Slavic legend of the vampire.

In 1462 the forces of the Ottoman Sultan Mehmed II were approaching the city of Tîrgoviste, capital of their enemy, Vlad Dracul, prince of Transylvania. At a distance of sixty miles from the city the Turkish advance guard encountered one of Vlad's most terrible scenes of horror – a forest of impaled bodies. Stretching for more than a mile in front of them and as far as the eye could see to left and right were thousands of sharpened stakes holding the bodies of upwards of twenty thousand Turkish prisoners, who had been left to die in agony there. The bodies were in various stages of decomposition and in the summer heat the stench was indescribable. On particularly tall stakes were impaled the bodies of Turkish nobles and generals, and in many places birds were nesting in the skulls and ribcages. As the Turks moved closer clouds of ravens and numerous other birds of prey rose up from the corpses they had been pecking. So appalling was the scene that even as ferocious a conqueror as Mehmed was deeply shocked. Calling off his invasion, he ordered a very deep ditch to be dug around his camp, to keep out the dreaded 'Vlad the Impaler', the original Dracula.

187 MILITARY DISCIPLINE

Military discipline in the British Army of the 18th century was notoriously strict. In this incident a British officer acts first and asks questions later.

The captain of the guard had received orders to hang any man he caught out of the line. A certain William Cross Taylor, a grenadier, having heard a great cry in the woods, went there and found another British soldier about to ravish a lady. Taylor set the woman free, while her attacker took to his heels. However, the captain, hearing a noise, found Taylor and, without listening to his explanation, hanged him from one of the trees without any more ado, to the extreme distress of the woman he had rescued. In a flood of tears she told the captain that the hanged soldier should have been rewarded for his kindness – but now it was too late.

188 THE 54TH MASSACHUSETTS AT FORT WAGNER

Many black soldiers fought in the Union Army during the American Civil War. They often faced extreme prejudice not only from white soldiers but from the white population of Northern cities. The most famous black regiment, the 54th Massachusetts, fought heroically during the siege of Fort Wagner in 1863 and suffered heavy casualties there.

One of the black soldiers wounded during the heroic assault on Fort Wagner was First Sergeant Robert J. Simmons, whose arm was shattered by a ball from a Confederate rifle. Fortunately Simmons, as he lay injured, could not have known that only three days before there had been a race riot in New York City during which a white mob had attacked his mother and sister and clubbed to death his seven-year-old nephew. Although Simmons managed to regain Union lines, his arm was too badly injured to be saved and had to be amputated. Simmons died several weeks later in a Charleston hospital, having given his life for the very same people who had murdered his nephew.

189 GERM WARFARE – 15th-CENTURY STYLE

In his epic struggle against the Turks in the 1460s, Vlad Dracul – Vlad the Impaler, prince of Transylvania - used the unusual weapon of disease.

He assembled all those in his lands who were affected by lethal infectious disease, such as leprosy, tuberculosis, plague and virulent syphilis, dressed them in Turkish fashion and infiltrated them into the Turkish camp. If a diseased man managed to infect a Turk, and the Turk died from the disease, he had only to return to Dracula's camp with the dead man's turban to earn a substantial reward.

190 FOLLOWING THE LEAD

The Albigensian Crusade against the Cathar heretics of southern France was noted for its savagery.

In 1209, the Crusader army led by Arnald-Amaury, the Archbishop of Narbonne, had no sooner camped outside the Cathar city of Béziers when the gates opened and a horde of Cathars from within the walls poured out and killed a number of knights. So infuriated were the servants and camp followers, who were in the process of pitching tents for their masters, that they seized tent poles, kitchen utensils and wooden staves and rushed into the attack. The defenders were unprepared, clearly not expecting an assault quite so soon. While the Crusaders sat outside watching in astonishment, their ragged servants stormed over the walls driving the defenders before them. Within a short space of time the city was taken.

But now that their blood was up it became impossible to control the ragged heroes. Convinced by the words of their preachers that the people of Béziers were servants of the devil they killed without mercy, entering the churches and slaughtering everyone who sought sanctuary there. When asked by his men how they could tell the heretic from the true Christian, the Archbishop replied, 'Kill them all; God will recognize his own.'

191 GRAND GUIGNOL

The battle of Pavia in 1525, between the French under King Francis I and the Imperial troops of Charles V, commanded by the renegade Frenchman, the Duke of Bourbon, was the decisive event of the early part of the struggle between the Valois and the Habsburgs. It also marked a watershed in military history, marking the end of the supremacy of the armoured knight in the face of cannon and firearms.

During the battle many heavily armoured French knights were toppled from their horses and met unpleasant ends at the hands of Spanish fusiliers. La Trémoille was particularly unfortunate. A Spaniard lifted the iron flaps guarding his thighs and thrust in an arquebus, blowing him to pieces inside his armour. After the battle it was found to be impossible to separate the old man's body from his armour and pieces had to be hooked out one at a time. Saint-Sevrin, the Master of the King's Horseguards, had the top of his head severed by a sword blow but remained fixed in his saddle, already dead, while his horse raced madly about the stricken field. His body was riddled with over a hundred shots but nothing could dislodge him. It seemed like a miracle and the superstitious Spanish soldiers crossed themselves in fear as the indestructible Frenchman rode by.

192 MURDER IN THE STREETS

Even in 1940 the RAF was a multi-national unit, with Czechs, Poles, Free French and Americans adding their skills to the British and Empire flyers. Unfortunately, the general public was unaware of this.

In 1940 a pilot was forced to bale out of a fighter plane over Wapping and came down by parachute, landing in the crowded streets. The man was injured and had apparently been partially blinded by a fire in his cockpit. He jabbered away in some foreign tongue to the people who gathered around him and they quickly reached the conclusion that he was a German. Infuriated by recent raids on civilian targets in London they beat him to death. Tragically, they learned too late that he was Polish, and a member of the RAF.

193 CANNON FODDER

After the British defeat at the battle of Bemis Heights in 1776, General John Burgoyne withdrew his troops to Saratoga. Here they sustained a siege by General Horatio Gates's American forces. The wife of the German general von Reidesel describes the fate of one British soldier.

Eleven cannon balls went through the house and we could plainly hear them rolling over our heads. One poor soldier whose leg they were about to amputate, having been laid upon a table for this purpose, had the other leg taken off by another cannon ball in the very middle of the operation. His comrades all ran off and when they again came back they found him in one corner of the room where he had rolled in his anguish, scarcely breathing.

Source: Baroness von Reidesel, *Letters and Memoirs Relating to the American War of Independence* (1827)

194 CENSORSHIP

During the Second Boer War (1899–1902) in South Africa, the British army suffered a disastrous defeat at the battle of Spion Kop in 1900. British generalship was poor and casualties heavy. Had the soldiers' sacrifices been in vain?

One British soldier had been shot in the face by a piece of shell which had carried away his left eye and the upper jaw with the corresponding part of the cheek, and had left a hideous cavity at the bottom of which his tongue was exposed. He had been lying hours on the hill. He was unable to speak and as soon as he arrived at the hospital he made signs that he wanted to write. Pencil and paper were given him and it was supposed he wished to ask for something but he merely wrote, 'Did we win?' None of the doctors had the heart to tell him the truth.

195 THE FORBIDDEN FEAST

During the siege of Leningrad in 1941–44, the Russian defenders were reduced to living at a level hardly better than animals. In the struggle to survive, normal human standards were suspended and the dreadful word 'cannibalism' began to be mentioned as a reality rather than just a possibility.

In November 1941 meat patties, made from minced human flesh, were on sale at the Leningrad Haymarket. Many bodies brought to the frozen cemeteries for burial were found to have the fleshy parts removed from upper arms, thighs and buttocks. Sometimes only the heads were left behind after the whole body had been taken. Soviet sources have been notably silent about this aspect of the siege.

196 FLYING BOMBS

In the difficult conditions the British encountered in fighting the Japanese in Burma, supplies had to be brought in by air and dropped by parachute.

On one unfortunate occasion during the airlift in Burma, two Indian soldiers, who got too near to the dropping area, were killed when they were hit on the head by tins of bully beef.

197 MAN MANAGEMENT

The Wars of the Roses, between the Houses of York and Lancaster, lasted for some thirty years from 1455 to 1485. They were marked by a savage rivalry among the leading families of England.

At the battle of Tewkesbury in 1471 Lord Wenlock, not having advanced to the support of the first line but remaining stationary contrary to the expectations of the Lancastrian commander, the Duke of Somerset, the latter in a rage rode up to him, reviled him and beat his brains out with an axe.

Source: Lord de Ros, *The Young Officer's Companion* (1868)

198 KICKING AGAINST THE PRICKS

Discipline in the British Army in the First World War was by far the most severe in that of any of the combatant states. Several offences, including desertion, cowardice and striking an officer, carried the death penalty. Over 330 British soldiers were officially executed in the period 1914–18 and the number was probably much higher. Sometimes the culprit had extenuating circumstances for his 'crime', but these were rarely sufficient to save him.

A private in a Highland regiment . . . was . . . executed on a charge of 'striking his super-

After the suppression of the Indian Mutiny, many rebel sepoys were executed by tying them across the mouth of a gun and firing it. This appears to have given much satisfaction to the onlookers (see number 200).

ior officer' . . . After his platoon commander had reprimanded him for having a dirty rifle and dirty boots he had stepped forward from the ranks and kicked the officer twice on the knee. In his defence the man said that he had served in the BEF since November 1914 (two years) without being granted any leave. His mother had died two months before and he was worried about his crippled sister who had nobody to look after her.

Source: Anthony Babington, *For the Sake of Example* (1983)

199 MUD

Conditions for fighting on the Western Front in the First World War were often very bad, particularly in the region of Flanders where the British troops were based. During the bombardment that preceded the third battle of Ypres in 1917 the drainage system broke down and the whole area was flooded. The heavy shells churned the ground up into liquid mud and thousands of men were drowned in it or dragged down into bomb craters. Without a firm foothold it was frequently impossible to rescue them.

A party of men passing up to the front line found a man bogged to above the knees. The united efforts of four of them with rifles beneath his armpits made not the slightest impression, and to dig, even if shovels had been available, was impossible, for there was no foothold. Duty compelled them to move on up to the line, and when two days later they passed down that way the wretched man was still there; but only his head was now visible and he was raving mad.

200 RED VENGEANCE

The hysterical reaction among Europeans in India to the Mutiny of 1857 – particularly to the massacre of women and children by the mutineers at Cawnpore – resulted in reprisals that sullied the reputation of British justice.

During the Indian Mutiny the penalty inflicted on the Mutineers was terrible indeed – blowing from a cannon. In the period immediately after the suppression of the revolt, an execution at Barrackpore was accompanied by a remarkable if tasteless demonstration by two British women. Dressed entirely in white, and riding white horses, they deliberately rode towards the place of execution at the moment the cannon was fired. The executed Sepoy's head flew thirty feet vertically in the air and landed between his feet, which were lashed to the wheels of the gun. His body burst open, spewing his entrails skywards, where vultures and falcons whirled in to grasp some of the pieces before they even hit the ground. His blood and flesh had showered the two lady spectators, leaving them to ride away triumphantly, coated from head to toe in red.

201 REMNANTS II

After the battle of the Miami river in 1813, the Indians, allies of the British, plundered the American camp with some bizarre and gruesome results.

On the evening of the second day after this event, I accompanied Major Muir of the

41st, in a ramble throughout the encampment of the Indians, distant a few hundred yards from our own. The spectacle there offered to our view was at once of the most ludicrous and revolting nature. In various directions were lying the trunks and boxes taken in the boats of General Clay's division, and the plunderers were busily occupied in displaying their riches, carefully examining each article, and attempting to divine its use. Several were decked out in the uniforms of the officers; and although embarrassed to the last degree in their movements, and dragging with difficulty the heavy military boots with which their legs were for the first time covered, strutted forth much to the admiration of their less fortunate comrades. Some were habited in plain clothes; others had their bodies clad in clean white shirts, contrasting in no ordinary manner with the swarthiness of their skins; all wore some article of decoration, and their tents were ornamented with saddles, bridles, rifles, daggers, swords and pistols, many of which were handsomely mounted and of curious workmanship. Such was the ridiculous part of the picture; but mingled with these, and in various directions, were to be seen the scalps of the slain drying in the sun, stained on the fleshy side with vermilion dyes, and dangling in the air as they hung suspended from the poles to which they were attached; together with hoops of various sizes on which were stretched portions of human skin, taken from various parts of the body, particularly the hand and foot, and yet covered with the nails of those parts; while, scattered along the ground, were visible the members from which they had been separated, and serving as a nutriment to the wolf-dogs by which the Indians were accompanied.

Source: Major John Richardson, *War of 1812* (1842)

202 THE FOUR CORPORALS

A cause célèbre in the French Army in 1915 was the case of the 'Four Corporals of Suippes', which became the subject of Stanley Kubrick's film, Paths of Glory.

In March of that year the 336th Regiment was fighting in trenches near Perthes-les-Hurlus in Champagne. Successive attacks had failed to pierce the German lines, and casualties had been high. Even the German barbed wire had not been cut by the French artillery. As exhaustion set in among the troops, General Reveilhac became furious and determined to break through at any cost. The 21st Company was ordered to try again, even though they had suffered heavy casualties in an abortive attack only two days before, and could clearly see the bodies of their comrades unburied in no-man's-land. When the whistle to attack was blown, only a few officers went over the top, leaving the enlisted men rooted in their trenches.

The few attackers fell back; it was clear that even if the poilus had joined them success would have been impossible. But Reveilhac did not see it this way; to him it had been mutiny. He ordered artillery commander, Colonel Bérube, to open fire on the French positions where, he claimed, only the officers were obeying orders and the men were in a state of mutiny. Bérube refused on the grounds that it would constitute murder and he would need written and signed orders from the general.

Thwarted for the time being, Reveilhac did not give up his intention to gain his revenge on the 21st Company. He ordered its commanders to send out into no-man's land a small patrol of four corporals and sixteen private soldiers to cut the German barbed wire by hand. In broad daylight it was a sentence of death. The men selected duly clambered out of the trenches but were pinned down by heavy fire. To advance at all was impossible and they stayed where they were until after dark, when they were able to fall back. Reveilhac now decided to use this failure to punish the 21st Company, and the members of the patrol were court martialled. However, the general decided that the lesson could be just as emphatic if only the four corporals were executed and the privates acquitted on the grounds that they had not received the orders. The four corporals were duly sentenced to be shot, but the injustice of the case was such that the whole regiment now came close to mutiny and had to be quelled by a cavalry detachment.

The executions were bungled as the firing squad was so unwilling to cooperate that two of the corporals were only wounded and had to be shot by the supervising officer. Ironically the whole operation was completed only minutes before a stay of execution signed by Reveilhac himself was brought to the parade ground. The case of the 'Four Corporals of Suippes' was not an isolated one and it did much to fuel hostility between the French soldier and his often incompetent commanders – hostility that was to break out in wholesale mutinies in 1917.

Conditions for Soviet POWs in German camps in the Second World War were well below the requirements of the Geneva Convention (see number 203).

203 IRON RATIONS

Operation Barbarossa in June 1941 had immense early success and a million and a half Soviet soldiers were taken prisoner. The POW camps set up by the Germans in the east were extremely primitive, in keeping with Hitler's view of the Russian people as 'untermenschen'.

Stray dogs were legion, among them were the most unbelievable mongrels; the only thing they were all alike in was that they were thin. The sheikh said one could have learned to play the harp on their ribs. That was no hindrance to the prisoners. They were hungry, so why not eat roast dog? They were always trying to catch the scary beasts. They would also beg us with gestures and *bow-wows* and *bang-bangs* to kill a dog for them. There it was, shoot it! And we almost always did; it was a bit of sport anyway and at the same time it delighted those human skeletons. Besides, those wild dogs were a regular pest.

When we brought one down, there followed a performance that could make a man puke. Yelling like mad, the Ruskies would fall on the animal and tear it in pieces with their bare hands, even before it was quite dead. The pluck [heart, liver and lungs] they would stuff their pockets with, like tobacco, whenever they got hold of any of that – it made a sort of iron ration. Then they would light a fire, skewer shreds of the dog's meat on sticks and roast it. There were always fights over the bigger bits. The burned flesh stank frightfully; there was almost no fat in it.

But they did not have roast dog every day. Behind the huts there was a big midden, a regular mountain of stinking waste, and if we did not look out they would poke about in it and eat such things as decaying onions, the mere sight of which was enough to turn you up. If one of us came near they would scatter like dung-flies. I once found one roasting dried pig's dung.

Source: Benno Zieser, *In Their Shallow Graves* (1956)

204 BEAUTY AND THE BEAST

The German people were quick to insist that responsibility for the Holocaust rested with a few members of the Gestapo and the SS. However, it was soon obvious to Allied commanders that many more Germans had known about and participated in the horrors of the extermination camps.

As the war drew to a close in Europe an American officer summoned a lovely young German hospital nurse to his office. He showed her horrific photographs of the inmates of the concentration camp at Buchenwald. She looked horrified at first but then her face relaxed and she said, 'But it's only the Jews.'

205 JERUSALEM THE GOLDEN

In 1099 the warriors of the First Crusade reached the walls of Jerusalem and laid siege to the city. Not until Godfrey of Bouillon erected a huge, movable siege tower did the crusaders gain a foothold on the battlements. What followed, however, was one of the most terrible massacres in

*history, with the Christians destroying all the infidels as well as their possessions in a fury of
senseless killing.*

At noon, the hour Christians traditionally associate with the crucifixion of Jesus Christ,
the movable siege tower of Godfrey of Bouillon was in position at the eastern end of the
northern walls of Jerusalem. At this point, east of Herod's Gate, the walls were some
fifty feet high and the tower overlooked them by some seven to ten feet. In the upper
section of the tower were Duke Godfrey himself, his brother Eustace of Boulogne and a
company of knights; while in the middle section were Ludolph and Engelbert of
Tournai. Amidst the noise of war – the crashing of great boulders on the timber of the
tower, the crackling sounds of burning thatch, the curious whirring and hissing noises as
the pots of Greek fire flew through the air like shooting stars, emitting fiery tails – the
grim Crusaders had little time for reflection. As they crouched low to the floor the siege
tower was moved to within a few feet of the walls of Jerusalem. The goal of their journey and all their suffering was now just feet away; and yet these last few steps would be
the hardest of any they had taken since they left France two years before. Crouching,
and occasionally crossing themselves or wiping the sweat from their eyes in the burning
heat, the Frankish knights could sometimes make out the faces of the Muslims on the
walls, faces contorted by fear and hatred, just as theirs must have seemed to their
enemies. They were hardened soldiers, bred to their trade, veterans of a dozen such
sieges and many battles in the field, and yet this was different. They had fought for their
faith at Dorylaeum and Antioch, but it had not been like this. The Muslims who manned
these walls seemed in their eyes less than human, mere servants of antichrist who were
fighting now to prevent true believers from inheriting the city of God. Here, in Jerusalem, there was to be salvation for all, forgiveness for sins, cures for physical and mental
ills, and in the Church of the Holy Sepulchre a tangible link with their Saviour Jesus
Christ. In the heart of the Crusaders there was a hatred more bitter than any they had
known before . . .

The Muslim defenders made a final effort to halt the inexorable progress of
Godfrey's tower. Ropes were thrown over the wooden leviathan and efforts made to
topple the whole structure while rocks and pots of naphtha crashed onto its walls of
hide. But the Crusaders managed to keep the tower intact by scything through the ropes
which threatened it, and by using vinegar to extinguish the flames of a combustible log
swung out against the tower by the defenders. In the smoke and confusion opposite
them the Franks began to detect a slackening resistance. At once, Ludolph and Engelbert
pushed out tree trunks from the middle section of the tower to the top of the walls and
clambered onto the battlements, soon followed by Duke Godfrey and his knights. With
a shout of triumph from the waiting troops below, a dozen ladders were placed against
the walls and selected soldiers now scaled them to join the Lorrainers on the battlements. It was hand-to-hand fighting now in which there was little skill. Men wrestled
with each other, sometimes toppling together from the battlements, sometimes gouging
at each other's eyes or tearing at throats. The press was too close for sword strokes and
handles were used like hammers. But the longer Duke Godfrey and his men held the
wall, the longer it gave the Lorrainers and Normans to use their ladders, while across the

perilous bridge of logs first tens and then hundreds of warriors flooded onto the walls. Soon, by sheer weight of numbers, the Muslims were pressed back and then turned to flee. At last Godfrey of Bouillon raised his banner above the walls as a signal that the city had been entered . . .

For the rest of the day and through the night the killing went on as the Crusaders hunted down every living thing: man, woman, child, even animal. Much of the slaughter was carried out by the pilgrims who had accompanied the Crusade and who now fell to their work with any weapon that came to hand: axes, clubs, and even sharpened staves. Almost intoxicated by the killing, they hacked at everything in their path. By torchlight the Muslims of Jerusalem were hunted down, some dying by fire, some by the sword and others, abandoning hope, chose to leap to their deaths from the highest buildings. To the disgust of the knights, the Christian Tafurs – followers of the Norman knight known as 'King Tafur' – even slaughtered the beautiful Arab stallions which were kept in the city. It was as if they could not rest until everything that had profaned the holy places had been slain. These terrible fanatics, who fought naked with faith alone as their shield, and ate the flesh of their victims, drove the Muslims before them in greater terror than even the armoured knights of Duke Godfrey or Raymond of St Gilles. As they moved through the city it was as if the Angel of Death had passed by leaving nothing living. Even the pots and jars of oil and grain were smashed, and sacks of corn ripped open like the bellies of their human victims.

In the Muslim holy places of the al-Aqsa Mosque and the Dome of the Rock, the bodies lay so thickly that they formed a veritable mound of flesh. Moreover, the Christians had hacked their victims horribly, slashing open their stomachs in search of the gold coins that, it was rumoured, the Muslims had swallowed to avoid losing them to the invaders. The result was that the blood was literally ankle-deep in some areas of the city, where drainage was impossible. For the Jews a different fate was reserved. They were herded together into their chief synagogue and burned alive in the great conflagration that followed the assault on that building. It was as bloodsoaked butchers that the Crusaders eventually went to the Church of the Holy Sepulchre to celebrate their victory and to thank God for his great goodness, while around them in the streets were the unburied corpses of the Muslim population of Jerusalem, the first martyrs in the *Jihad* that was to rage for the next two centuries.

Source: Geoffrey Regan, *Saladin and the Fall of Jerusalem* (1987)

206 THE HONOURS OF WAR

The fate of garrisons that refused to surrender to their assailants was generally cruel in the 17th century.

In the war between the Dutch and the Spaniards, the captain of Weerd Castle, having previously refused to surrender to Sir Francis de Vere, begged at last for a capitulation with the honours of war; Vere's answer was, that the honours of war were halters for a garrison that had dared to defend such a hovel against artillery. The commandant was killed first, and the remaining twenty six men, having been made to draw black and white straws, the twelve who drew the white straws were hanged, the thirteenth only escaping by consenting to act as executioner for the rest.

Source: J.L. Motley, *United Netherlands* (1860–68)

207 OLD FRIENDS

The warfare of the 16th and 17th centuries was fought with a ruthlessness not seen again in Europe until the Second World War. A characteristic incident of this sort is connected with the famous pacification of Guienne by Montluc in 1562.

Montluc had won Montsegur by storm, and its commander had been taken alive. The latter was a man of notorious valour, and in a previous campaign had been Montluc's fellow-soldier and friend. For that reason many interceded for his life, but Montluc decided to hang him, and simply on account of his valour. 'I well knew his courage,' he says, 'which made me hang him . . . I knew him to be valiant, but that made me the rather put him to death.'

Source: J.A. Farrer, *Military Manners and Customs* (1885)

A GALLERY OF ECCENTRICS

208 A NATURALIST ON THE BATTLEFIELD

Lieutenant Henry Charles Harford was an unusual British officer in Victorian times, being at least as interested in insects and birds as he was in battles and military honour. Although eccentric he was prodigiously brave. The following incident occurred at the battle of Victory Hill in the Zulu War of 1879.

The British redcoats were under a blistering fire from the Zulus when Lieutenant Harford suddenly let out a loud exclamation and fell to the ground, dropping his sword and revolver. 'Good God, Harford,' said his commanding officer, 'you are hit!' 'No, sir,' he replied, 'not hit but I have caught such a beauty.' And there, in full view of the enemy, Harford had captured a butterfly or moth, and was blowing its wings out, as unconscious of the bullets striking the rocks all round him as if he had been in his garden at home. He began explaining the importance of his find, and reeling off Latin names, until his exasperated commander ordered him to get as quick as he could to the right flanking company and hurry them up before the Zulus wiped out the entire command. Looking disappointed, Harford put his prize into a tin box and was off like a shot.

209 THE DANCING GENERAL

Prussian generals believed they were capable of doing anything required of them. Sometimes the results could be quite surprising.

The success of General Moltke in the wars against Austria in 1866 and France in 1870 was enough to convince many Germans that the army had all the answers. As a result, it became accepted that not only was the army officer the only person fit to judge matters of defence, but further that he was more versatile than members of other professions. In fact, the German officer was capable of any duty – including the direction of the Prussian royal theatres. The officer in question, General von Hülsen, even made the supreme sacrifice in the cause of entertaining his royal master: he dressed himself as a ballerina and performed a pas de ballet in the presence of the Kaiser. Unfortunately, his 56 years caught up with him and he suffered a fatal heart attack at the height of his performance.

210 HOME FROM HOME III

A British divisional intelligence officer on the Western Front in 1917 built a home from home.

I was told that he lived somewhere near me on the Ypres salient but I had never been able to find him. One evening I struck a patch of fresh vegetables and flowers in the midst of a desolate shelled area. I found him sitting up in bed, a shelf full of books beside him. He had built up for himself a life completely detached from the war and to this he returned every evening after his work. His pride was his vegetable garden. He was perhaps the only man in the salient who supplemented his rations with home-grown vegetables.

Source: Paul Maze, *A Frenchman in Khaki* (1934)

211 POMPO'

The latter part of Queen Victoria's reign saw a flourishing of eccentric admirals, some of whom even survived to lead Britain's navy into war with Germany in 1914. And if the Royal Navy ruled the waves during the 19th century then men like Admiral Sir Algernon Charles Fiesché Heneage ruled the Royal Navy.

Sir Algernon was the most pompous and preposterous admiral of them all, rightly earning his sobriquet Pompo'. Throughout his career at sea Pompo' set a pattern of eccentricity that he seemed to believe, and some observers ignorantly agreed, was the correct one for a British admiral.

Pompo' was fastidious to the point of obsession, refusing to allow his shirts to be washed at sea by seamen he considered to be some kind of lower life form. He took a stock of twenty dozen to sea, wore a clean one each day and sent them back by the first available ship to England to be washed. This took some organizing and may indicate that Pompo' had qualities that would have been eminently suitable had he been running a laundry. On one occasion, a ship's carpenter entered his cabin without being introduced by the appropriate officer and was immediately placed under arrest and clapped in irons for his pains. In fact the carpenter had gone there only to shut the stern ports to keep out a heavy sea. Pompo' refused to listen and kept the carpenter under arrest, so the ports remained open and the sea came in, soaking Pompo' and all his host of clothes. Even now Pompo' decreed that nobody less than a petty officer could be trusted to bale out his suite. For days afterwards there were clothes lines between the main and mizzen rigging loaded with his shirts. Aboard the other ships in Pompo's squadron there was puzzlement and consternation at the curious signals displayed aboard the flagship.

212 THE LEGENDARY GENERAL SUVOROV

The famous General Suvorov, who led Russian armies successfully against both the Turks and the soldiers of revolutionary France, was renowned for both his brutality and his eccentricities, which became legendary.

At the head of his army or on parade Suvorov could stand for half an hour on one leg, shouting or singing. In a salon, in the midst of a most numerous company, he was liable to jump onto a table or chair, or throw himself flat on the floor. On one occasion he gave vent to lamentations on the death of a turkey, which had been decapitated by a soldier. He kissed the defunct fowl and tried to set the head back on the neck.

213 THE SHOWMAN

It was said that every French soldier carried a marshal's baton in his knapsack. Yet as Captain La Salle shows in this episode it was necessary not only to do great things but to be seen – by Napoleon himself – to be doing them.

The review took place at the gates of Verona. Complete full-dress had been ordered, and the care taken to execute the order caused all the more surprise at the appearance of La Salle, who, usually the most brilliant as he was the handsomest officer in the army, turned up in an old pelisse, pantaloons, and dirty boots, and riding an Austrian hussar's horse, on which he had been careful to leave its saddle, its bridle, and even its rope-halter.

The surprise caused by this get-up was universal, and the commander-in-chief's first question was: 'What horse have you got there?' The answer was ready: 'A horse I have just taken from the enemy!' 'Where?' 'At Vicenza, general.' 'Are you mad?' 'I have just come thence; indeed I bring news from thence, which you will, perhaps, deem not unimportant.'

Bonaparte at once took him aside, talked with him for a quarter of an hour and came back to the group formed by Generals Berthier, Masséna and Augereau, and by the staff officers present, announcing that he had just promoted La Salle major. Here is the rest of the story.

La Salle, who was a man of many accomplishments and a highly susceptible temperament, found, amid all his enthusiasm for his military duties, some time at his disposal for love affairs. He was carrying on one of these with a Marchesa di Sale, one of the cleverest and most charming women of Upper Italy, who afterwards poisoned herself in despair at the loss of him. She lived at Vicenza, and the withdrawal of our army across the Adige had interrupted the *liaison*. The lovers had found means to correspond across the Austrian army, but correspondence was not enough for La Salle, and he resolved on one of those enterprises which success alone will justify. Selecting twenty-five men from the 1st Regiment of Cavalry – one of the best that we then had – he assembled them after nightfall and set out at once, without orders, without letting anyone know, without even a show of authority. He passed the enemy's vedettes unperceived, escaped his pickets, got through the hills to the rear of the Austrian army, and, marching without cockades and with cloaks unfolded, by mountain roads which he knew, reached Vicenza, where he knew there was no garrison, toward midnight, concealed his little troop, and hastened to the Marchesa.

About half past two in the morning, as he was preparing to be off, some pistol shots were heard. He mounted at once and rejoined his escort, learning then that he had been discovered and surrounded. The most direct roads were strongly guarded but he recollected one point which was likely still to be open and hastened thither. Thirty-six Hussars were occupying it; he charged them without knowing their numbers, overturned them, captured and brought away nine horses; then he returned by a different road which involved a long way round, avoided cantonments, spoke German, and passed himself off for an Austrian to the men of a picket through which he had to pass. Lastly, marching as fast as possible, he fell upon the rear of the last Austrian advanced post, sabred all that he could get at, and returned by daylight to San Martino D'Albaro, whence he had started without having lost a single man.

But the fleeting moments which La Salle had passed at Vicenza were not devoted solely to making love. The Marchesa, prepared for the interview, had procured some valuable information which she had passed on to him. Moreover, he had chosen for his prank the night preceding the commander-in-chief's review. On his return he had avoided showing himself, so as not to have to report to anyone, and then had waited for the moment when, by appearing before Bonaparte in the get-up and on the horse which I have mentioned, he might make the most he could of an attempt which would have either to be punished or rewarded.

Source: General Thièbault, *Memoirs* (Trans. A.J. Butler, 1896)

214 CHOOSE YOUR WEAPONS

During the Seven Years War British officers in the American colonies often found it difficult to accept the more relaxed attitudes towards discipline held by colonial officers.

On one occasion the American Israel Putnam was challenged to a duel by a British officer. Fearing that he stood no chance with traditional weapons against a professional soldier, the ingenious Putnam came up with a solution. As a test of courage he and his opponent would sit on kegs of gunpowder into which had been inserted burning fuses. As the fuse grew shorter and shorter the British officer became increasingly uncomfortable, particularly as Putnam simply sat on his keg smoking his pipe contentedly. The watching crowd began to scatter as the explosions became imminent and at last Putnam's opponent lost his nerve and ran for cover, acknowledging Putnam the winner. It was only then that Putnam revealed that the kegs contained not gunpowder but onions.

215 SIR ARTHUR ASTON

When Cromwell besieged Drogheda in 1649 the town was defended by Sir Arthur Aston, a Royalist commander of the Catholic faith, who had had a stormy military career in his youth.

In October 1644 he had been confined to his room for thrashing the mayor of Oxford, while a few months later he was thrown from his horse, while trying to impress a group of ladies with his horsemanship. Unfortunately he broke his leg, which turned gangrenous and had to be amputated. His Puritan enemies apparently claimed this as an act of divine vengeance for Aston's action in ordering one of his own men to have his hand sawn off in punishment for some minor indiscretion. Aston furiously maintained that he was as good on one leg as any man on two, but when Cromwell's men sacked Drogheda he had his brains knocked out by a soldier wielding his own wooden leg.

216 WRANGEL AND THE DIPLOMAT

During the war between Prussia and Denmark in 1864 the Prussian commander Field Marshal Count Frederick von Wrangel combined extreme old age with an eccentricity bordering on madness.

Wrangel had a particular aversion to diplomats. When the foreign office minister von Holstein was sent to visit the front lines during the Danish War, Wrangel was instructed to arrange a safe tour for him. Instead the cantankerous old man told his men to take von Holstein to a position where the Danes could shoot at him.

217 VAUBAN'S CARRIAGE

The great master of fortifications in Louis XIV's time, Sebastien le Prestre de Vauban, was a man with a bizarre sense of humour.

On one occasion in Paris, having dined well, Vauban emerged into the street at the precise moment that the funeral procession of a famous financier and tax-collector was passing by. Clearly somewhat the worse for drink Vauban jumped on top of the hearse and shouted 'Home'. It is said that many of the mourners, including the priest who was to conduct the funeral, could not contain their laughter.

218 A NERVE TONIC

The British retreat from Mons in 1914 stretched the nerves of officers and men to breaking point. There were occasions when chaos reigned, as in the town of Landrecies on 25 August.

A senior British officer apparently took leave of his senses and began firing his revolver down a street. When a nearby military policeman was asked why he did not try to stop him, he was told that as the officer was a full colonel and that the only things that were in danger down the street were horses, including the Colonel's own, he thought it was better to let the old gentleman get it out of his system.

219 RABID WOLFE

General James Wolfe was considered mad by some of his rivals in the army and this, of course, gave rise to George II's famous quip: 'Mad is he? Then I hope he will bite some of my other generals.'

At a banquet in his honour the night before sailing for America in 1759 Wolfe's behaviour shocked even his patron, William Pitt. At the end of the meal Wolfe leapt to his feet, drew his sword and rapped on the table to attract everyone's attention. He then began striding round the room, flourishing his sword, and boasting of what he was going to do to the French when he met them. Then, without another word, he marched abruptly out of the room and was gone.

Pitt was horrified. 'Good God!' he said. 'And I have entrusted the fate of the country to that man.' What Pitt did not know was that Wolfe was an abstainer and the wine he had had with the meal had gone straight to his head.

220 THE BOOK CRITIC

During the Mexican War of 1846 the American general Zacharay Taylor achieved a number of remarkable victories. However, Taylor was an essentially simple man who felt uneasy in the presence of learning. His views were shared by some of his senior officers including Colonel William Whistler.

As the American column was about to begin its march from Texas a young officer of pronounced literary tastes, Lieutenant Graham, dared to load one of the wagons with a case of books. Whistler was horrified and told the young man, 'We can't encumber our train with such rubbish as books.' Another young lieutenant, Charles Hoskins, standing nearby overheard the colonel's words and hastened to tell him that he had consigned a keg of whisky in the wagon without permission. 'Oh that's all right, Mr Hoskins,' said the affable colonel, 'Anything in reason. But Graham there wanted to carry a case of books!'

221 OLD KILLICK

Wolfe's successful attack on Quebec in 1759 required the British to navigate a difficult passage of the St Lawrence River. The local pilots felt it was an impossible task for such ships, but they had reckoned without old Killick.

Aboard the leading transport *Goodwill* one enraged pilot vowed that Canada would be the graveyard of the British army and the walls of Quebec would be hung with English scalps. Captain Killick, the ancient master of the *Goodwill*, angrily pushed the Canadian aside and went forward to the forecastle to guide the ship through himself. The pilot shouted that the ship would be wrecked for no French ship had ever attempted the Traverse without a pilot. 'Aye, aye, my dear,' old Killick shouted back, fiercely shaking his speaking-trumpet, 'but damn me, I'll convince you that an Englishman shall go where a Frenchman dare not show his nose.' Behind *Goodwill* the captain of the following ship was alarmed to learn that *Goodwill* had no pilot. 'Who's your master?' he yelled, and

The British capture of Quebec in 1759 was largely due to the navigational skills of 'Old Killick' (see number 221).

Killick replied, 'It's old Killick, and that's enough.'

Leaning over the bow the old man chatted gaily with the soldiers in the sounding boats, giving his orders easily while pointing out the different shades of blue and grey indicating the depth of the water, warning of submerged ridges marked by telltale ripples or the sudden disturbance of smoothly flowing waters. Eventually *Goodwill* emerged from the zig-zag Traverse into easier water. Killick put down his trumpet and handed the ship over to his mate. 'Well, damn me,' he snorted, 'damn me if there are not a thousand places in the Thames more hazardous than this. I'm ashamed that Englishmen should make such a rout about it.'

222 FOR THE FALLEN

John Nicholson was a legend in his lifetime among the Pathan tribesmen of the Punjab. He combined a fierceness in battle with a respect for his fallen foes. Ensign Wilberforce observed Nicholson in action during the Indian Mutiny in 1857.

All the Sepoys but one in charge of that gun died at their posts. The one who ran away was pursued by Nicholson, who overtook him, and rising in his stirrups dealt him such a mighty blow that he actually severed the man in two! It is curious to relate that Nicholson, who hated Sepoys with a hatred no words could describe, not only had them buried according to the rights of the Moslem religion, but actually raised a monument on the spot where the defenders of the gun fell, and placed an inscription on it, testifying his regard for their valour.

Source: Ensign R.G.Wilberforce, *An Unrecorded Chapter of the Indian Mutiny* (1894)

223 WOOD'S LARGESSE

At the end of the Ashanti Campaign of 1874 Colonel Evelyn Wood decided to reward the native chiefs Essevie and Andoo for their assistance.

I said to my friend Essevie, 'You have done very well throughout the four months you have served with me and I should like to send you a present from England. Have you any preference?' After a moment's reflection, he replied, 'Well I should like a tall black hat.' Before the ship sailed, however, he wrote me a letter asking if I would sell him one of my umbrellas. I sent him both as a present, but the request put another idea into my head, and on reaching London, having ordered him a 23/- Lincoln and Bennett black hat of the largest size ever made, I called on Mr Lawson, secretary of the Army and Navy Co-operative Society and said I wanted him to make the biggest umbrella ever seen, the sort of thing that would take two men to carry and with a different and startling colour between every rib. 'Do you know that will cost you over twenty guineas?' 'Possibly, but I should like to send a black man something of which he may be proud,' and he booked the order. A few days later he wrote to me that, as I probably knew, my idea was not original, and he had found in the city an umbrella such as I desired, which had been ordered by the Colonial Office for a chief on the Gambia River three years previously but the sable potentate, having misbehaved, the umbrella was still for sale, for as Mr Lawson quaintly wrote, 'there is no demand.' He bought it for me for twelve pounds and also made for me a ten guinea walking stick, ornamented with gold bosses and the hat, umbrella and stick, on receipt at Cape Coast Castle, were handed over to Essevie and Andoo in a full dress parade of the garrison, who marched past these somewhat unusual emblems of honour.

Twenty-two years afterwards, my eldest son took part in the next expedition to Ashanti and was sitting one day in the market place, when he saw a native carrying a handsome gold stick. He, like most Englishmen, thinking that money would buy any-thing that a black man possessed, called to him, 'Hey, sell me that stick.' The man replied, 'I cannot. It belongs to my chief.' 'Oh, he'll take five pounds for it.' 'No,' said the man, 'he would not take any money for it.' And somewhat unwillingly he handed it over for closer inspection. My son read on it, 'Presented to Chief Andoo by Colonel Evelyn Wood, 1874.' Essevie was dead but Andoo still lives, and was in Coomassie with the Expedition of 1895–6.

Source: Sir Evelyn Wood, *From Midshipman to Field Marshal* (1906)

224 BATHING ALFRESCO

During the Boer War one of the most eccentric of the British commanders was General Sir Charles Warren. He it was who believed in entertaining his troops by bathing in public.

On one particularly hot day he was taking a lengthy soak in his mackintosh bath outside his tent, with many of his soldiers crowded round, when General Buller and his staff rode up to discuss the military situation. Draping a towel round his waist Warren rose to greet the commander with the words, 'I feel I have done what I can for today to amuse the troops.'

225 STONEWALL JACKSON GETS A NEW UNIFORM

Thomas Jackson, as well as being the South's most able general, was also probably its most eccentric soldier. Caring little for worldly affairs, such as his personal appearance, he made no concessions to the notion of the Southern gentleman, something his compatriot Jeb Stuart hoped to put right with a gift.

From a long rest, after the dissipations of the past night, I was roused about noon by General Stuart, with orders to ride, upon some little matters of duty, to the camp of General Jackson. I was also honoured with the pleasing mission of presenting to old Stonewall, as a slight token of Stuart's high regard, a new and very 'stunning' uniform coat, which had just arrived from the hands of a Richmond tailor. The garment, neatly wrapped up, was borne on the pommel of his saddle by one of our couriers who accompanied me; and starting at once I reached the simple tent of our great general just in time for dinner. I found him in his old weather-stained coat, from which all the buttons had been clipped long since by the fair hands of patriotic ladies, and which, from exposure to sun and rain and powder-smoke, and by reason of many rents and patches, was in a very unseemly condition.

When I had despatched more important matters, I produced General Stuart's present,

Many stories are told of Thomas 'Stonewall' Jackson. His lack of concern for his personal appearance was just one of his eccentricities (see number 225). At the battle of Fredericksburg he came up with a plan for the whole army to strip naked and swim the Rappahannock River in a surprise night attack on the Union lines. Fortunately – as it was the middle of winter – Lee vetoed the plan. Even as a junior officer Jackson had behaved strangely: he once wore his greatcoat through a long, sweltering summer because he had received no orders to change it.

in all its magnificence of gilt buttons and sheeny facings and gold lace, and I was heartily amused at the modest confusion with which the hero of many battles regarded the fine uniform from many points of view, scarcely daring to touch it, and at the quiet way in which, at last, he folded it up carefully, and deposited it in his portmanteau, saying to me, 'Give Stuart my best thanks my dear Major – the coat is much too handsome for me, but I shall take the best care of it, and shall prize it highly as a souvenir. And now let us have some dinner.' But I protested energetically against this summary disposition of the matter of the coat. Deeming my mission indeed but half executed I remarked that Stuart would certainly ask me how the uniform fitted its owner and I should therefore take it as a personal favour if he would put it on.

To this he readily assented with a smile and having donned the garment he escorted me outside the tent to the table where dinner had been served in the open air. The whole of the staff were in a perfect ecstasy at their chief's brilliant appearance and the old Negro servant, who was bearing the roast turkey from the fire to the board, stopped in mid career with a most bewildered expression and gazed in wonderment at his master as if he had been transfigured before him. Meanwhile the rumour of the change ran like electricity through the neighbouring camps and the soldiers came running by hundreds to the spot, desirous of seeing their beloved Stonewall in his new attire. And the first wearing of a fresh robe by Louis XIV at whose morning toilet all the world was accustomed to assemble never created half the sensation at Versailles that was made in the woods of Virginia by the investment of Jackson in this new regulation uniform.

Source: Major Heros von Borcke, *Memoirs of the Confederate War for Independence* (1938)

226 MAJOR FOLEY DE ST GEORGES

During the Crimean War the bureaucratic methods of the Commissariat Department inflicted unbelievable suffering on the British soldiers. Sometimes, however, the department met its match.

Major Foley de St Georges, the rich and amusing aide-de-camp to General Rose, was not deterred when he encountered Commissariat red tape. He visited Balaclava to buy a few nails only to be told that they were issued by the ton. 'Very well,' he said, 'I'll take a ton,' and paid for them forthwith.

227 MRS NASH

Homosexuality was a not uncommon feature of life in the American cavalry in the Wild West.

One story tells of a 'Mrs Nash', who was company laundress in the 7th Cavalry. Mrs Nash was always heavily veiled and remained with the regiment, 'married' to a succession of husbands from the ranks of the 7th. As each successive husband was discharged, Mrs Nash bid them goodbye and 'married' the next man. In 1878, at Fort Meade, she was living with a corporal, but while he was on campaign she fell ill and died. When the garrison women were preparing her for burial they discovered the shocking truth that Mrs Nash was in fact a man. When the corporal returned he received such a barracking from his men that he retired to his room and blew his brains out.

228 JOHN BURNS GETS EVEN

Lee's invasion of Pennsylvania in 1863 brought on the crisis of the whole war. This is how one particular Northerner reacted.

One day during the campaign a little old man, named John Burns, came up to an advanced company of Union infantry, wearing a swallow tailed coat with smooth brass buttons, indicating that he was a veteran of the 1812 War. He had a rifle on his shoulder. The Union soldiers began to poke fun at him, thinking no civilian in his senses would show himself in such a place but finding that he had really come to fight, they offered him a cartridge box. Burns shook his head and slapped his pantaloon pocket saying, 'I can get my hands in here quicker than in a box. I am not used to them new fangled things.' When asked why he had come out there in the middle of a battle he replied that the rebels had either driven away or milked his cows and that he was going to be even with them. About this time the enemy began to advance. Bullets were flying thicker and faster and everyone hugged the ground, but not Burns; he got behind a tree and surprised everyone by being as calm and collected as any veteran there. John Burns stayed behind that tree until he was three times wounded – but when he saw Lee's Confederates in retreat, he knew that it had been worth it.

229 MARSHAL STOCKPOT

During the Peninsular War in Spain discipline was difficult to maintain in both French and Allied armies. Baron de Marbot relates the story of 'Marshal Stockpot'.

A French sergeant, wearied of the misery in which the army was living, resolved to decamp and live in comfort. To this end he persuaded about a hundred of the worst characters in the army, and going with them to the rear, took up his quarters in a vast convent deserted by the monks, but still full of furniture and provisions. He increased his store largely by carrying off everything in the neighbourhood that suited him; well-furnished spits and stew-pans were always at the fire, and each man helped himself as he would; and the leader received the expressive if contemptuous name of 'Marshal Stockpot'. The scoundrel had also carried off numbers of women; and being joined before long by the scum of the three armies attracted by the prospect of unrestrained debauchery he formed a band of some 300 English, French and Portuguese deserters, who lived as a happy family in one unbroken orgy. The brigandage had been going on for some months, when one day, a foraging detachment having gone off in pursuit of a flock as far as the convent which sheltered the so-called 'Marshal Stockpot', our soldiers were much surprised to see him coming to meet them at the head of his bandits, with orders to respect his grounds and restore the flock which they had just taken there. On the refusal of our officers to comply with this demand, he ordered his men to fire on the detachment. The greater part of the French deserters did not venture to fire on their compatriots and former comrades, but the English and Portuguese obeyed, and our people had several men killed or wounded. Not being in sufficient numbers to resist, they were compelled to retreat, accompanied by all the French deserters who came back with them to offer their submission. Masséna pardoned them on condition that they should march at the head of the three battalions who were told off to attack the convent. That den having been carried after a brief resistance, Masséna had 'Marshal Stockpot' shot, as well as the few French who had remained with him . . .

Source: Baron de Marbot, *Memoirs* (Trans. A.J. Butler 1893)

230 FACING THE BATTLESHIPS

Early in 1915 the German High Seas Fleet carried out a series of bombardments on seaside towns on the east coast. Much civilian damage was caused. This is how one Yorkshire family reacted.

The man told his wife to go next door and help their neighbour to pacify her children. She went to go out of the back door but he locked it and said, 'I am an Englishman and a Yorkshireman, and they'll not make us go the back way!' He then walked to the end of the terrace and stood defiantly facing the battleships.

231 DIGGING FOR GOLD

War brings great opportunities for undertakers, particularly when the battles are on his doorstep, as was the case with the battle of Gaines Mill in 1862 during the American Civil War.

In one of the outhouses a grim embalmer stood amid a family of nude corpses. He dealt with the bodies of high officers only for, said he, 'I used to be glad to prepare private soldiers. They were wuth a five dollar bill a-piece. But Lord bless you a colonel pays a hundred and a brigadier-general two hundred. There's lots of them now and I have cut the acquaintance of everything below a Major. I might,' he added, 'as a great favour do a captain, but he must pay a major's price. I insist upon that! Such windfalls don't come every day. There won't be another such killing for a century.'

Source: George Alfred Townshend, *Campaigns of a Non-combatant* (1866)

232 THE FISHERMAN

Soldiers in every war will try to avoid the dangers inherent in military service by feigning ill health or even insanity. The following story comes from the American Civil War.

One night there was a very heavy rain and in the morning before the other soldiers began to stir about camp, this fellow tied a string to his bayonet, took a position on the parapet, began fishing in a shallow pool and to all appearances became entirely unmindful of his surroundings. An hour passed, no one interrupted him and still he could be seen quietly but regularly lifting his gun with the string from the pool as though the gun were a fishing pole and that he had a bite. By and by the sun came up and while the other boys were going about camp, preparing for breakfast, the fisherman still kept up his weary stroke, lifting his supposed fishing tackle from the water almost as regularly as though it were done by a clock.

The surroundings and occasion were such that it was only necessary for a sane man to look once in order to be convinced that something was lacking about the 'headwork' of the machine that was fishing in the pool.

The boys all began to talk about the matter, many of them jesting in a manner wholly amusing. But no cessation in the regular stroke of the fisherman. Finally, the matter came to the notice of the captain, who at once proceeded to the interesting scene of operations. 'What are you doing there?' he demanded. No response. The gun and string were lifted with the same regularity as ever. 'Halt!' commanded the captain. Not a single movement of the fisherman. Up went the pretended fishing tackle again. 'Shoulder arms!' again commanded the captain, thinking that hearing an accustomed order might bring the soldier to his senses.

But the warrior's countenance was as rigid as ever and the fixed stare seemed riveted on the string which hung from the point of his bayonet and dropped carelessly down into the small pool before him.

The captain now concluded to report the matter to the colonel and started off on the errand at once. He suddenly met the colonel who had also beheld the fisherman and was coming to investigate. The captain then returned to the scene with the colonel when the same experience was repeated.

The colonel concluded to call the surgeon who came and examined the fisherman – as well as possible – while the incessant raising and lowering of his gun was being carried on – and recommended that the insane fisherman be given a discharge, which was accordingly written out and handed to the captain; but before it was given to the soldier the colonel asked, 'What are you fishing for?' No reply. 'Well, I guess you can give him the document,' continued the colonel and the captain handed it over to the fisherman, saying loudly, 'Here, take this!' 'That's what I was fishing for,' replied the fisherman as he threw down his gun, pocketed the discharge and immediately left camp, much to the amazement of the colonel, the captain and the surgeon, and very much to the amusement of all others who had heard the conversation.

Source: Colonel Thomas B. Van Buren, quoted in Washington Davis, *Campfire Chats of the Civil War* (1888)

233 SOME INTERESTING SENTENCES

A noted eccentric of the early 19th century was General Sir Robert Wilson. As a regimental commander some of his punishments were highly original.

On one occasion four of his men were sentenced to a thousand lashes. Wilson had this sentence commuted to a 'booting' from their comrades, 'who had been disgraced by the transaction'. When one of the cooks stole regimental liquor, namely Madeira and porter, he was sentenced to receive a strong emetic and to have the word 'Rogue' written on his left sleeve. While the cook was being violently sick, Wilson instructed the regimental band to play 'The Rogue's March'.

234 **A BERSERKER**

Napoleon's Grand Armée was officered by many men who would not have risen so highly in the other European armies of the ancien régime. But what many lacked in education and finesse they more than made up for in leadership qualities. There was even room for men like General Macard.

In some of these fights I had occasion to see Brigadier-General Macard, a soldier of fortune, who had been carried by the whirlwind of the Revolution, almost without intermediate steps, from the rank of trumpet major to that of general officer. He was an excellent specimen of the officers who were called into existence by chance and their own courage, and who, while they displayed a very genuine valour before the enemy, were none the less unfitted by their want of education for filling exalted positions. He was chiefly remarkable for a very quaint peculiarity. Of colossal size and extraordinary bravery, this singular person, when he was about to charge at the head of his troops, invariably cried, 'Look here! I'm going to dress like a beast.' Therewith he would take off his coat, his vest, his shirt, and keep on nothing except his plumed hat, his leather breeches, and his boots. Stripped thus to the waist, General Macard offered to view a chest almost as shaggy as a bear's, which gave him a very strange appearance. When he had once got on what he very truly called his beast's clothing, General Macard would dash forward recklessly, sabre in hand, and swearing like a pagan, on the enemy's cavalry. But he very seldom got at them, for at the sight of this giant, half-naked, hairy all over, and in such a strange outfit, who was hurling himself at them, and uttering the most fearful yells, his opponents would bolt on all sides, scarcely knowing if they had a man to deal with or some strange wild animal.

Source: Baron de Marbot, *Memoirs* (Trans. A.J. Butler 1893)

235 **COLD COMFORT**

The commander-in-chief of the British army in the second half of the 19th century, the Duke of Cambridge (a grandson of George III), was not renowned for his intelligence. He had served as a divisional commander in the Crimean War, from which period this story comes.

Accompanying the legendary Florence Nightingale around the wards of a hospital in the Crimea, Cambridge recognized a sergeant who had served in his division. The man had suffered appalling wounds and, addressing him by name, the Duke jokingly inquired, 'Aren't you dead yet?' After the Duke had left the man told Miss Nightingale, his eyes brimming with tears of affection, 'So feeling of 'is Royal 'ighness, wasn't it, ma'am? Bless 'is 'eart, 'e wondered why I ain't dead yet!'

236 **GODDAM!**

It is impossible to overestimate the contribution to the success of the American troops in the War of Independence of Baron Friedrich von Steuben, who had originally claimed to be a lieutenant-general in the Prussian Army of Frederick the Great, though in fact his rank had

Field Marshal His Royal Highness the Duke of Cambridge, cousin of Queen Victoria and commander-in-chief of the British Army from 1856 to 1895. A man renowned neither for his intelligence nor for his bedside manner (see number 235), he once complimented one of his generals by exclaiming 'Brains! I don't believe in brains. You haven't any, I know, sir.' When he made appointments and promotions, social position and seniority counted for everything and ability for nothing. He fiercely resisted all attempts to reform the army in the wake of the Crimean fiasco, and was eventually forced to resign at the age of 76.

been that of captain. He was no great military thinker but as a master of drill he had few peers. On his arrival in America his English was limited to a single word – Goddam – and he used a man named Ben Walker to do his cursing for him. He was enormously effective and won the admiration of the American soldiers by his curious capacity to curse them in any number of languages. The following was overheard as the baron left the scene of one of his confrontations with American recruits.

'Viens, Walker, mon ami, mon bon ami! Sacré! Goddam de gaucherie of dese badouts! Je ne puis plus. I can curse dem no more!'

237 GENTLE JULIUS

Some Renaissance popes were less renowned for their learning than for more worldly accomplishments.

Vasari, in his 'Life of Michel Angelo' has a good story, which is not only highly typical of this martial Christianity, but may be also taken to mark the furthest point of divergence reached by the Church in this respect from the standpoint of her earlier teaching.

Pope Julius II went one day to see a statue of himself which Michel Angelo was executing. The right hand of the statue was raised in a dignified attitude, and the artist consulted the Pope as to whether he should place a book in the left. 'Put a sword into it,' quoth Julius, 'for of letters I know but little.' This was the Pope of whom Bayle says that never man had a more warlike soul, and of whom, with some doubt, he repeats the anecdote of his having thrown into the Tiber the keys of St Peter, with a declaration that he would thenceforth use the sword of St Paul.

Source: J.A. Farrer, *Military Manners and Customs* (1885)

WAR AND WEATHER

238 DIVINE DISCONTENT

General Raimund Montecuccoli was ordinarily a pious Catholic, but circumstances during the Thirty Years War occasionally made it difficult to keep up standards.

Stopping one Friday at an inn the ravenous general ordered an omelette with a little ham sliced up in it. As the dish was presented to him there was a sudden, unheralded clap of thunder and a storm began. Without a second thought the general got up, went to the window and threw the ham omelette out into the rain. Looking up at the storm clouds overhead he commented, 'What a lot of fuss over a piece of ham.'

239 ARMIES IN THE SKY

In 1590, just before the battle of Ivry in France, a strange phenomenon was observed in the sky.

A French eyewitness named Davila described it in this way: 'The thunder and lightning, sometimes mingled with horrid darkness, added to their terrors; and such a flood of rain poured suddenly down, that the whole army was alarmed. A prodigious apparition, which appeared in the sky as soon as it had ceased to rain, increased the general dismay; for during the noise of the thunder, at which the boldest among them trembled, two great armies were distinctly seen in the air, that, after continuing some time engaged in fight, disappeared, covered with a thick cloud; so that the event [outcome] of the battle was not seen.'

240 RED STICKS

Tecumseh, war-chief of the Shawnee, is one of the most famous Indians of the 19th century. He fought against the Americans for much of his life, sometimes in alliance with the British forces in Canada. His influence on other Indian tribes - and the forces of nature – was most considerable, as this story shows.

He had been down south, to Florida, and succeeded in instigating the Seminoles in particular, and portions of other tribes, to unite in the war on the side of the British. He gave out that a vessel, on a certain day, commanded by red coats, would be off Florida, filled with guns and ammunition, and supplies for the use of the Indians. That no mistake might happen in regard to the day on which the Indians were to strike, he prepared bundles of sticks – each bundle containing the number of sticks corresponding to the number of days that were to intervene between the day on which they were received, and the day of the general onset. The Indian practice is, to throw away a stick every morning – they make, therefore, no mistake in the time. These sticks Tecumseh caused to be painted red. It was from this circumstance that, in the former Seminole war, these Indians were called 'Red Sticks' . . . On his return from Florida, he went among the

Creeks in Alabama, urging them to unite with the Seminoles. Arriving at Tuckha-batchee, a Creek town on the Tallapoosa river, he made his way to the lodge of the chief called the Big Warrior. He explained his object; delivered his war talk – presented a bundle of sticks – gave a piece of wampum and a war hatchet; all which the Big Warrior took. When Tecumseh, reading the spirit and intentions of the Big Warrior, looked him in the eye, and pointing his finger towards his face said, 'Your blood is white. You have taken my talk, and the sticks, and the wampum and the hatchet, but you do not mean to fight. I know the reason. You do not believe the Great Spirit has sent me. You shall know. I leave Tuckhabatchee directly – and shall go straight to Detroit. When I arrive there, I will stamp the ground with my foot, and shake down every house in Tuckhabatchee.' So saying, he turned, and left the Big Warrior in utter amazement, at both his manner and his threat, and pursued his journey. The Indians were struck no less with his conduct than was Big Warrior, and began to dread the arrival of the day when the calamity would befall them. They met often, and talked over this matter – and counted the days carefully, to know the day when Tecumseh would reach Detroit. The morning they had fixed upon as the day of his arrival at last came. A mighty rumble was heard – the Indians all ran out of their houses – the earth began to shake; when, at last, sure enough, every house in Tuckhabatchee was shaken down! The exclamation was in every mouth, 'Tecumseh has got to Detroit.' The effect was electric. The message he had delivered to the Big Warrior was believed, and many of the Indians took their rifles and prepared for war.

Source: Thomas L. McKenney and James Hall, *History of the Indian Tribes of North America* (1842)

241 SECOND THOUGHTS

More rumblings of divine discontent.

When Donald Balloch, the general of the last Lord of the Isles, made his great raid into Atholl in 1462, and carried off the Earl and Countess from the castle of Blair, he also desecrated the Chapel of St Bridget. On his way back to Islay with his prisoners, a terrible storm of thunder and lightning burst over his galleys, several of which, being heavily laden with spoil, foundered. This visitation so impressed Balloch that, besides at once returning to do penance at the plundered and partially burnt chapel, he also released the Earl and Countess of Atholl from their dungeon.

Source: Richard Bentley, 'Weather in War-Time' (From the *Quarterly Journal of the Royal Meteorological Society* 1907)

242 THE FLEET SURROUNDED BY CAVALRY

Probably unique in military annals . . .

It was the hardest winter for a century in Holland, and a force of cavalry and flying artil-lery, after their horses had been roughed, even got across the salt water of the Zuyder Zee on the stout ice in January 1795, and summoned the Dutch fleet lying helplessly

'Capture of a Dutch Fleet by Hussars of the French Republic, January 1795' (see number 242).

frozen up in the Texel to surrender. The commanders of the vessels were as astonished at the new form of warfare as they were helpless to resist it, and capitulated to the plucky French cavalrymen riding round the ships.

Source: Richard Bentley, 'Weather in War-Time' (From the *Quarterly Journal of the Royal Meteorological Society* 1907)

243 **HOT AIR**

The Russo-Japanese War of 1904–5 was fought partly on land, in Manchuria, and partly at sea.

During the battle of Yoshirei in Manchuria in 1904, Colonel Hume relates that a pause took place at 10.30 a.m., and he noticed a curious palpitating tremor, across the valley, which seemed to pulsate up and down the Japanese firing line. On looking more closely he found that each of the Japanese soldiers who composed it had pulled out his fan and was using it vigorously. 'It certainly was an appalling hot day,' said Hume.

244 **SMOKE SCREEN**

Lighting fires to create a smoke screen is an ancient ruse in military tactics.

On land the wind has been sometimes turned to special account, as at the passage of the Dvina by the Swedes in 1701. The Saxons being encamped on the south side of the river, use was made of the strong north wind by the firing of vast quantities of the straw, duly wetted, in the Swedish camp. A dense smoke swept across the river, completely hiding the movements of the Swedish troops. Under cover of this dense cloud several boats sneaked across loaded with still more straw, which was then ignited on the south bank and nearer the enemy, completely blinding and stifling them and rendering it impossible for them to know if the passage of the river was being attempted or not. When the Swedes at last did cross, the enemy's forces were so confused and blinded by the smoke that their guns were worked at random and with little effect. Indeed, as soon as their aim was discoverable the Swedes were able to avoid their fire in their advance.

Source: Richard Bentley, 'Weather in War-Time' (From the *Quarterly Journal of the Royal Meteorological Society* 1907)

245 KINGS ARE NEVER DROWNED

Less than a century after King Canute . . .

When William Rufus hurried across the Channel to suppress a rebellion in Normandy in 1099, the master of the ship he was embarking upon remonstrated, saying that the weather was 'too stormy to put out'. 'Hold thy peace, knave,' said William, 'kings are never drowned.'

246 THE ROAD TO HELL

Stonewall Jackson was famous for his decisive flank marches, which won a number of battles for his commander, Robert E. Lee. His troops believed there was nowhere he would not go to pursue the Yanks.

The night of January 1st, 1862, was the most dismal and trying night of this terrible expedition of Jackson's to Bath and Romney. It had been and was still snowing lightly and the small army was in uncomfortable bivouac. A squad of soldiers in the Stonewall Brigade had built a large fire and some of them were standing and some lying about it, wrapped up in their thin and inadequate blankets. The sharp wind was blowing over the hills and through the trees with a mocking whistle, whirling the sparks and smoke in eyes and over prostrate bodies.

A doleful defender, who had been lying down by the fire with one side to it just long enough to get warm and comfortable while the other got equally cold and uncomfortable, rose up and, having gathered his flapping blanket around him as well as possible, stood nodding and staggering over the flames. When the sparks set his blanket on fire it exhausted his patience and in the extremity of his disgust he exclaimed, 'I wish the Yankees were in hell!'

As he yawned this with a sleepy drawl, around the fire there went a drowsy growl of approbation. One individual, William Wintermeyer, however, lying behind a fallen tree, shivering with cold but determined not to get up, muttered, 'I don't. Old Jack would follow them there, with our brigade in front!'

Source: Major Henry Kyd Douglas, quoted in *History of the Corn Exchange Regiment* (1888)

247 THE 'RAIN MIRACLE' BATTLE

In AD 173, during the reign of the Emperor Marcus Aurelius, a Roman army was surrounded by a Germanic tribe, the Quadi, and, without water, was dying of thirst.

For when the Romans were in peril in the course of the battle, the divine power saved them in a most unexpected manner. The Quadi had surrounded them at a spot favourable for their purpose and the Romans were fighting valiantly with their shields locked together; then the barbarians ceased fighting, expecting to capture them easily as the result of the heat and their thirst. So they posted guards all about and hemmed them in to prevent their getting water anywhere; for the barbarians were far superior in numbers. The Romans, accordingly, were in a terrible plight from fatigue, wounds, the heat of the sun, and thirst, and so could neither fight nor retreat, but were standing in the line and at their several posts, scorched by the heat, when suddenly many clouds gathered and a mighty rain, not without divine interposition, burst upon them. Indeed there is a story to the effect that Arnuphis, an Egyptian magician, who was a companion of Marcus, had invoked by means of enchantments various deities and in particular Mercury, the god of the air, and by this means attracted the rain . . .

   When the rain poured down at first all turned their faces upwards and received the water in their mouths; then some held up their shields and some their helmets to catch it, and they not only took deep draughts themselves but also gave their horses to drink. And when the barbarians now charged upon them, they drank and fought at the same time; and some, becoming wounded, actually gulped down the blood that flowed into their helmets, along with the water. So intent, indeed, were most of them on drinking that they would have suffered severely from the enemy's onset, had not a violent hailstorm and numerous thunderbolts fallen upon the ranks of the foe. Thus in one and the same place one might have beheld water and fire descending from the sky simultaneously; so that while those on the one side were being drenched and drinking, the others were being consumed by fire and dying; and while the fire, on the one hand, did not touch the Romans, but, if it fell anywhere among them, was immediately extinguished, the shower on the other hand, did the barbarians no good, but, like so much oil, actually fed the flames that were consuming them . . .

Source: Dio Cassius, *Roman History* (2nd/3rd century; trans. E. Cary 1927)

248 BLOCKING THE PATH

The French Alpine campaign of 1800 against the Austrians was fought in the most difficult conditions.

Another interesting use of ice was that by the Austrians to close the Tonal Pass in the Tyrol in 1800 against the advancing French. Three rows of fortifications were built of solid ice cut into regular square blocks, as if granite, but even more difficult to scale. The attacking force cut its way under fire through the abattis and palisades, when it found itself confronted by these massive walls, too treacherous to scale and too substantial to

Napoleon received by monks on the Great St Bernard Pass during his Alpine campaign. On another Alpine pass his welcome was to be less warm . . . (see number 248).

batter down, and in consequence was obliged to retire and report that the position was impregnable. A week later a second attack was delivered by General Vandamme; but in the interval still more ice forts had been constructed and this assault also was repulsed.

Source: Richard Bentley, 'Weather in War-Time' (From the *Quarterly Journal of the Royal Meteorological Society* 1907)

249 A STORMY PASSAGE

For the superstitious people of the Middle Ages storms could indicate God's wrath.

In the spring of 1360, when Edward III was in France at the head of his army, he encountered, near Chartres, one of the most dreadful storms recorded in history. The violence of the wind, the size of the hailstones, the incessant glare of the lightning and the sight of hundreds slain around him, greatly worried the king. In a fit of remorse, he sprang from the saddle and stretching his arms towards the cathedral of Chartres, vowed to God and the Virgin that he would no longer object to proposals of peace, provided that they were compatible with his honour.

250 THE MIRAGE

Napoleon's Egyptian campaign of 1798 asked too much of the long-suffering French soldier.

The sufferings from heat of the French army under General Kléber when in the Egyptian desert in 1798 are historic. Even Lannes and Murat threw themselves on the sand and gave way to despair. In the midst of the general depression a sudden hope illuminated the countenances of the soldiers: a lake appeared in the arid wilderness, with villages and palm trees reflected in its glassy surface. The parched troops hurried towards the enchanting object, but it receded from their steps; in vain they pressed on with burning impatience, it fled again at their approach, and the fevered troops had the mortification of discovering that they had been deceived only by a mirage of the desert.

Source: Richard Bentley, 'Weather in War-Time' (From the *Quarterly Journal of the Royal Meteorological Society* 1907)

251 THE GENERAL'S NOT FOR BURNING

The person of George Washington took on a symbolic importance for both Americans and British during the War of Independence. As this example shows, some of the Hessian mercenaries fighting on the British side began to associate Washington with more than earthly abilities.

On a summer evening in 1776, British and German troops had erected a huge bonfire on which they had decided to burn in effigy four of the most prominent American leaders: John Witherspoon and Generals George Washington, Israel Putnam and Charles Lee. As the dummies were thrown into the flames a sudden storm broke over the proceedings and sent everyone scampering for cover. After the downpour had abated, the soldiers returned to their bonfire to find that three of the dummies had been thoroughly burned, but that of Washington had miraculously survived. The superstitious soldiers, particularly the Hessians, were greatly affected by this inexplicable event and began to wonder whether the American leader had powers beyond those of mortal men.

252 THE CALLOUS KNIGHTS

In 1379, when a fleet of English knights, under Sir John Arundel, on its way to Brittany, was overtaken by a storm, and the jettisoning of other things failed to relieve the vessels, sixty women, many of whom had been forced to embark, were thrown into the sea.

Source: J.A. Farrer, *Military Manners and Customs* (1885)

WAR GAMES

253 THE EUROPEAN CUP

Most British officers of the First World War came from a public-school background and were accustomed to a healthy diet of team games. On 1 July 1916, at the start of the battle of the Somme, Captain W.P. Nevill of the 8th East Surreys, planned to use the British love of football to inspire his men when the time came to attack.

Nevill, while home on leave, had purchased four footballs – one for each of his platoons – and in the difficult moments before the signal to attack was given, he offered a prize to the first of the platoons that managed to kick their ball into the German trenches. The idea was adopted enthusiastically by his men and one platoon even inscribed their ball with this message:

The Great European Cup
The Final
East Surreys v. Bavarians
Kick Off at Zero.

At zero hour Nevill's men punted their footballs into 'no-man's-land' and hurtled after them (one of these footballs is preserved in the National Army Museum). As to which of the platoons won the game we will never know, nor was Nevill ever able to present his prize to the winners: he was killed, shortly after kicking off for one of the platoons.

254 A STING IN THE TALE

As a young officer Frederick the Great was as willing as the next man to play pranks.

While still a cadet, Frederick and his young officers once took revenge on a regimental chaplain who had criticized them. They first smashed the windows of his bedroom and then threw into the room a hive full of angry bees. The Chaplain and his pregnant wife were driven from their bed, across the courtyard and eventually ended up in a dunghill.

255 CHILDREN'S GAMES

During the Thirty Years War German schoolchildren often acted out war games as a childish reaction to the real fighting raging around them. Sometimes the results were not all that might have been desired.

During one such children's game at a small Catholic town in the Upper Palatinate the Burgomaster selected his son to play the star part of the Imperialist commander Tilly. Armed with a drum the boy marched around the town recruiting his 'soldiers' until he had more than 150 loyal Catholic warriors. Only then did the Burgomaster and town councillors face the problem of who was to play the enemy commander, King Gustavus Adolphus of Sweden. At first none of the boys was willing to take on the part of a hated Protestant heretic. Eventually a victim was found by casting lots, and this unfortunate boy was also given a drum and orders to collect his 'army', by force if necessary. The Swedish king succeeded in raising just fifty soldiers. The following day – Shrove Tuesday of 1632 – the Swedes were ordered to march out of the town, with drums beating and fifes playing, and take up their position. They were followed by the Catholic force, urged on by an interested audience of priests and parents.
    As soon as the young Tilly arrived on the chosen battlefield the boy playing the here-

The real Gustavus Adolphus dies at Lützen (1632). His schoolboy counterpart in a German town was to find discretion the better part of valour (see number 255).

tic Swede charged at him with his followers and drove the Catholic army in headlong retreat. But the Catholic priests were shocked at the outcome and demanded that the battle should be renewed as soon as the good Catholic fighters had been rounded up. Second time around the result was just the same, only this time Gustavus captured Tilly, tied him up and took him to his father's house, demanding a ransom before he would hand him over.

The priests were furious and next day they visited the school from which all of the 'actors' had come and ordered all boys who had been in the Swedish army to be soundly whipped. What they had in mind for the youthful – and victorious – Gustavus Adolphus, we will never know, for that brave prince showed that discretion is the better part of valour and ran away to hide until the priests had stopped looking for him.

256 TALLY HO!

The French could never take seriously the British approach to war.

In 1939 some officers of the BEF imported packs of foxhounds and beagles from Britain in just the same way as Wellington's officers had done in the Peninsular War. They were furious when the French authorities refused to allow them to import any foxes or to make the countryside available for hunting.

257 WINTER MANOEUVRES

After the battle of Fredericksburg in December 1862, the Confederate forces under Lee encamped on the high ground across the Rappahannock river. They found ways of passing the time in the wintry conditions, including fully organized snowball fights.

These contests were unique in many respects. In the first place, here was sport, or friendly combat, on the grandest scale, perhaps known in modern times. Entire brigades lined up against each other for the fight. And not the masses of men only, but the organized military bodies – the line and field officers, the bands and the banners, the generals and their staffs, mounted as for genuine battle. There was the formal demand for the surrender of the camp, and the refusal, the charge, and the repulse; the front, the flank, the rear attack. And there was intense earnestness in the struggle – sometimes limbs were broken and eyes, at least temporarily, put out; and the camp equipment of the vanquished was regarded as fair booty to the victors. . . . One would have supposed these veteran troops had seen too much of the real thing to seek amusement at playing at battle.

Source: Robert Stiles, *Four Years under Marse Robert* (1910)

258 WAR ON STILTS

Military celebrations at Namur in the early years of the 18th century provided entertainment for Colonel de la Colonie, as he relates.

But the play with which they wound up these games was the best, to my mind, to wit, a battle on the Grande Place of the town, which was produced in an altogether original manner. It represented a quarrel which formerly existed between the inhabitants of a suburb (now included within the walls) and the town itself. In the old days, each side, wearing a distinguishing uniform, assembled in equal strength in the town square to wipe out their differences, and fought the matter out sword in hand, as gunpowder had not been invented at that time. The party which drove the other to the extreme limit of the square was held to have proved their point by victory, under the control of properly appointed judges, who decided also as to the fairness of the blows. To commemorate this battle the inhabitants divided into two parties, one of which called themselves Meylans, the other Aures. They were formed into companies and were drilled in the art of walking on stilts, on which they maintained as solid a footing as if they had been on their own feet. They had their officers and drummers, as in the regular army; the Aures carried blue and white plumes and cockades, and the Meylans red and white. Officers were not appointed by favour. To become a captain it was necessary to have vanquished five competitors; and it would be a good thing for many States if they enforced the same regulations, things would go much better then.

The height of the stilts was an advantage from the spectator's point of view, which might be described as a combat between two giant forces. At the time appointed each side arrives at opposite ends of the square, where they form up in battle array with the utmost precision. The most famous fighters are distributed along each line to receive the brunt of the shocks and the most violent attacks, and bodies in reserve are placed ready to support the points that may show signs of weakness in the course of the action. These two little armies then solemnly advance against one another with well-dressed and locked-up ranks, until they arrive near the place marked out for the combat, which is exactly half-way across the square. Then their march quickens its pace, the two sides close with each other, and the fight begins in earnest. The elbows of the combatants are their only weapons, for their hands are engaged with the butts of their stilts, which reach up to their thighs, so that their elbows stick out like the handles of a pot, and they work these with such rapidity to upset their adversaries that they look for all the world like teetotums. They are so adroit in this exercise that they can use one shoulder instantaneously after another, and can stoop and recover themselves in a second. The blows given and taken are extremely brisk, and one must have a robust constitution to enlist in these troops. When one side has been so often floored that it can no longer offer any resistance the other occupies the ground of the defeated ones, forms up in battle array and shouts victory. Then the vanquished retire stunned and confused and dare not put in an appearance during the subsequent fête held by the victors, which lasts about three days.

When the two sides advance to the attack their fathers, mothers, sisters, wives or near relatives follow in their steps and during the action encourage them in the liveliest tones. They keep close behind them to support them less they kill themselves by falling upon the stone pavement, to give them refreshment, to reanimate their strength and to help them remount their stilts and make them return to the charge. There is something very comic to see these women following up the giants, trembling, gesticulating and screaming all at the same time to animate their husbands or relations. The cry one hears oftenest is, 'A chasse! A chasse!' which is addressed to those who have been upset and is intended to encourage them to be quick in remounting their stilts to rejoin the fray.

I was a witness of this famous battle and so was the Elector with his whole court. It went on for nearly three hours before one side had made much impression on the other for as soon as the one gained any ground so soon did the other regain it, and the reserves which came to the rescue restored the balance of affairs over and over again. However, the combatants were upset with greater ease towards the end of the conflict than had been the case at the beginning. One saw these colossi one moment prostrated by their falls then reappearing as if Mother Earth had given new birth to them. This spectacle was altogether most amusing, the bullfights, contests between various animals and other shows of this kind were nothing in comparison; it was a true picture of war.

Source: Jean M. de la Colonie, *Chronicles of an Old Campaigner* (1904)

259 PARTISANS

To break the monotony on the long marches through the Near East, the Macedonian army of Alexander the Great invented their own entertainments.

Now Alexander having conquered all Asia on this side of the river Euphrates, he went to meet with Darius, that came down with ten hundred thousand fighting men. It was told him by some of his friends to make him laugh, that the slaves of his army had divided themselves into two parts, and had chosen them a General of either part, naming the one Alexander and the other Darius: and that at the first, they began to skirmish only with clods of earth, and afterwards with fists, but at the last, they grew so hot, that they came to plain stones and staves, so that they could not be parted. Alexander hearing that, would needs have the two Generals fight hand to hand one with the other: and Alexander himself did arm him that was called Alexander, and Philotas the other which was called Darius. All the army thereupon was gathered together to see this combat between them, as a thing that did betoken good or ill luck to some. The fight was sharp between them, but in the end, he that was called Alexander overcame the other: and Alexander to reward him, gave him twelve villages, with privileges to go after the Persian manner.

Source: Plutarch, *Life of Alexander* (1st century; trans. Sir Thomas North, 1579)

260 THE BIG MATCH

At Christmas 1914, an unofficial truce came into operation at many points on the Western Front. Between Frelinghien and Houplines the Saxons and the Seaforth Highlanders played football, as Leutnant Johannes Niemann observed.

I grabbed my binoculars and looking cautiously over the parapet saw the incredible sight of our soldiers exchanging cigarettes, schnapps and chocolate with the enemy. Later a Scottish soldier appeared with a football which seemed to come from nowhere and a few minutes later a real football match got underway. The Scots marked their goal mouth with their strange caps and we did the same with ours. It was far from easy to play on the frozen ground, but we continued, keeping rigorously to the rules, despite the fact that it only lasted an hour and that we had no referee. A great many of the passes went wide, but all the amateur footballers, although they must have been very tired, played with huge enthusiasm. Us Germans really roared when a gust of wind revealed that the Scots wore no drawers under their kilts – and hooted and whistled every time they caught an impudent glimpse of one posterior belonging to one of 'yesterday's enemies'. But after an hour's play, when our Commanding Officer heard about it, he sent an order that we must put a stop to it. A little later we drifted back to our trenches and the fraternization ended.

The game finished with a score of three goals to two in favour of Fritz against Tommy.

Source: Leutnant Johannes Niemann, quoted in Lyn Macdonald, *1914–1918 Voices and Images of the Great War* (1988)

261 GAME FOR ANYTHING

Many of the aristocratic British officers did not lose their love of shooting for the pot even while in the trenches in France in 1914–18. Although officially frowned upon, because of the waste of bullets incurred, the practice was widespread.

One officer, a noted marksman, achieved a 'double' in the space of thirty minutes, potting four pheasants and an incidental seven Germans as they passed across his sights. When night fell he retrieved the pheasants, presenting a brace to battalion headquarters and dining well on the remainder.

262 THE BATTLE THAT WASN'T

The English invasion of France in 1339, at the start of the Hundred Years War, was not without its lighter side.

On 22 October 1339, near La Capelle, the English king Edward III sent a herald to challenge the French king Philip VI to give battle on the following day. The French accepted the challenge and on 23 October both armies assembled in battle formation. However, no agreement had been made on who was to attack first. Clearly Edward III expected to be attacked, but as the French made no obvious move the situation entered a stalemate. Suddenly a great roar was heard from the English ranks, together with the clamouring sound of swords beating shields. To the waiting French it seemed that the English were beginning their attack. In panic one of the leading French commanders knighted several of his senior officers – a ceremony often preceding a battle – only to discover that the English had not moved. Apparently the 'halloas' that the French had heard had started up when two hares had been sighted in the midst of the English lines; and the English soldiers – being the sportsmen they were – had abandoned thoughts of battle and pursued the wretched quarry until both animals had been bagged. The new French knights became the butt of many a joke, earning notoriety as the Knights of the Order of the Hare. In the event no battle took place and both sides withdrew – the casualties being limited to two dead hares and some soldierly reputations.

263 DEPARTING WITH GRACE

When events in Europe in 1939 began to interfere with the cricket season everyone knew that things were getting serious.

On the day Hitler invaded Poland I was in the Long Room at Lords. There were balloons in the sky, but although a game was being played there were no spectators in the stands.

As I watched the ghostly movements of the players outside, a beautifully preserved member of Lords, with spats and rolled umbrella, stood near me inspecting the game. He did not speak, of course; we had not been introduced. Suddenly two workmen entered the Long Room in green aprons and carrying a bag. They took down the bust of W.G. Grace, put it in the bag and departed with it. The noble lord by my side watched their every move, then he turned to me. 'Did you see that, sir?' he asked. I told him I had seen. 'That means war,' he said.

Source: Neville Cardus, *A Cardus for all Seasons* (Ed. Margaret Hughes 1985)

264 BIG GAME, SMALL WAR

During the East African campaign of 1914–18, hostilities were not carried out as ruthlessly as they were in other parts of the world.

A sergeant was taking three German prisoners back to base when they came upon some eland. The sergeant halted his party and took several shots, but he missed badly. One of the prisoners, forgetting his position for a moment, asked if he could have a shot. The sergeant promptly gave him the rifle and the prisoner succeeded in bringing down an eland at a distance of about 500 yards – a feat which called forth much applause from the entire party. He gave the sergeant his rifle back and the party marched on.

Source: Gordon Makepeace, *Safari Sam* (1933)

THE NAVAL ANGLE

265 ADMIRAL SUFFREN SOLVES A PROBLEM

This anecdote conveys an impression of life in an 18th-century French man-of-war. The French admiral Suffren had an earthiness that many of his highborn officers found offensive. Nevertheless, Suffren was an able commander and kept his men happy.

Life was hard in the navies of the 18th century and the French admiral, Pierre André de Suffren, had his own ideas on how to make his men more comfortable. With the sailors forced through lack of space to sleep two to a bunk Suffren promoted the idea of campaign marriages, matching the sailors according to age and experience, pairing a veteran with a novice as the Greek generals used to do. Suffren insisted that his matrimonial bureau was a perfect arrangement and far better for his men than hasty visits to brothels when in port. He insisted that his married lads fought better in battle and were always cheerful.

For those who resisted the appeal of Suffren's matchmaking service, the admiral ordered three well-greased barrels full of tallow to be set up in a corner near the toilets. The barrels were to have holes of three diameters – 'Grandmother', 'Girl,' and 'Nymphet' – bored into them at varying heights. In Suffren's words his flagship could 'offer a ride on horseback in mid-ocean, and with no horse on board.'

266 ADMIRALS BY THE SCORE

During the wars between England and the Dutch Republic during the mid-17th century the Dutch suffered from a lack of central control.

Within the seventeen provinces there were five separate admiralties, including three from the province of Holland alone and two fiercely independent rivals from Zeeland and Frieseland. The rivalry was often so intense that when a senior officer was promoted by one admiralty the others responded by promoting their own officers until there were far more admirals than there were ships for them to command. The Dutch fleet that set sail in 1665 contained as many as 21 admirals, each vying for command. In order to give each admiral due prominence, the fleet was divided into seven squadrons, with each of these further divided into three parts. Confusion reigned after they encountered the English fleet, particularly when the flagship *Eendracht* blew up with a loss of the overall Dutch commander and 400 of his crew. The Dutch fleet then scattered, pursued back to harbour by the English.

The Dutch authorities were furious after the fiasco. The admiral of the Zeeland squadron was thrown into a river by the enraged populace of Brielle, while a number of other admirals were found guilty of cowardice and incompetence, and some were even shot.

267 PEPYS'S PASTY

The job of Secretary to the Navy was a trying one for Samuel Pepys, particularly during the summer of 1666.

At noon home to dinner, and then to the office, the yard being very full of women (I believe above 300) coming to get money for their husbands and friends that are prisoners in Holland; and they lay clamouring and swearing, and cursing us, that my wife and I were afeared to send a venison-pasty that we have for supper tonight to the cook's to be baked, for fear of their offering violence to it – but it went, and no hurt done. Then I took an opportunity, when they were all gone into the fore-yard, and slipped into the office and there busy all afternoon. But by and by the women got into the garden, and came all to my closet window and there tormented me; and I confess, their cries were so sad for money, and laying down the condition of their families and their husbands, and what they have done and suffered for the King, and how ill they are used by us, and how well the Dutch are used here by the allowance of their masters, and what their husbands are offered to serve the Dutch abroad, that I do most heartily pity them, and was ready to cry to hear them – but I cannot help them; however, when the rest was gone, I did call one to me, that I heard complain only and pity her husband, and did give her some money; and she blessed me and went away.

Source: Samuel Pepys, *Diaries* (1666)

268 TOO LITTLE, TOO LATE . . .

Even during the Second World War racial prejudice was present in the United States armed forces.

On 7 December 1941, 'Dorie' Miller, a black mess attendant, second class, was working on the battleship USS *West Virginia* at Pearl Harbor. When the Japanese bombers began their attack, Miller put down the pots and pans he was cleaning and ran up to the burning bridge to rescue the wounded captain and take him to safety. Miller then manned a machine gun, which had been abandoned by other sailors, and shot down four Japanese planes. Dorie's heroism was so great that under pressure from civil rights groups, he was decorated with the Navy Cross for gallantry and was promoted to mess attendant, first class, a year later. In 1944, Miller died when the aircraft carrier on which he was working as mess attendant was torpedoed by a Japanese submarine. Incredibly the story of Dorie Miller's heroism might have been lost right there but for the constant campaigning of civil rights groups, determined that the navy should acknowledge the courage of a black American. At last, in the 1970s, the US Navy named one of their destroyers after the mess attendant, who had shown in America's darkest moments what raw courage could achieve.

269 WOMEN AT SEA

During the Napoleonic Wars it was not unknown for Nelson's warships to carry women among the crew, some of whom even took part in his most famous battles. At the battle of the Nile in 1798, John Nichol on board the Goliath *recorded events between decks.*

My station was in the powder magazine with the gunner. As we entered the bay, we stripped to our trousers, opened our ports, cleared, and every ship we passed gave them a broadside and three cheers. Any information we got was from the boys and women who carried the powder. The women behaved as well as the men and got a present for their bravery from the Grand Signior. When the French admiral's ship blew up the *Goliath* got such a shake we thought the after part of her had blown up until the boys told us what it was. They brought us, every now and then, the cheering news of another French ship having struck and we answered the cheers on deck with heartfelt joy. In the heat of the action a shot came right into the magazine but did no harm as the carpenters plugged it up and stopped the water that was rushing in. I was much indebted to the gunner's wife who gave her husband and me a drink of wine every now and then which lessened our fatigue much. There were some women wounded and one woman, belonging to Leith, died of her wounds and was buried on a small island in the bay. One woman bore a son in the heat of the action. She belonged to Edinburgh.

Source: John Nicol, *Memoirs of John Nicol, Mariner* (1822)

270 THE CALL OF DUTY

Aboard Nelson's ships courage was taken for granted, as this episode from the battle of the Nile reveals.

A lad who had a match in his hand to fire his gun, in the act of applying it a shot took off his arm. It hung by a small piece of skin. The match fell to the deck. He looked to his arm and seeing what had happened seized the match in his left hand and fired the gun before he went off to the cockpit to have it dressed.

Source: John Nicol, *Memoirs of John Nicol, Mariner* (1822)

271 A HUNDRED FATHERS

In an engagement off the French coast in 1812 between the Swallow *and the* Reynard *a tragic incident tested the resourcefulness of the British sailors. It is pleasing to note how effectively they rose to the challenge.*

In this gallant and sanguinary action there was a seaman named Phelan aboard the *Swallow* who had his wife on board; she was stationed to assist the surgeon in the care of the wounded.

From the close manner in which the *Swallow* engaged the enemy, yard-arm and yard-arm, the wounded as may be expected were brought below very fast; amongst the rest, a messmate of her husband's, who had received a musket ball through his side. Her exertions were being used to console the poor fellow, who was in great agonies and nearly breathing his last, when by some chance she heard her husband was wounded on deck; her anxiety and already overpowered feelings could not one moment be restrained; she rushed instantly upon deck and received the wounded tar in her arms; he faintly raised his head to kiss her; she burst into a flood of tears, and told him to take courage, as 'all would yet be well'; but had scarcely pronounced the last syllable when a shot took her head off. The poor fellow, who was closely wrapt in her arms, opened his eyes once more and then closed them forever. What rendered the circumstance more affecting was, the poor woman had only three weeks before given birth to a fine boy, who was thus in a moment deprived of both father and mother. As soon as the action was over, and nature again began to take its course, the feelings of the sailors, who wanted no unnecessary incitement to stimulate them, were all interested for poor Tommy, for so he was called. Many said, and all feared, he must die; they all agreed that he should have a hundred fathers, but what could be the substitute for a nurse and a mother? However, the mind of humanity soon discovered there was a Maltese goat on board, the property of the officers, which gave an abundance of milk and, as there was no better expedient, she was resorted to for the purpose of suckling the child, who, singular to say, is thriving and getting one of the finest little fellows in the world; and so tractable is his nurse, that she lies down when little Tommy is brought to be suckled by her. Phelan and his wife were sewed up in one hammock and it is needless to say were buried in one grave.

Source: Edward Giffard, *Deeds of Naval Daring* (1910)

272 TURNING A BLIND EYE

At the battle of Copenhagen in 1801, Nelson in the Elephant *led the attack on the Danish fleet, though he was acting under orders from Admiral Sir Hyde Parker, a rather cautious commander. This first-hand account records Nelson's famous disobedience.*

Lord Nelson was at this time, as he had been during the whole action, walking the starboard side of the quarterdeck, sometimes much animated and at others heroically fine in his observations. A shot through the mainmast knocked a few splinters about us. He observed to me with a smile, 'It is warm work and this day may be the last to any of us at a moment.' And then, stopping short at the gangway, he used an expression never to be erased from my memory and said with emotion, 'But mark you, I would not be else-where for thousands.' When the signal number 39 was made the signal lieutenant reported it to him. He continued his walk and did not appear to take notice of it. The lieutenant, meeting his lordship at the next turn, asked whether he should repeat it. Lord Nelson answered, 'No, acknowledge it.' On the officer returning to the poop his lord-ship called after him, 'Is number 16 (for close action) still hoisted?' The lieutenant answering in the affirmative, Lord Nelson said, 'Mind you keep it so.' He now walked the deck considerably agitated which was always known by his moving the stump of his right arm. After a turn or two he said to me in a quick manner, 'Do you know what's shown on board of the commander in chief, number 39.' On asking him what he meant, he answered, 'Why, to leave off action.' 'Leave off action!' he repeated, and then added with a shrug, 'Now damn me if I do.' He also observed, I believe, to Captain Foley, 'You know, Foley, I have only one eye. I have a right to be blind sometimes.' And then with an archness peculiar to his character, putting the glass to his blind eye, he exclaimed, 'I really do not see the signal.'

Source: Lieutenant-Colonel William Stewart, quoted in *Dispatches and Letters of Vice-Admiral Lord Viscount Nelson* (Ed. Sir Nicholas Harris 1845)

273 WASTE

Each of the British ships at Copenhagen carried a detachment of soldiers. During the naval battle there was nothing for these men to do and they were generally kept below decks for safety. On board the Bellona, *however, the army commander showed an idiotic and reckless lack of concern for his men.*

The commanding officer asked where his men should be stationed. He was told that they could be of no use, that they were not near enough for musketry and were not wanted at the guns. They had therefore better go below. This, he said, was impossible. It would be a disgrace that could never be wiped away. They were, therefore, drawn up upon the gangway to satisfy this cruel point of honour and there without the possibility of annoy-ing the enemy they were mown down.

Source: Robert Southey, *Life of Nelson* (1813)

274 ENGLAND CONFIDES

Nelson's famous – indeed timeless – signal at the battle of Trafalgar in 1805 might have read rather differently if his lordship had enjoyed more time.

His Lordship came to me on the poop and said, 'I wish to say to the fleet ENGLAND CONFIDES THAT EVERY MAN WILL DO HIS DUTY.' And he added, 'You must be quick, for I have one more to make which is for Close Action.' I replied, 'If your Lordship will permit me to substitute *Expects* for *Confides* the signal will soon be com-pleted because the word *expects* is in the vocabulary and *confides* must be spelt.' His Lord-ship replied in haste and with seeming satisfaction, 'That will do, Pascoe, make it directly!' Nelson was greatly pleased by the signal but it received a mixed reception among the fleet.

Source: Lt. John Pascoe, quoted in *Dispatches and Letters of Vice-Admiral Lord Viscount Nelson* (Ed. Sir Nicholas Harris 1845)

The royal barge conveying the body of Lord Nelson from Greenwich to Whitehall Stairs on 8 January 1806. What state the corpse was in at this stage history does not record, the great admiral's body having had an adventurous – and protracted – journey home in a cask of brandy (see number 275).

275 NELSON PRESERVED

After the battle of Trafalgar Nelson's body was placed in a cask of brandy prior to returning to England for burial. However, this entailed more difficulty than might have been imagined.

In the evening after this melancholy task was accomplished, the gale came up with violence, and continued that night and the succeeding day without any abatement. During this boisterous weather Lord Nelson's body remained under the charge of a sentinel on the middle deck. The cask was placed on its end, having a closed aperture at its top and another below; the object of which was, that as a frequent renewal of the spirit was thought necessary, the old could thus be drawn off below and a fresh quantity introduced above, without moving the cask or occasioning the least agitation of the body.

On the 24th there was a disengagement of air from the body to such a degree that the sentinel became alarmed on seeing the head of the cask raised.

The spirit was drawn off at once and the cask filled again, before the arrival of the *Victory* at Gibraltar on October 28th, where spirit of wine was procured; and the cask, showing a deficit produced by the body's absorbing a considerable quantity of the brandy, was then filled up with it.

Source: Sir William Beatty, *Authentic Narrative of the Death of Lord Nelson* (1807)

276 THE SECOND BATTLE OF BEACHY HEAD

Admiralty efforts to counter the German U-boat menace in the First World War were particularly inept, which made their refusal to adopt the convoy system even more difficult to understand. Conventional attempts to find and destroy the enemy were clearly failing by 1916.

Admiralty efforts had been enormous but totally misplaced. Their philosophy had been that they must destroy U-boats faster than Germany could build them, rather than that they should prevent U-boats sinking British merchant ships. In the vastness of the seas it was infinitely more difficult to find a single U-boat than it was to defend a merchant ship. This is illustrated by the farcical 'Second battle of Beachy Head' fought over a week in September 1916. Three U-boats, operating between Beachy Head and the Eddystone, an area commanded by the naval bases of Portsmouth, Portland and Plymouth, were hunted by 49 destroyers, 48 torpedo boats, 7 'Q' ships and 468 armed auxiliaries. Yet in seven days, the U-boats sank 30 merchant ships and escaped unscathed.

Source: Geoffrey Regan, *Someone Had Blundered* (1987)

277 A CLOSER LOOK

British naval gunnery proved disappointing in both world wars.

During the final battle in 1941 between the German battleship *Bismarck* and the British battleships *Rodney* and *King George V*, 719 heavy shells were fired by the British guns, many at close range, but the number of hits was derisory. Admiral Tovey was so exasperated that he told his fleet gunnery officer that he would have a better chance if he threw his binoculars at the *Bismarck*.

278 THE REVENGE

The last fight of the Revenge, *commanded by Sir Richard Grenville, against a whole fleet of Spanish warships in 1591, is one of the greatest epics in British maritime history. Grenville's cousin, Sir Walter Raleigh, immortalized both ship and admiral with his account of Grenville's determination never to surrender.*

All the powder of the *Revenge* to the last barrel was now spent, all her pikes broken, forty of her best men slain, and the most part of the rest hurt. In the beginning of the fight she had but one hundred free from sickness, and four score and ten sick, laid in hold upon the ballast. A small troop to man such a ship, and a weak garrison to resist so mighty an army. By those hundred all was sustained, the volleys, boardings, and enterings of fifteen ships of war, besides those which beat her at large. On the contrary, the Spanish were always supplied with soldiers brought from every squadron: all manner of arms and powder at will. Unto ours there remained no comfort at all, no hope, no supply of either ships, men, or weapons; the masts all beaten overboard, all her tackle cut asunder, her upper work altogether razed, and in effect evened she was with the water, but the very foundation or bottom of a ship, nothing being left overhead for fight or defence. Sir Richard, finding himself in this distress, and unable any longer to make resistance, commanded the Master gunner, whom he knew to be a most resolute man, to split and sink the ship; that thereby nothing might remain of glory or victory to the Spaniards, seeing in so many hours fight, and with so great a navy they were not able to take her, and persuaded the company, or as many as he could induce, to yield themselves unto God, and to the mercy of none else; but as they had like valiant resolute men repulsed so many enemies, they should not now shorten the honour of their nation, by prolonging their own lives for a few hours, or a few days. The Master gunner readily condescended, and divers others; but the Captain and the Master were of another opinion, and besought Sir Richard to have care of them.

And as the matter was thus in dispute, and Sir Richard refusing to hearken to any of those reasons, the Master of the *Revenge* (while the Captain was unto him the greater party) was convoyed aboard the *General*, [commanded by] Don Alonso Bassan. Who finding none overhasty to enter the *Revenge* again, doubting lest Sir Richard would have blown them up and himself, and perceiving by the report of the Master of the *Revenge* his dangerous disposition: yielded that all their lives should be saved, the company sent for England, and the better sort to pay such reasonable ransom as their estate would bear, and in the mean season to be free from galley or imprisonment. To this he so much the rather condescended as well, as I have said, for fear of further loss and mischief to themselves, as also for the desire he had to recover Sir Richard Grenville; whom for his notable valour he seemed greatly to honour and admire.

When this answer was returned, and that safety of life was promised, the common sort being now at the end of their peril, the most drew back from Sir Richard and the Master gunner, being no hard matter to dissuade men from death to life. The Master gunner finding himself and Sir Richard thus prevented and mastered by the greater number, would have slain himself with the sword had he not been by force withheld and locked into his cabin. Then the *General* sent many boats aboard the *Revenge*, and divers of our men fearing Sir Richard's disposition stole away aboard the *General* and other ships. Sir Richard, thus overmatched, was sent unto by Alonso Bassan to remove out of the *Revenge*, the ship being marvelous unsavoury, filled with blood and bodies of dead and wounded men like a slaughter house. Sir Richard answered that he might do with his body what he list, for he esteemed it not, and as he was carried out of the ship he swooned, and reviving again desired the company to pray for him. The *General* used Sir Richard with all humanity and left nothing unattempted that tended to his recovery, highly commending his valour and worthiness, and greatly bewailed the danger wherein he was, being unto them a rare spectacle, and a resolution seldom approved, to see one ship turn towards so many enemies, to endure the charge and boarding of so many huge Armadoes, and to resist and repel the assaults and entries of so many soldiers . . .

Sir Richard died, as it is said, the second or third day aboard the *General*, and was by them greatly bewailed. What became of his body, whether it were buried in the sea or on the land we know not; the comfort that remaineth to his friends is, that he hath ended his life honourably in respect of the reputation won to his nation and country, and of the same to his posterity, and that being dead, he hath not outlived his own honour.

Source: Sir Walter Raleigh, *A Report of the Fight about the Isles of the Azores* (1591)

279 AN UNHAPPY ENDING

Life in the Royal Navy of the 18th century had its ups and downs . . .

In the London Gazette of 18th December, 1769, the following singular and splendid trait of magnanimity and courage was printed, although the name of the hero was not given, by Captain Dalrymple, from whose published account of the storm and capture of the Spanish fort of St Fernando de Omoo, on the Mosquito Coast, it has been extracted.

It happened that during the assault on this fort, which was taken by a well-concerted night attack, a sailor, who had scrambled over the walls, had in the confusion become separated from the main body of the assailants. Jack, like a true British tar, had provided himself with two cutlasses, one in each hand, in case of emergency, and, thus armed, met a Spanish officer, who, under the same circumstances of darkness and confusion, and suddenly roused from sleep, had rushed out unarmed. Our brave countryman without hesitation presented his opponent with one of the cutlasses, observing that he scorned to take any advantage of an enemy, and that now they were on equal terms. The Spaniard, amazed at this elevation of mind, yielded himself to so gallant a foe; and Captain Dalrymple adds, that the incident gave them a very high idea of English valour. This intrepid fellow was rewarded by promotion to the rank of boatswain by Admiral Sir Peter Parker; but a few years after, in a fit of madness caused by intoxication, he struck the lieutenant of his ship, was tried by court martial, sentenced, and executed.

Source: Edward Giffard, *Deeds of Naval Daring* (1910)

280 BOARDING PARTY

The Victorian age saw enormous changes in the technology of shipbuilding and naval warfare, but many officers – notably senior men – felt there was no need to change the values and methods that had served them and their country in their youth.

When Sir John Commerell, soon to become Admiral of the Fleet, inspected the cruiser HMS *Northampton* he saw an officer not carrying a sword. When asked why, the officer replied that he was the Chief Engineer and that there was not enough room for a sword in the engine room. 'What do you mean?' demanded Sir John, 'If the enemy has the good fortune to overpower us all on deck, how will you kill him when he comes down here if you have no sword?' In fact with guns now able to fire over ten thousand yards all this was ridiculously antiquated.

Source: Geoffrey Regan, *Someone Had Blundered* (1987)

281 A SPIRITED ASSAULT

Most of us when we feel groggy look for the nearest chair or bed – not so Able Seaman Strahan, as this incident from the early 18th century shows.

During the tranquil state of the camp, one Strahan, a common sailor, belonging to the *Kent*, having just received his allowance of grog, found his spirits too much elated to think of taking any rest; he therefore strayed by himself towards the fort, and imperceptibly got under the walls. Being advanced thus far without any interruption, he took it into his head to scale the breach that had been made by the cannon of the ships, and having fortunately reached the bastion, he there discovered several Moors sitting upon the platform, at whom, nothing daunted, he flourished his cutlass, and then fired his pistol, and having given three loud huzzas, cried out, 'The place is mine.' The Moorish soldiers immediately attacked him, and he defended himself with incredible resolution, but in the encounter had the misfortune to have the blade of his cutlass cut in two, about a foot from the hilt; this, however, did not happen until he was warmly supported by two or three other sailors who had accidentally straggled to the same part of the fort on which the other had mounted; they, hearing Strahan's cries, immediately scaled the breach likewise, and with their triumphant shouts roused the whole army, who, taking the alarm, presently fell on pell-mell, without order and without discipline, following the example of the sailors. Luckily, the enemy was equally ill-prepared for this sudden and ill-disciplined attempt, and fled from the fort upon the opposite side, as the attacking party poured in, leaving the works, with twenty cannons and a large store of ammunition, in the hands of the English, whose only loss was that of a Captain Dougall Campbell, of the East India Army, who was accidentally killed by a musket discharged by one of his own party. On the following day, Strahan, the hero of this adventurous action, was brought before the Admiral, who, with assumed anger inquired – 'Strahan, what is this you have been doing?' The sailor made his bow, scratched his head, and replied, 'Why to be sure, sir, it was I that took the fort; but I hope, your honour, as how there was no harm in it.' This was almost irresistible; but the Admiral restrained himself sufficiently to expatiate on what might have been the fatal results of his irregular conduct, and dismissed him with hints at punishment at some other time for his temerity. Poor Strahan, astonished at the results of his interview, receiving blame where he expected praise, muttered to himself on leaving the cabin, 'Well if I am flogged for this here action, I will never take another fort by myself as long as I live.'

Source: Edward Giffard, *Deeds of Naval Daring* (1910)

282 DIEGO GARCIA

The German cruiser Emden *achieved more in its short life than any other German surface raider of the First World War.*

On 9 October 1914 the German cruiser *Emden* arrived at a small coral island in the Indian Ocean, known as Diego Garcia. It was a lonely place, so much so that word of the outbreak of war in Europe had not even reached it and the German captain, Müller, decided that he would be unlikely to find a better place to complete some repairs, recoal and give his men shore leave in these idyllic tropical surroundings.

When the English manager of the coconut plantation, along with his Creole assistant, visited the ship, the Germans hurriedly concealed newspapers which might have given away the fact that war had broken out. The visitors told the Germans that a schooner called every three months with news and supplies, and the last visit had been in July.

The First World War German raider Emden, *whose captain left the British representative on Diego Garcia with a very red face (see number 282).*

Plied with copious quantities of whisky and soda the two islanders overlooked the obvious questions like what was a battered German cruiser doing coaling in such an isolated place. The German officers lied skilfully, convincing the two men that they had been involved in the suppression of a native revolt in German East Africa. The manager soon lost any doubts and was delighted when Müller sent two of his engineers to repair the Englishman's defunct motor-boat. In response to this gesture, the manager sent a boat to the *Emden* loaded with fresh fruit, fish, vegetables and a pig, Captain Müller sending by return wine, whisky and cigars. International goodwill and friendship was the order of the day on Diego Garcia – while in Flanders Briton and German were slaughtering each other in thousands.

On 10 October the *Emden* pulled out of the harbour at Diego Garcia to the sad farewell waves of their friends at the coconut plantation. Only two days later the British auxiliary cruiser, *Empress of Russia*, sailed into the same harbour to ask the English manager if he had seen or heard anything of Müller's ship. The British newspapers wrote of a 'high comedy on the high seas' and the general reaction was to laugh it off as a bizarre farce – though one very much at the expense of His Britannic Majesty's official representative on Diego Garcia, the manager of the coconut plantation, who had unwittingly helped the enemy and prolonged his active career.

283 THE EMPIRICIST

The British sailor had no truck with scientists.

One of the men who had been round the world with Commodore Byron soon after his return to England visited his native place, where he was considered as a very extraordinary sort of person, and was invited to a club of his townsmen, who expected to be greatly edified by his conversation. It was plain that a man who had been round the world must know more of it than Jenkins who had only been round London, and Wilkins who had never been out of it; but the circumnavigator could give them but very little information with respect to what he had seen in his voyage; and seemed to have very little to say for himself, till some of the club began to question him about the world being round: and only then did he open with a tone of authority; 'As to that I'll tell you what it is: they say the world is round; but I have been all round it and by God it is as flat as this table!'

Source: *Naval and Military Anecdotes* (1824)

284 THE SHIP THAT BROUGHT THE BOMB

In July 1945 the American cruiser USS Indianapolis *was responsible for delivering to Guam the atomic bombs that were later dropped on Hiroshima and Nagasaki. Little did the crew know that they were themselves to face disaster on their return journey.*

On 29 July 1945 the *Indianapolis* was torpedoed by a Japanese submarine. In spite of her distress signals, no American vessels appeared to be aware of her plight, and so no rescue operation was mounted. More than 800 of her crew survived the initial explosions and were pitched into the sea. The next morning, with the survivors now spread over a large area, they were attacked by dozens of sharks. Those who had kept together, or were hanging from the liferafts, survived far longer than the solitary swimmers. Before long many of the men resorted to drinking seawater and soon yielded to madness and death. For five days the men remained in the water, with the sharks decimating their numbers and many succumbing to exposure and exhaustion, before they were spotted by an American aircraft. Incredibly, the *Indianapolis* had not even been listed as missing, and so there was still no coordinated rescue mission. Only 318 of the crew survived their experience, the remainder having drowned or been eaten by sharks. It was the greatest loss suffered by the American navy at sea.

285 'Q' SHIPS

The German submarine threat in the First World War came closer to defeating Britain than is generally realized. Up to 1917 the Admiralty concentrated on destroying U-boats rather than protecting merchant shipping through convoys. The 'Q' ship was one of its most potent weapons. An apparently innocuous merchant vessel would, in fact, be heavily armed and would try to persuade the U-boat to surface so that it could spring its surprise and destroy it. It was a dangerous job, requiring nerve and split-second timing. Sometimes, as in this case, the U-boat fired first before surfacing to investigate its prey.

The sea was calm, it was a nice fine day, and everything looked peaceful. Suddenly a torpedo was seen approaching from our starboard side: it was fired at a great range and we would have had time to avoid it, but (as had been prearranged) we wanted to make sure it hit. Nothing, therefore, was done till it was close to the ship and coming straight for the engine-room. At the last moment, when it would be too late for the enemy to see our movement, I put the helm over to avoid unnecessary loss of life and brought the torpedo just abaft the engine-room, but it caught us on the bulkhead and flooded, in consequence, two thirds of the ship.

Whilst the torpedo was approaching, I sang out to the Navigator, who was in the chart-house working out his morning observations, 'Look out, we are going to get it all right.' He only bobbed his head outside and said, 'Aye, aye, sir; just time to finish this sight,' and back he went, quite disinterested except to complete his job, which was to have our position always accurate in case we wanted it.

The torpedo exploded with a great crash and knocked several of us down, including myself. Smith, who was on watch in the engine-room and nearest to the explosion, had the worst shaking, but he quickly recovered himself and went to his panic-party station in charge of a boat. After getting up, I observed a thing which I hadn't foreseen and I couldn't help laughing at. It will be remembered that we had drilled for nearly every emergency, and how I would say 'Torpedo coming,' and then 'Torpedo hit' or 'Torpedo missed.' Now the torpedo had hit and I saw the men rushing for the boats, but on looking over the front of the bridge I saw a group of men still smoking and lolling over the ship's side when they ought to have been 'panicking'. I shouted out to know why the something something they weren't rushing for the boats. The reply was, 'Waiting for the order, sir, "Torpedo Hit".' They then joined in the pandemonium, and whilst the panic-party were getting away in the boats, the submarine was seen watching us through his periscope about two hundred yards off the ship. This will show the necessity of even the 'panic' being done in correct detail, and sure enough it was. The boats were lowered in a fashion enough to give any Commander seven fits, and the crew got in anyhow; one boat was only partially lowered and then allowed to 'jam' so that a rush was made for the next one, but two lifeboats and a dinghy eventually shoved off with 'all' of the crew, Lieutenant Hereford with my M.O.B.C. hat getting down last. An unrehearsed incident added to the panic, and this was through my friend the Chief Steward (who was a very fat man) getting pushed over the side with the crowd; his weight was too much for his arms to support from the rope and he landed with a great thud in the boat, squashing two or three men who were already in.

Whilst this pantomime was going on, things were happening on board. The ship had only two bulkheads and the torpedo had burst the after one, so that she was free to the water from the fore side of the boiler room right to the stern, and she rapidly began to settle by the stern – so rapidly that our black cat, which had either been blown off the fo'c'sle by the explosion or had jumped over in fright, swam down the ship's side and inboard over the stern.

The Chief Engineer reported that the engine-room was flooded, and I ordered him and his men to hide, which they did by crawling on the top gratings: the ship being abandoned they couldn't come out on deck – again an unrehearsed incident, but Loveless and all of them knew the game we were out to play.

As soon as the boats were away, the submarine went close to them only a few yards off; she was obviously going to leave nothing to chance, and it was as well that the crew were carefully dressed to their part with no service flannels. One of the crew in the boats was heard telling another, as the periscope was looking at them, 'Don't talk so loud; he'll hear you!'

The submarine now came and inspected the ship at very close range, some ten or fifteen yards – so close that from my look-out at the starboard end of the bridge I could see the whole of his hull under water. The temptation to open fire on the periscope was very great, though obviously not the thing to do, as it would have done no harm. But it looked at the time as if, after getting deliberately torpedoed we were going to have nothing to show for it since he appeared to be moving off.

The Chief had reported the ship sinking by the stern; still, there was nothing for it but to wait and watch the submarine move slowly past the ship and way ahead. All this time the men on board were lying hidden, feeling the ship getting deeper by the stern – in fact, the men at the after gun were practically awash – but they all stuck it and never moved a muscle. Each one had a responsibility. Had one man got in a real panic and showed himself, the game would have been up; the scrutiny of the submarine was indeed a severe one. The wireless operator, locked up in his cabin by himself, had to sit still and do nothing; he must have been aching to send out an S.O.S. and have his picture in the illustrated papers next day as 'The man who sent out the S.O.S.' but he knew we wanted no one to interfere with our cold-blooded encounter with the enemy.

After the submarine had passed up the starboard side, he crossed our bow and went over towards port; the signalman and I therefore did our 'belly-crawl' and swopped places. At 10.05 a.m. the enemy broke surface about 300 yards on our port bow, but not in the bearing of any of the guns. Anyhow, things were looking more hopeful and I was able to tell the men that all was going well. The boats had by this time got to our port quarter, and towards them the submarine now proceeded. We heard afterwards that their intention had been to take the 'Master' prisoner and also get some provisions. It was only a matter of waiting now, as the submarine was right up with the conning tower open. It was obvious that she would pass very close to the ship, and we might just as well have all guns bearing so as to make sure of it. As she came abreast of the ship the Captain was seen coming out of the conning tower. At this moment I gave the order to open fire – at 10.10 – twenty five minutes after we had been torpedoed. The White Ensign fluttered at the mast head, and three 12 pounders, a 6 pounder, the Maxim guns and rifles all opened fire together. What a shock it must have been for the Captain, suddenly to see our wheelhouse collapse, our sides to fall down, and the hen-coop to splutter forth Maxim shots! But he had not long to think, as the first shot, which was from the 6 pounder, hit him, and I believe the first intimation the submarine crew had that anything was wrong was seeing their captain drop through the conning tower.

The range was only about a hundred yards, so the submarine never had a chance to escape. It seemed almost brutal to fire at such close range, but we had taken a sporting chance ourselves in decoying him to such an ideal position that one really had no other thought than destruction. The submarine never seemed to recover from her surprise as she lay on the surface upon our beam whilst we pumped lead and steel into her. Forty five shells were fired in all, practically every one being a hit, so that she finally sank with the conning tower shattered and open, the crew pouring out as hard as they could. About eight men were seen in the water, which was bitterly cold and thick with oil. I ordered the boats to their assistance and they were just in time to rescue one officer and one man – as the panic-party called them, a 'sample of each.' Thus ended U-83.

Source: Gordon Campbell, *My Mystery Ships* (1928)

286 A SIGNAL ERROR

The job of the naval signaller was a vital if occasionally amusing one.

An admiral was approaching Malta on his flagship after a lengthy spell at sea with a lot of dirty washing on board. As was his custom he ordered the yeoman of signals to have the washer woman picked up. The yeoman showed the admiral the signal he had sent. 'On arrival please send admiral's woman aboard.' Incensed by this idiotic mistake the admiral ordered the yeoman to send an immediate correction. It read, 'Re last signal, please insert washer between admiral and woman.'

Source: Godfrey Smith, *Sunday Times*, 1 March 1987

287 WALKING OUT WITH A SAILOR

Naval ports are notorious for certain activities . . .

Lady Astor canvassing for her first parliamentary seat in Plymouth, because of her status and because she was new to the town, was allotted a senior naval officer as a minder, and together they went round knocking on doors. 'Is your mother at home?' asked Lady Astor imperiously when one door was opened by a small girl. 'No', replied the child, 'but she said if a lady comes with a sailor they're to use the upstairs room and leave ten bob.'

Source: Sue Arnold, *Observer Magazine*, 16 June 1985

288 THE LIGHT OF REASON

Second only to God on their flagships, admirals are unreceptive to orders from anyone.

An American admiral, spotting a blip on the radar screen, ordered his radio operator, 'Tell that ship to alter course fifteen degrees.' The word came back, 'You change your course fifteen degrees.' When a more heavily phrased message met with the same response he snatched the microphone and bawled, 'You change your course fifteen degrees. I am an admiral in the United States navy.' A calm voice replied, 'And I am a lighthouse.'

Source: *Profile* magazine, quoted in *The Times*, 3 September 1986

289 REPORTS AND RETORTS

If you can keep your head when all around are losing theirs . . .

Admiral Lord Howe, when a captain, was once hastily awakened in the middle of the night by a lieutenant of the watch, who informed him with great agitation, that the ship was on fire near the magazine. 'If that be the case,' said he, rising leisurely to put on his clothes, 'we shall soon hear a further report in the matter.'

Source: *The Percy Anecdotes* (Ed. S. & R. Percy 1823)

MEDICAL MATTERS

290 FAT FREE

Medical knowledge in Renaissance times was in its infancy.

During the fighting in the Netherlands in the late 16th century surgeons came to the conclusion that human fat was an efficacious salve for wounded men. After the ill-fated Spanish siege of Ostend in 1602, during which over 2000 Spaniards and Italians were killed in a single night, 'the ground was strewn everywhere with arms, legs and hands'. This proved an irresistible source of raw material for the medical fraternity, who flocked from the city after dark to scrape the fat from the bodies and bring it back in bags.

291 REGIMENTAL HONOUR

The 'honour of the regiment' can be an immense burden for a young officer to bear.

Colonel Guise, going over one campaign to Flanders, observed a young raw officer, who was in the same vessel with him, and with his usual humanity told him that he would take care of him, and conduct him to Antwerp, where they were both going; which he accordingly did, and then took leave of him. The young fellow was soon told by such arch rogues, whom he happened to fall in with, that he must signalise himself by fighting some man of known courage, or else he would soon be despised in the regiment. The young man said, he knew no one but Colonel Guise, and he had received great obligations from him. It was all one for that, they said in these cases; the colonel was the fittest man in the world as everybody knew his bravery. Soon afterwards, up comes the young officer to Colonel Guise, as he was walking up and down the coffee room, and began in a hesitating manner to tell him how much obliged he had been to him, and how sensible he was of his obligations. 'Sir,' replied Colonel Guise, 'I have done my duty by you, and no more.' 'But colonel,' added the young officer faltering, 'I am told that I must fight some gentleman of known courage, and who has killed several persons and that no-body –' 'Oh, sir,' interrupted the colonel, 'your friends do me too much honour; but there is a gentleman (pointing to a fierce-looking black fellow that was sitting at one of the tables) who has killed half the regiment.' So up goes the officer to him and tells him he is well-informed of his bravery, and that for that reason he must fight him. 'Who, I, sir?' said the gentleman, 'why, I am the apothecary.'

Source: *Naval and Military Anecdotes* (1824)

292 **AN UNUSUAL REMEDY**

Sometimes fate has a curious way of repeating itself.

On 21 June 1803, the British succeeded in capturing the French island of St Lucia, in the Caribbean. During the fighting Captain Edward Pakenham, later to be brother-in-law to the Duke of Wellington, received a curious wound, which baffled medical opinion at the time. A spent bullet hit him in the neck and apparently damaged a nerve so that he was forced to carry his head at an unusual angle. A few years later, fighting on the island of Martinique, Pakenham was hit by a spent bullet on the other side of his neck, which had the effect of straightening it out and allowing him to carry his head normally.

However, Pakenham's luck ran out in 1815, when he was killed during the British defeat at New Orleans.

293 **SELF HELP**

Military prisons in the 18th century were breeding grounds for disease, particularly the hulks used by the British to house American soldiers taken in the War of Independence. As this example shows, inoculation against smallpox was an acknowledged procedure by 1780.

As I had never had the smallpox it became necessary that I should be inoculated and there being no proper person on board to perform the operation I concluded to act as my own physician. On looking about me I soon found a man in the proper stage of the disease and desired him to favour me with some of the matter for the purpose. He readily complied, observing that it was a necessary precaution on my part and that my situation was an excellent one in regard to diet as I might depend upon finding that extremely moderate. The only instrument that I could procure for the purpose of inoculation was a common pin. With this, having scarified the skin of my hand between the thumb and forefinger, I applied the matter and bound up my hand. The next morning I found that the wound had begun to fester, a sure symptom that the application had taken effect.

Many of my former shipmates took the same precaution and were inoculated during the day. In my case, the disorder came on but lightly and its progress was favourable and without the least medical advice or attention, by the blessing of divine providence, I soon recovered.

Source: Captain Thomas Dring, *Recollections of the Jersey Prison-ship* (Re-written by Albert Greene, Ed. Henry Dawson 1865)

294 **THE SOGGY END**

The British regular soldier in the Napoleonic Wars had a toughness that was proverbial. He was intolerant of those who did not share his stoicism in the face of suffering.

One such soldier, awaiting treatment in a British field hospital was angry at the screams of a French casualty lying alongside him. As soon as the Frenchman's arm had been amputated, the British soldier seized the severed limb by the wrist and hit the Frenchman a sharp blow with it, saying 'Here, take that, and stuff it down your throat and stop your damned bellowing.'

295 MERCIFUL END

Mercy killings in wartime, though frowned upon by both the legal and the medical professions, are nevertheless far more common than is generally realized. Nor is the practice a modern one as this story shows.

As the French army broke into Turin in 1536 the famous French surgeon, Ambrose Paré, saw three badly burned soldiers, suffering in terrible agony. Watching them with pity an old soldier asked Paré if there was any means of curing them. Paré replied that there was none. At once the soldier approached them and cut their throats gently. Paré shouted at him that he was a villain, but he replied that he prayed to God that should he be in such a state he might find someone who would do the same for him, so that he would not be in pain.

296 SHELL-SHOCK

In the First World War little was known of the psychological effects of exposure to prolonged or extreme artillery bombardment. Men who broke down were often regarded as cowards.

I saw a man, a regular officer, who went out to Gallipoli and went mad on the beach. He saw the whole beach covered with jewelled spiders of enormous size. They did not know what to do with the man so put him on one of the boats, and as the barges came up with the wounded he saw his wife and child on a barge, cut in pieces.

Source: Medical Officer's Report to War Office Committee of Inquiry into 'Shell Shock' (1920)

297 BITING THE ALMOND

William Grattan describes an operation carried out by an army surgeon in the Peninsular War.

A little further on, in an inner court, were the surgeons. They were stripped to their shirts and bloody: – curiosity led me forward; a number of doors, placed on barrels served as temporary tables, and on these lay the different subjects upon whom the surgeons were operating; to the right and left were arms and legs, flung here and there, without distinction, and the ground was dyed with blood. Doctor Bell was going to take off the thigh of a soldier of the 50th, and he requested I would hold down the man for him; he was one of the best-hearted men I ever met with, but, such is the force of habit, he seemed insensible to the scene that was passing around him, and with much composure was eating almonds out of his waistcoat pockets, which he offered to share with me but, if I got the universe for it, I could not have swallowed a morsel of anything. The operation upon the man of the 50th was the most shocking sight I ever witnessed; it lasted nearly half an hour but his life was saved.

Source: William Grattan, *Adventures with the Connaught Rangers 1808–1814* (Ed. Sir C. Oman 1904)

298 CHRISTIAN UNDERSTANDING

During the Middle Ages Arab medicine was far in advance of that used in the West. This was obvious during the Crusades, when the Muslims came to regard Christian doctors as ignorant butchers, as this Arab doctor relates.

They took me to see a knight who had an abscess on his leg. I applied a poultice to the leg and the abscess opened and began to heal. Then there appeared a Frankish doctor who said, 'This man has no idea how to cure this person!' He turned to the knight and said, 'Which would you prefer, to live with one leg or to die with two?' When the knight replied that he would prefer to live with one leg, he sent for a strong man and a sharp axe. They arrived, and I stood by to watch. The doctor supported the leg on a block of wood and said to the man, 'Strike a mighty blow, and cut cleanly!' And there before my eyes, the fellow struck the knight one blow and then another for the first had not finished the job. The marrow spurted out of the leg, and the patient died instantaneously.

Source: Usama ibn Munqidh, *Autobiography* (Trans. H. Derenbourg 1893)

299 PROFESSIONAL TRUST

Alexander the Great was a good judge of men.

This furthermore made him bold also, when he saw that Alexander remained a good while in Cilicia, supposing it had been for that he was afraid of him. Howbeit it was by reason of a sickness he had, the which some say he got, by extreme pains and travel, and others also, because he washed himself in the river of Cydnus, which was cold as ice. Howsoever it came, there was none of the other physicians that durst undertake to cure him, thinking his disease incurable, and no medicines to prevail that they could give to him, and fearing also that the Macedonians would lay it to their charge, if Alexander miscarried. But Philip the Acarnanian, considering his master was very ill, and bearing himself of the love and good will towards him, thought he should not do that became him, if he did not prove (seeing him in extremity and danger of life) the utmost remedies of physic what danger soever he put himself into: and therefore took upon him to minister physic unto Alexander, and persuaded him to drink it boldly if he would quickly be whole, and go to the wars. In the meantime, Parmenio wrote him a letter from the camp, advertising him, that he should beware of Philip the physician, for he was bribed and corrupted by Darius, with large promises of great riches, that he would give him with his daughter in marriage, to kill his master. Alexander when he had read this letter, laid it under his bed's head and made none of his nearest familiars acquainted therewith. When the hour came that he should take his medicine, Philip came into his chamber with other of the king's familiars, and brought a cup in his hand with the potion he should drink.

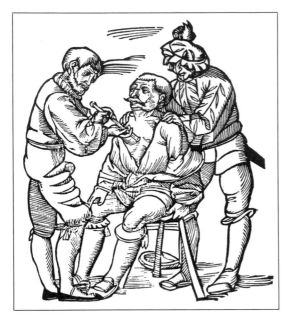

In this German woodcut of 1530 a soldier has an arrow extracted from his chest. Surgery – particularly on the field – was very rough and ready until the advent of anaesthetics and antisepsis in the mid-19th century. Prior to that, surgeons prided themselves on the speed at which they could amputate a limb: the shortest time recorded for a leg amputation was 13–15 seconds by Napoleon's chief surgeon, Dominique Larrey. There is a story of one surgeon who in his haste managed to take off a finger of his assistant while sawing through a leg.

Alexander then gave him the letter, and withal cheerfully took the cup off him showing no manner of fear or mistrust of anything. It was a wonderful thing and worth the sight, how one reading the letter and the other drinking the medicine both at one instant, they looked one upon another, howbeit not both with like cheerful countenance. For Alexander looked merrily upon him, plainly showing the trust he had in his physician Philip, and how much he loved him: and the physician also beheld Alexander, like a man perplexed and amazed to be so falsely accused and straight lift up his hands to heaven, calling the gods to witness that he was innocent, and then came to Alexander's bedside, and prayed him to be of good cheer, and boldly to do as he would advise him. The medicine beginning to work, overcame the disease, and drave for the time, to the lowest parts of his body, all his natural strength and powers: insomuch as his speech failed him and he fell into such a weakness, and almost swooning that his pulse did scant beat and his senses were well near taken from him. But that being past Philip in a few days recovered him again. Now, when Alexander had gotten some strength, he showed himself openly unto the Macedonians: for they would not be pacified nor persuaded of his health, until they had seen him.

Source: Plutarch, *Life of Alexander* (1st century; trans. Sir Thomas North 1579)

300 CHANCE ENCOUNTER

During the Second Afghan War in 1878, war correspondent Frederic Villiers set off from the British base at Jellalabad to visit the famous Colonel Smyter, VC, who commanded a Gurkha regiment in an advanced position. Villiers took with him just two Muslim servants, and set off through the rocky paths of the Khyber Pass. As night fell he realized that he was lost.

Presently a light leapt out of the blackness. I immediately whispered a halt, now that like 'will-o'-the-wisps' flecks of fire danced about in front of us. Could this be a bivouac of the enemy? I told my servant to remain in position while I crept towards the distant lights. I stumbled down the face of a deep cut nullah [gorge], and on clambering up the opposite bank I could discern in the distant play of the fires a few white tents. It was the British encampment. I would have shouted for joy but that I knew that any noise would have brought a sharp fusillade in our direction. I stole back to my servant and we boldly marched towards the tents.

'Halt! Who come dah?' shouted the native sentry.

'Friend,' I replied.

'Parse, fren, alisvel!' answered the incoherent Gurkha.

The news of our approach rapidly spread. Out of a large marquee hurried two or three officers.

'Glad to see you,' said one, as I rolled out of my saddle.

'Qui hi,' shouted another, 'brandy peg low. Geldi Ghow.'

In the twinkling of an eye a servant appeared with cooling draught, a big soda and brandy with a dash of snow in it from the Safed Koh, or White Mountain, which loomed over the valley. I greedily drained the peg.

'That's only to moisten your throat,' said they. 'Have another just to quench your thirst – and then we will allow talking. You are the first we have seen for an age.'

'Well,' thought I, 'this is indeed hospitable.'

'So good of you to come!'

'Why, it's Villiers – good fellow! Just in time for dinner,' cried the officers in chorus.

My men went off with their kind, and I was hustled into the mess tent. As I seated myself at the table, faces, beaming with good nature, turned to mine. I inwardly congratulated myself. I had never met with more cordial hospitality in my life.

As I commenced to eat an orderly entered the tent and whispered to one of the officers, who immediately got up and followed him. Then another orderly spoke to the man on my left.

'Excuse me, Villiers,' and he hurriedly disappeared. Soon the one sitting opposite me was summoned in the same mysterious way. By and by the first who had quitted the tent came back. All eyes were anxiously turned on him.

'Any more?' asked one.

'How many?' enquired another.

The answer slowly came: 'Two, worse luck.'

'Oh, that's nothing! We had three before the evening was through last night.'

I turned to the man on my right. 'What are these good fellows talking about?'

'Fresh cases,' he replied.

'Cases?' I exclaimed, with no little astonishment. 'Cases of what?'

'Well,' he grimly smiled, 'not champagne – that's for certain.'

I must have still looked bewildered.

'Ah! ah! Good joke that,' I rather stupidly rejoined.

'You don't understand,' said he. 'Why cholera, of course.'

'Cholera! Oh, yes; I see,' I faintly murmured.

'Cholera!' I gazed in the kindly faces and then it struck me that their uniforms seemed very familiar to me. My genial friends were doctors – they were all medicine-men. Now I could understand their delight in seeing me – their sad lack of news. I had struck a cholera camp. These poor fellows had been isolated from the outer world for months. I almost choked with emotion. My heart seemed to sink into my boots. I tried to pull myself together, poured out another glass of wine and was about to swallow it, when the doctors lifted their glasses, and drank my health.

'So good of you to take pity on us – just like you war correspondents. Don't seem to care a fig for anything.'

'Well,' thought I, struggling against a chill that seemed to freeze my heart, 'Anyway, I must keep up the reputation with which our profession has been so cordially accredited.'

So I staggered to my feet and responded to the toast. I told them that as I was passing by I thought I would look them up – in my province as a war correspondent it was only right – in fact, my duty. I protested that I was never happier in my life, and they could look upon me as a veritable newspaper – in fact, a special edition. I would give them all the news I contained.

After a short conversation – but a very long one to me – I shared the tent of one of the doctors, but not his slumbers. I was never so wide awake in my life, and I vowed that if I found myself alive at dawn I would hurry from that pestilent, stricken camp before breakfast. During the night a hot wind sprang up, coming upon us like the breath from a baker's oven, choking us with dust and flaying our faces with burning particles of sand. Towards morning, lights flickered from tent to tent as the surgeons went about their work. The groans and wails of the doomed patients were heard above the sowing of the wind. The sun shot up from the horizon. It was day once more. But many brave men in that camp of misery had died in the gloom of the previous night. The stretcher-bearers were already carrying their inanimate burdens to the little cemetery on the parched-up plain as I turned my back on the cholera-stricken camp.

The sun was well up when we gained the main road to the Khyber. The rocks began to glow once more under the fierce rays, warming up the valley to a heat one would think would sterilise and disinfect the most pestilent-ridden country in the world. Yet, clinging to the shadow of the rocks by the roadside, where they had sought shelter from the merciless sun, were corpses of stricken hillmen, who had come down from their lairs to cut up any stragglers such as we, but who had been taken with the deadly sickness while waiting for their victims. Never shall I forget the horrible nausea which held me all the way on this ghastly journey across the plains of Chadéh.

It was nearing sunset once more and we had not yet gained Smyter's command, when presently we saw a cloud of dust on the road, coming in our direction.

'Well, sir, and where's your escort?' said an angry voice, as a tall, gaunt figure on a small grey horse rode towards me.

'I have no escort,' I replied, 'only my two servants.'

'What, sir! Do you mean to tell me you have ridden here from Jellalabad without protection?'

I was stammering out a reply, when the officer interrupted me, 'Damn! Don't think I'm anxious about your carcass, sir! It's my men I'm thinking about. If you were cut up it would be my duty to rescue your remains, and probably in doing so I might lose one or

THE BEST OF ENEMIES

two of my valuable little Gurkhas. Do you understand, sir? Now you have arrived, kindly keep in camp and report yourself to me this evening.' And the peppery officer rode on.

For the moment I had not the slightest idea who on earth he was, but after a wash and brush up I soon found out on my reporting myself to the general, and presenting my letter. It was Smyter, V.C., himself.

Source: Frederic Villiers, *Pictures of Many Wars* (1902)

301 CHILDISH AILMENTS

In August 1914 the Territorial Highland Division was moved from Scotland to billets in Bedford. Here the Scots experienced for the first time the potential problems of a highly populated area.

The Scots soldiers, fresh from the sparsely populated areas of the Highlands of Scotland, found that they had little immunity to the kind of childhood ailments almost universally experienced by children in urban areas. Many of them fell victim to epidemics of mumps, measles and chicken pox. Hospitals were flooded, not with the wounded men from Flanders and France, with bullet, shell and bayonet wounds, but with young territorials with swollen glands or rashes. Many cases were serious – 85 men died in three months and hundreds were out of action for lengthy periods. The strain on nurses and hospital wards was as severe as it was unexpected. However, it did serve as a gentle introduction to war work for hundreds of young voluntary nurses.

THE BEST OF ENEMIES

302 AN ANGLO-TURKISH ALLIANCE

Before the bungled landings at Gallipoli in April 1915 the Turks stood in awe of Britain's power, notably that of her navy. When offered the chance to cooperate even with an enemy some Turks were only too willing to oblige.

The first task for the British was to cut the links between Constantinople and the Turkish forces stationed in Arabia. It was decided to breach the Medina railway just north of Alexandretta, and a British cruiser landed sailors to carry out the work on 8 December 1914. The Britons were expecting some resistance and were surprised to find that, far from posing a threat, the Turks were only too willing to help them in their sabotage. While some of the cruiser's men wrecked a nearby station and bridge, Turkish soldiers helped by shunting up locomotives to be dynamited. The British officer in charge of the operation, a navy lieutenant, had the faintly disconcerting experience of carrying out the destruction in company with Turkish officers, who simply watched in silence having told him that they would like to have helped but feared that it would involve them in loss of 'face' to be commanded by a foreigner. If the lieutenant would agree to become a Turkish officer for the day, all objections would disappear. Nonplussed, the lieutenant agreed to become an 'Anglo-Turk', in the interests of doubling his workforce and getting his mission completed in half the time. The Turks now threw their weight behind the joint act of vandalism and soon the railway, complete with its locomotives and equipment, was completely wrecked. The British party withdrew unscathed and the lieutenant hastily resigned his Turkish commission, shaking hands with his erstwhile colleagues and retiring promptly to his boat. It had been a successful – if totally baffling – operation, completed in the best traditions of the senior service.

303 **SHOULDER BOTH ARMS**

Fraternization during the Peninsular War was more widespread than the officers would ever have liked to admit.

What Wellington would have said about the Irish sentry found with a French musket on one shoulder and his own on the other shoulder, keeping guard for both sides while the French sentry had gone into the village nearby to buy brandy for both of them to drink, is past repeating.

304 **POLES APART**

During Napoleon's invasion of Russia in 1812 there were numerous instances of fraternization between the French and the Russians. An officer from a regiment of Polish Lancers in the Grand Armée recorded the following incident.

Soon a Russian officer of dragoons rode forward a few paces, greeted us, and made signs with a bottle. I followed suit and placed myself in front of our line of tirailleurs [skirmishers]. In this way we approached to within thirty yards of one another, whereupon the Russian shouted in French, 'Mon camarade! It is useless to exhaust our horses and kill our men for nothing. Let us drink together instead. There will be plenty of time for fighting afterwards.'

We went nearer and enjoyed a friendly drink, while other troops continued fighting undisturbed in the distance. A few more Russian officers came up shortly. I wanted to withdraw, but the dragoon officer said: 'I promise you on my sword of honour that they will do you no harm.'

So I stayed where I was and we talked amicably. I found his rum good, but could not give him any in return. It was not long before other officers arrived from both sides. Our sutler, Frau Ehmke, a pretty woman who always rode around among the light infantrymen and had two little casks of brandy on her horse, came past and poured the Russians a free drink, though she charged us a high price for her liquor. A young lieutenant in our regiment named Piessac, who had an attractive, girlish face, was kissed by a bearded, elderly Russian. A Russian officer of uhlans, Polish by birth, who took us for Poles because we wore their uniform, wanted to make enquiries about his compatriots, and when he heard that a regiment of Polish lancers stood in the second line behind us, he rode confidently over to this regiment as fast as his horse would carry him. We thought he meant to desert, but this was not his intention at all. He merely wanted to see his fellow-countrymen and air his bitter views about the inglorious way in which Barclay de Tolly [the Russian commander] had chosen to wage war.

When he learned that we wanted nothing better than a full-scale battle which would decide the outcome of the war, and that we were heartily tired of wandering around a country so devoid of resources, he replied that if we hoped for such a battle at Smolensk, then we hoped in vain. He would lay heavy odds that the Russians would, as before, slip away without fighting.

Meanwhile General Bruyère, who was some distance away, had noticed this scene and sent an aide-de-camp to recall our officers to their posts and to indicate to the Russians that they should retire behind their line of sharpshooters, otherwise they would be fired on. He gave orders for the Polish officer who had ridden through to our second line to be arrested, but the aide rode so slowly – no doubt on purpose – that the Pole was warned by another officer and hurried away.

We remained opposite each other for several hours longer, until the evening, but the friendship which had been struck up lasted, and not another shot was fired until both sides withdrew.

Source: Count von Wedel, *History of an Officer in the War against Russia* (1897)

305 THE BLUE AND THE GREY

During the American Civil War fraternization was inevitably widespread.

It was the latter part of August 1863; orders were given to be prepared to go on picket early in the morning and until a late hour the men were busy cooking rations and cleaning equipment. Before the mists had been chased by the rising sun a company in close column of fours marched down the road . . . A sergeant and a squad of men were left at each post, the company being spread out several miles on the river banks to act as videttes whose duty it was to watch the enemy on the other side of the Rappahannock. The next day our squad, Sergeant Joe Reid in command, sauntered down the bank . . .

'Johnny Reb, I say, J-o-h-n-n-y R-e-b, don't shoot.'

Joe Reid shouted back, 'All right.'

'What command are you?'

'The Black Horse cavalry. Who are you?'

'The Second Michigan cavalry.'

'Come out on the bank,' said our spokesman, 'and show yourselves. We won't fire.'

'On your honour, Johnny Reb?'

'On our honour, Billy Yank.'

In a second a large squad of bluecoats across the way advanced to the water's brink. The Southerners did the same. Then the former put the query, 'Have you any tobacco?'

'Plenty of it,' went out our reply.

'Any coffee and sugar?' they questioned.

'Not a taste nor a smell.'

'Let's trade,' was shouted with eagerness.

'Very well,' was the reply, 'we have not much with us but we will send to Fredericksburg for more so meet us here this evening.'

'All right,' they answered, then added, 'Say, Johnny, want some newspapers?'

'Y-e-s.'

'Then look out, we're going to send you some.'

'How are you going to do it?'

'Wait and see.' The Rebs watched the group on the other side curiously, wondering how even Yankee ingenuity could devise a way of sending a batch of papers across the river two hundred yards wide and in the meantime each man had his own opinion.

'They will shoot arrows over,' said Martin. 'Arrows the devil,' replied the Sergeant, 'There never was a bow bent which could cast an arrow across this river.'

'Maybe they will wrap them around a cannon ball and shoot them across. We'd better get away from here,' hastily answered a tall, slim six-footer, who was rather afraid of big shots.

A roar of laughter followed this suggestion but the originator was too intent on his own awakened fears to let the slightest movement of the enemy pass unscanned. Eagerly he watched while the others were having all the fun at his expense. Presently he shouted, 'Here they come,' and then in a tone of intense admiration, 'I'll be doggoned if these Yanks are not the smartest people in the world.'

On the other side were several miniature boats and ships, such as schoolboys delight in, with sails set; the gentle breeze impelled the little crafts across the river, each freighted with a couple of newspapers. Slowly but surely they headed for the opposite bank as if some spirit Oberon or Puck sat at the tiller and in a few minutes had accomplished their voyage and were drawn up to await a favourable wind to waft them back.

Drawing lots Joe Boteler, who found luck against him, started to town with a muttered curse to buy tobacco, leaving his comrades to seek some shady spot and with pipes in our mouths sink deep in the latest war news from the enemy's standpoint, always interesting reading . . .

Joe returned in the evening with a box of plug tobacco about a foot square, but how to get it across was the question. The miniature boats could not carry it and we shouted over to the Yanks that we had about twenty pounds of cut plug and asked them what we must do. They hallooed back to let one of us swim across and declared that it was perfectly safe. We held a council of war and it was found that none of the Black Horse could swim beyond a few rods, then I volunteered having lived on the banks of the Potomac most of my life, I was necessarily a swimmer. Sergeant Reid went to a house not far off and borrowed a bread trough and placing it on a plank the box of tobacco was shipped and disrobing I started pushing my queer craft in front of me. As I approached the shore the news of my coming had reached camp and nearly all the Second Michigan were lined up along the bank. I felt a little queer but I had perfect faith in their promise and kept on without missing a stroke until my miniature scow grounded on the beach. The bluecoats crowded round me and gave me a hearty welcome and relieving the trough of its load heaped the craft with offerings of sugar, coffee, lemons and even candy, till I cried out that they would sink my transport. I am sure they would have filled a rowboat to the gunwhale had I brought one.

There was no chaffing or banter only roistering welcomes. Bidding my friends the enemy goodbye I swam back with the precious cargo and we had a feast that night.

Source: Alexander Hunter, *Johnny Reb and Billy Yank* (1905)

306 SHORT BACK AND SIDES

The most famous example of fraternization between combatant troops occurred on the Western Front at Christmas in 1914. What is not so well known is the fact that such local truces continued at Christmas throughout the war in some areas. In 1915, Bruce Bairnsfather relates one incident resulting in Anglo-German cooperation.

We parted but there was a distinct and friendly understanding that Christmas day would be left to finish in tranquillity. The last I saw of this little affair was a vision of one of my machine-gunners, who was a bit of an amateur hairdresser in civil life, cutting the unnaturally long hair of a docile Boche, who was patiently kneeling on the ground whilst the automatic clippers crept up the back of his neck.

Source: Bruce Bairnsfather, *Bullets and Billets* (1916)

307 CLOSE RELATIONS

Many prominent Scottish nobles fought with the French during the Hundred Years War, as well as having kinsmen in the English army.

After the battle of Poitiers in 1356, Archibald Douglas, having been made prisoner along with other Scottish lords, appeared in more sumptuous armour than his fellows and therefore was supposed, by the English, to be a noble of great importance. Late in the evening, after the battle, when the English were about to remove Douglas's armour, Sir William Ramsay of Colluthy, seeing the Scotsman, flew into a rage and cried out, 'You cursed, damnable murderer. How comes it, in the name of mischief, that you are thus proudly decked out in your master's armour. Come hither and pull off my boots.' Douglas approached, trembling, knelt down and pulled off one of Sir William's boots. Ramsay, taking up the boot, beat Douglas around the head with it. The English bystanders, imagining him to be out of his senses, interposed and rescued Douglas. They said that the person whom he had beaten was certainly of great rank and a lord. 'What? He, a lord?' cried Ramsay, 'He is a scullion and a base knave and, as I suppose, has killed his master. Go, you villain, to the field. Search for the body of my cousin, your master, and when you have found it come back that at least I may give him a decent burial.' Then he ransomed the feigned serving man for forty shillings and having buffeted him smartly he cried, 'Get you gone; fly!'

Douglas put up with this charade from Ramsay, who unknown to the other English soldiers, was a kinsman of his and soon he was out of reach of his enemies.

Source: Lord Hailes, *Annals of Scotland* (1819)

308 AN OFFICER AND A GENTLEMAN

The first day of the Somme offensive – 1 July 1916 – was the blackest day in the history of the British Army. As is well known, nearly 60,000 casualties were suffered on that one day and the gains made were minimal.

On 2 July 1916, in many places where the assaults had failed, the area of no-man's-land was thick with dead or seriously wounded British soldiers. Some unofficial truces were in operation and British survivors were not fired on by the Germans as they tried to carry back the injured men. One young soldier, crawling out under the cover of mist to rescue a fallen comrade found himself, when the mist lifted, only a few feet from the German positions. Expecting to be shot at any moment, he was surprised when a German officer climbed onto the parapet and said, in excellent English, 'You can't stop there with that man. Either bring him into our trench and we will look after him or hurry on back to your own side. We will not fire.' 'I will go back to my own trench, sir,' said the soldier, standing at attention, and gulping down his embarrassment. As he scuttled back, helping his wounded friend, the Germans were as good as their word and no shots were fired.

309 THE CHRISTMAS TRUCE

For most people the word fraternization suggests the truce that occurred on the Western Front at Christmas in 1914. There was nothing official about it and it happened spontaneously at many points along the front line between individual groups of Germans and Britons.

At 8.30 a.m. I was looking out, and saw four Germans leave their trenches and come towards us; I told two of my men to go and meet them, unarmed (as the Germans were unarmed), and to see that they did not pass the half-way line. We were 350–400 yards apart at this point. My fellows were not very keen, not knowing what was up, so I went out alone, and met Barry, one of our ensigns, also coming out from another part of the line. By the time we got to them, they were three quarters of the way over, and much too near our barbed wire, so I moved them back. They were three private soldiers and a stretcher bearer, and their spokesman started off by saying that he thought it only right to come over and wish us a happy Christmas, and trusted us implicitly to keep the truce. He came from Suffolk, where he had left his best girl and a 3.5 hp motorbike! He told me that he could not get a letter to the girl, and wanted to send one through me. I made him write out a postcard in front of me, in English, and I sent it off that night. I told him that she probably would not be a bit keen to see him again. We then entered on a long discussion on every sort of thing. I was dressed in an old stocking cap and a man's overcoat, and they took me for a corporal, a thing which I did not discourage, as I had an eye to going as near their lines as possible. I asked them what orders they had from their officers as to coming over to us, and they said none, they had just come over out of good will . . .

I kept it up for half an hour, and then escorted them back as far as their barbed wire, having a jolly good look round all the time, and picking up various little bits of information which I had not had an opportunity of doing under fire! I left instructions with them that if any of them came out later they must not come over the half-way line, and appointed a ditch as the meeting place. We parted after an exchange of Albany cigarettes and German cigars, and I went straight to headquarters to report. On my return at 10 a.m. I was surprised to hear a hell of a din going on, and not a single man left in my trenches; they were completely denuded (against my orders) and nothing lived! I heard strains of 'Tipperary' floating down the breeze, swiftly followed by a tremendous burst of 'Deutschland über alles' and as I got to my own company headquarters' dugout, I saw, to my amazement, not only a crowd of about 150 British and Germans at the half-way house which I had appointed opposite my lines, but six or seven such crowds, all the way down our lines, extending towards the eighth division on our right. I bustled out and asked if there were any German officers in my crowd, and the noise died down (as this time I was myself in my own cap and badges of rank).

I found two but had to talk to them through an interpreter, as they could neither talk English nor French . . . I explained to them that strict orders must be maintained as to meeting half-way, and everyone unarmed and we both agreed not to fire until the other did, thereby creating a complete deadlock and armistice (if strictly observed) . . .

Meanwhile Scots and Huns were fraternizing in the most genuine possible manner. Every sort of souvenir was exchanged, addresses given and received, photos of families shown etc. One of our fellows offered a German a cigarette; the German said, 'Virginian?' Our fellow said, 'Aye, straight-cut.' The German said, 'No thanks, I only smoke Turkish.' It gave us all a good laugh.

A German N.C.O. with the Iron Cross – gained, he told me, for conspicuous skill in sniping – started his fellows off on some marching tune. When they had done, I set the note for 'The Boys of Bonny Scotland, where the heather and the bluebells grow', and so we went on, singing everything from 'Good King Wenceslaus' down to the ordinary

Heilige Nacht: the spontaneous Christmas truce of 1914. One officer recounted his own experiences of the truce in his section (see number 309), which seems to have been initiated by ordinary soldiers. Gifts and jokes were exchanged, and songs sung, ending with 'Auld lang syne'. In other sections, football matches were played. Needless to say, the military commanders on both sides did not approve of such fraternization, but in some areas local Christmas truces continued throughout the war (see number 306).

Tommies' song, and ended up with 'Auld lang syne', which we all, English, Scots, Irish, Prussians, Wurtembergers etc, joined in. It was absolutely astounding, and if I had seen it on a cinematograph film I should have sworn that it was faked!

Source: Captain Sir Edward Hulse Bart, *Letters from the English Front in France* (1918)

310 FOR OLD TIME'S SAKE

The Civil War in the United States between the North and South divided families and broke up friendships – but not always permanently.

On the birth of Confederate general George Pickett's first baby, on 17 March 1864, Union commander Ulysses S. Grant – a friend of Pickett's since the days of the Mexican War twenty years before – lit celebratory bonfires along the Union lines. Later he sent a baby's silver service engraved with the names of Ulysses S. Grant and two other officers – Rufus Inglas and George Suckley – over to the Confederate lines to be presented to General Pickett and his wife.

THE FORTUNES OF WAR

311 THE DUELLISTS

In the 18th century duels between officers were often savage affairs. This one continued even beyond the grave.

Two French captains, La Fenestre and d'Agay, had been deadly enemies for 28 years, and had fought seven duels. Although La Fenestre had his head blown off at the battle of Vellinghausen, his friends were pleased to observe that a fragment of his skull hit d'Agay in the right eye and partially blinded him.

312 HOME FOR HEROES

As the war came to an end in 1918 millions of British servicemen returned to the 'land fit for heroes' promised by Prime Minister David Lloyd George. Invariably they faced bitter disappointment. There were few houses . . .

We'd had a war wedding before he left, so we didn't have a house of our own. After a few months we were given a railway carriage to live in. That was the Home for Heroes. It was the best they could do. So we started our married life in a converted railway carriage.

Source: Mrs I. McNicol

The fortunes of many ex-servicemen after the First World War were distinctly low (see numbers 312 and 313). This demonstration against their treatment took place in 1923.

313 WHEN THE WAR WAS OVER

There were even fewer jobs in 1919 . . .

I had a walk around and eventually sat on a seat on the Embankment. I must have dozed off, because it was dark when I woke up, so I decided to stay put until the morning. I woke as the dawn was breaking, and what a sight it was. All the seats were full of old soldiers in all sorts of dress – mostly khaki – and a lot more were lying on the steps, some wrapped up in old newspapers. Men who had fought in the trenches, now unwanted and left to starve, were all huddled together.

Source: Trooper Sydney Chaplin

314 THE UNKNOWN SOLDIER

During the Seven Years War Austria, France and Russia were at war with Prussia and England.

A young Walloon soldier in the Austrian service was killed near Breslau in 1757. His father wanted to have the body, but the Austrian authorities faced the problem of finding it among the grave pits where corpses had been thrown in thousands at a time. The father was six hundred miles away, and the request was made some two months after the battle was fought. As fate would have it the Austrians were encamped not far from the battlefield and the officer entrusted with the task took the first body he came upon, which happened to be the corpse of a Prussian soldier. The body was duly sent to Namur, where a thousand masses were offered uselessly for its benefit. A splendid marble tomb was erected – for the wrong man.

315 **GRATITUDE**

Frederick II of Prussia was a philosopher-king as well as a great military leader. As a result he was never surprised by the way men behaved, knowing that a coward one day might be a hero the next.

Frederick the Great had been inspired at the battle of Mollwitz in 1741 by the example of a wounded footsoldier, a grenadier, who seized a riderless horse, mounted it, rode into battle and returned with an Austrian officer as a prisoner. The King ordered the man's wounds to be tended and when he had recovered he was made an officer and transferred to the cavalry. But on his first day of duty with an élite cavalry unit he deserted to the enemy. Frederick often quoted this particular case when philosophers argued with him about human nature.

316 **STRANGE BEDFELLOWS**

The campaign in Belgium leading to the battle of Waterloo in 1815 was particularly dislocating and many military units – both British and French – were broken up and scattered over a wide area. As a result, some men were separated from their units and unsure of the outcome of the battle.

During the retreat from the field of Waterloo in 1815, Lieutenant Jean-François Faure de Saint Romand sought refuge at an inn at Philippeville, 40 miles from the battlefield, when his horse gave out on him. When he asked for a room, the innkeeper said he could share one with an officer who had arrived earlier and was in bed. The Frenchman was too tired to argue and went upstairs and fell asleep immediately. At dawn he found he was sharing a bed with a British officer who had become detached from his unit and thought the French had won the battle.

317 **NATURAL CAUSES**

In the early stages of the French Wars of Religion, Anthony of Bourbon joined the Catholic Triumvirate in fighting against the Huguenots.

A man cut off in his prime on the battlefield can rarely be considered to have died of natural causes, but such was the fate of Anthony of Bourbon, King of Navarre, during the siege of Rouen in 1562. Waiting his turn to ascend a scaling ladder into the city, Anthony's excitement got the better of him and he felt the call of nature. Unlacing part of his armour to facilitate the process he was struck by a musket ball *'et mourut en pissant'*.

318 **THE CONSTABLE ARRESTED**

The Constable Anne de Montmorency had been one of France's foremost soldiers during the Habsburg-Valois wars of the first half of the 16th century. Unfortunately he continued to base his tactical philosophy on the headlong charge, with himself at the head of his cavalry, which had more than once left him a prisoner in enemy hands and his army a leaderless rabble. Even at 74 he did not seem to have learned the discretion appropriate to his age.

At the battle of St Denis in 1567 he was knocked from his horse by a Scottish adventurer named Robert Stuart, who called on the old man to surrender. Montmorency responded by hitting Stuart in the face with his sword hilt, knocking out three of the Scotsman's front teeth. Temporarily allowing his anger to overcome his greed for ransom, Stuart pulled out his pistol and shot the Constable in the chest, killing him instantly.

319 THIEVES FALL OUT

The sack of Rome in 1527 was an atrocious act of vandalism by the Imperial army, left leaderless by the death of their commander the Duke of Bourbon.

During the sack of Rome in 1527 by Imperial troops, a group of Spaniards broke into a shop and discovered what they took to be a sackful of freshly minted gold coins. Determined to hold on to their booty, particularly against the acquisitive German landsknechts, they barricaded the doors and sat down to count their loot. Unfortunately for them a band of passing Germans heard of their lucky find and started banging at the door of the shop, trying to burst in and share the spoils. Fighting broke out and the Germans were driven back. Complaining that they did all the fighting while the Spaniards got the gold the Germans set fire to the shop and all the Spaniards inside were burned to death. Once the flames had died down the landsknechts broke into the smouldering ruins and retrieved the now blackened coins, only to find that they were not gold but low-value copper.

320 SWORDS INTO PLOUGHSHARES

After the end of the American Civil War in 1865 it was often difficult for returning Confederate soldiers to find employment in some devastated parts of the South.

One farmer near Appomattox in Virginia offered to supply work to any of Robert E. Lee's veterans. To save the embarrassment of the officers, who were unused to manual labour, the kindhearted farmer divided his workers into squads according to their military rank. A passing neighbour enquired of him one day, 'Who are those men working over there?'

'Them is privates, sir, of Robert E. Lee's army. Very fine men, sir, first-rate workers.'

'And who are those in that second group?'

'Them is lieutenants and captains. They work quite well, but not so well as the private soldiers.'

'I see you have a third squad. Who are they?'

'Them is the colonels.'

'And how do the colonels work?'

'Well, neighbour, you won't be hearing me say anything ag'in a man who fought under Bobby Lee. But I tell you one thing: I ain't gonna hire me no generals.'

Source: General John B. Gordon, *Reminiscences of the Civil War* (1903)

*'His Army Broke Up and Followed Him,
Weeping and Sobbing.' Many could not believe
that the great Robert E. Lee had surrendered at
Appomattox in 1865 (see number 321).
Paradoxically the Confederacy's finest general
believed neither in slavery nor in secession: in
1860 he had written that if 'strife and civil war
are to take the place of brotherly love and
kindness, I shall mourn for my country and for the
welfare and progress of mankind'. After the war
he became president of Washington College in
Virginia, proving to be a surprisingly enlightened
educationalist.*

321 THE OTHER LEE

*Robert E. Lee was such a famous general that it is easy to overlook the fact that there was
another General Lee in the South.*

After General Robert E. Lee surrendered at Appomattox in 1865, his nephew General
Fitzhugh Lee rode away from the courthouse and met an old North Carolina soldier on
the dusty road. Hailing the soldier, Lee asked where he was going.

'I've been on leave,' said the soldier, 'And I'm going back now to join General Bobby
Lee.'

'You needn't waste your time,' said Lee, 'Throw your rifle away and go home. Lee's
surrendered.'

'Lee surrendered?' asked the soldier incredulously.

'That's what I said.'

'It must have been that damned Fitzhugh Lee, then,' said the soldier contemptuously.
'Bob Lee would never surrender.' And he walked on.

Source: *Louisville Courier-Journal*, as quoted in *Confederate Veteran* (1896)

322 A COOL HEAD

*The Austro-Prussian war of 1866 was the decisive struggle for the future of Germany. At
Königgrätz, all Bismarck's work towards unification hung in the balance.*

At the battle of Königgrätz in 1866, Prussian success depended on the precise timing of the movement of separate armies. For Bismarck and Moltke there was an anxious moment when it seemed that the crown prince might not arrive in time with his army and the separate Prussian armies might be defeated in detail. One general remarked to Bismarck, 'Excellency, you are now a great man. But if the crown prince had come too late you would now be the greatest villain.' It was certainly a close-run thing, but Bismarck relates that Moltke had not been worried by the thought of failure. Bismarck had thought to test the commander and rode up to him to offer him a cigar. Moltke willingly accepted. Bismarck presented an open case in which there were just two cigars left, one top quality Havana and another of a much poorer type. Moltke apparently studied them both carefully, fingering each, before selecting the Havana. This action reassured Bismarck enormously. If Moltke was able to bestow so much of his attention on the choice of a cigar then clearly the military situation could not be disturbing him. Within minutes the sound of the crown prince's guns could be heard in the distance and the flank of the Austrian army began to waver. The battle was won.

323 THE NERVE OF FAIRFAX

Sir Thomas Fairfax was the highly respected and moderate leader of the northern Parliamentary army during the English Civil War.

In 1643 the Parliamentarian commander, Sir Thomas Fairfax, was at the head of his men as they galloped into the Yorkshire town of Wakefield, then held by troops loyal to King Charles I. So recklessly did Fairfax charge that having first captured two Royalist colonels he suddenly found himself alone in the market place, facing a whole regiment of Royalist foot. Fairfax kept his nerve and began a conversation with his two captives as if he were simply passing the time of the day. When other officers approached the captive colonels neither man gave Fairfax away, having apparently promised to be his 'true prisoners'. However, Fairfax knew his identity would be discovered at any moment, so he leapt on his horse and rode straight through the startled Royalist ranks and made good his escape. Within minutes he had returned with his men and a cannon, and had taken 1400 Royalist prisoners, including the two colonels – for the second time.

324 DIVINE JUSTICE

The Fairfaxes, father and son, were Godfearing men who would not let the soldiers under their command break the laws of Moses.

In 1643 Lord Fairfax and his son Sir Thomas met the Royalists under the Earl of Newcastle at Adwalton Moor. In spite of being heavily outnumbered the Fairfaxes won a startling victory, during which two of the enemy commanders, Colonels Howard and Heron, were killed. Lord Fairfax was horrified when he found that four of his men had looted and stripped the body of Colonel Heron. No sooner had he expressed his anger than a cannon ball struck the four villains, killing two and severely wounding the others. Fairfax was delighted at this evidence of divine justice, pointing out to his men that where men were unable to punish a sinful act, God himself could be relied upon to do it for them.

325 DEATH BY POST

Prince Eugène of Savoy, the Imperial commander-in-chief during the War of the Spanish Succession, was quite accustomed to the risks involved in being a commander – and not only on the battlefield.

In 1708, during the siege of Lille, Prince Eugène received a letter and on opening it found that it contained just a single piece of greasy paper, which he threw on the ground without a thought. His adjutant, a man of suspicious nature, picked up the paper and smelled it, whereupon he first became giddy and then fell unconscious to the ground. Only the swift administration of a general antidote saved him. When the poisoned paper was hung around the neck of a dog it was effective in killing the animal after a few hours' suffering. Eugène was the least disturbed of all the onlookers, commenting 'You need not wonder at it, gentleman. I have several times before now received letters of this nature.'

326 A LUCKY WAY TO GO

Death – even for generals – is as unwelcome as it is inevitable.

During the siege of Philipsburg in 1734 the famous French marshal, the Duke of Berwick, was accustomed to inspecting the trenches every morning at the same time. At one point in the line a sentry had been placed to warn people that the area was particularly dangerous as it was frequently under fire from both sides. Berwick apparently dismissed the sentry's warning and continued his inspection with his son, the Duke of FitzJames. As father and son wandered into the danger zone the cannons opened fire and a cannon ball neatly decapitated the old marshal. When the news of his death was received by his old comrade-in-arms, Marshal Villars, who was dying of a painful disease, Villars remarked, 'Ah, Berwick, that man always was luckier than me.'

327 THE MIGHTY FRUNDSBURG

The German landsknechts of George Frundsburg, Prince of Mindelheim, were a notoriously undisciplined force during the Italian Wars of the early 16th century. Fighting for money rather than loyalty to the Habsburg cause, they frequently mutinied when their pay was in arrears. Only the personality of their gigantic leader was ever able to overcome their greed for gold.

During the grim days of March 1527, marching in heavy rain and with hunger pangs tugging at their loyalty, the landsknechts threatened to break ranks and march back home. On 11 March patience finally snapped and they set off towards the tent of the Imperial commander, the Duke of Bourbon, determined to get the back pay that they were owed. Only a single figure opposed them, Frundsburg himself, now a very old man in spite of his great strength and stature. Frundsburg bellowed at them, called them his children, reminded them of their loyalty to the Habsburg emperor. But the magic had gone. He had quelled them many times in the past but this time he failed. Several landsknechts waved their halberds at him, forcing Frundsburg to wield his enormous double-handed sword to keep them back. What might have happened next we can only guess for sud-

George Frundsburg, Prince of Mindelheim. The disloyalty of the landsknechts that he had led for so long was to break his heart (see number 327).

denly Frundsburg, purple with fury, began to choke and then toppled over onto a drum, gasping for breath. The mutiny ended in a moment for this giant man was like a father to all of them and they loved him. They picked up his body and carried him to his tent where the doctors declared there was little they could do. Frundsburg had clearly had a stroke and never recovered. His men placed him on a stretcher and then in a carriage and took him back home, through Lombardy and across the Alps to his castle of Mindelheim where he died at the age of 82. This veteran of a hundred fights had finally died of a broken heart brought on by the disloyalty of those he had trusted and loved – an unusual fate for so grim a warrior.

328 DROWNING HIS SORROWS

In 1527 the Imperial soldiers occupied Rome for nearly ten months before they withdrew. Many terrible tales of revenge were told.

A certain rich merchant had seven German landsknechts billeted on him throughout the occupation, ruining his business and eating him out of house and home. As they were preparing to leave he offered them one final dinner from food that he had been saving for the occasion. The Germans happily ate the food, planning at the end of the meal to force the old man to disclose the whereabouts of the treasure they were convinced he still had hidden. Threatened with torture, he eventually admitted that he had a hoard of treasure buried on an artificial island in the River Tiber near the Ostian Gate. Under threat he agreed to let his son take the seven men to the treasure trove. The boy and the soldiers set out in a small boat with the boy rowing, but as soon as he was in midstream the boy threw the oars overboard and swam to the shore, leaving the helpless Germans to be swept into a downstream whirlpool, where they were all drowned.

329 A PALPABLE HIT

During the Austrian siege of Turkish-held Belgrade in 1717 a young Polish engineer claimed that he could explode the magazine of the city and promised the Imperial commander, Prince Eugène, that he would pay with his head if he failed to secure a hit with his first three shots.

The cocky young Pole was so unpopular with the German gunners that he could only win their help by bribing them with a cask of wine. Nevertheless, eventually everything was ready and the Pole fired the first shot, which was a miss. Unperturbed, he again fired and missed. Now the tension was electric. Everyone knew of his wager with the Prince and wondered how matters would go if he missed again. The Pole turned to an old sergeant who was helping him and admitted, 'If I don't land the bomb on the roof this time I shall have to make myself scarce.' He fired the mortar and to everyone's astonishment scored a direct hit. There was a tremendous explosion and the Pole, Eugène and the whole Imperial army were deluged in rocks, stones, shattered timbers and pieces of the unfortunate Turkish defenders. The bomb had exploded the main Turkish magazine, killing over 3000 people and destroying many of the city's minarets.

330 ALL IN A DAY'S WORK

The cavalrymen of the 19th century formed a band of brothers, crossing national divisions.

During the battle of Inkermann in 1855 Major the Hon. Hugh Clifford, acting as ADC to General Buller, leapt some high bushes on his horse only to find himself confronted by two Russian cavalrymen. He knocked down one with his horse and then slashed the other across the arm with his sword, before making his escape. Two days later he was visiting his brigade hospital when he noticed some prisoners, one of whom had had his arm amputated. On seeing Clifford the Russian smiled and waved with his uninjured arm, explaining through an interpreter that Clifford was the man who had cut off his arm. Apparently he bore the major no ill will at all.

331 GREAT MINDS . . .

As the Allied troops advanced through Italy in 1943 they discovered that the retreating Germans had left them some nasty surprises.

British troops once came upon a highly desirable billet abandoned by the Germans, its front door invitingly half-open. Entering cautiously through a window to avoid the likely booby trap they approached the front door from inside and found attached to it the expected explosive charge set to go off when the door was moved. They left the house carefully and tied a string to the outside knob of the front door taking cover in a slit trench across the road. When they were all in the slit trench they pulled the string. The slit trench exploded, killing them all.

332 THE FIRST TO FALL

Britain's first casualty of the Second World War occurred as a result of an air raid warning that turned out to be a false alarm.

PC George Southworth was killed falling from a third floor in Harley Street, London, in September 1939, after climbing up a drain pipe in an attempt to put out a light in one of the rooms there. He had been unable to get a reply when he knocked at the door.

333 RACIAL UNDERSTANDING

The racial mixture that was a part of the make-up of British forces in Africa in 1914–18 often resulted in the need for readjustments in the minds of the racially prejudiced white South Africans, who generally referred to their Indian colleagues as 'coolies' and expressed reluctance to fight alongside them.

In 1916, the 6th South African Infantry embarked for service in Kenya. On 12 February these young and inexperienced troops went into action for the first time at Salaita, and were put to flight by a bayonet charge by German askaris. While the white troops fled, the 130th Baluchis held their ground and saved the day. Later a mule was sent to the South African camp carrying the machine gun the white troops had abandoned, along with a note which said 'With the compliments of the 130th Baluchis. May we request that you no longer refer to our people as coolies.'

Indian troops with a French Hotchkiss machine gun on the Western Front, World War I. The effectiveness of Indian troops in the conflict undermined the racial prejudices of many (see number 333).

334 RILEY'S RENEGADES

During the Mexican War of 1846–8 the Americans relied on a mainly volunteer army to fight the troops of Mexican president Santa Anna. However, they were plagued with the problem of desertion, notably by Catholic soldiers responding to Mexican incitement to defect.

The Mexicans offered the American privates 320 acres of land and much more for non-commissioned and commissioned men. One of the foremost of the American defectors was a man named Riley, who had been a sergeant in the US Army but became a lieutenant in the Mexican one, gathering around him hundreds of deserters, so many of them Irish Catholics that a special unit named the Batallon San Patricio was set up, with its own standard bearing St Patrick himself, the harp of Erin and even the shamrock. Riley's men, known as the San Patricios, fought against the Americans throughout the war, at the siege of Monterrey, the battle of Buena Vista and the siege of Churubusco. It was at this last battle that some sixty of them were captured, including Riley, and sentenced to death at a court martial. US Colonel William Harney was put in charge of executing thirty of the San Patricios outside Churubusco. When only twenty-nine came out for execution Harney was furious and wanted to know where the missing man was. He was told that the wretched deserter had had both his legs blown off in the fighting and was already dying. Harney was not to be robbed of his victim and insisted, 'Bring the damned son of a bitch out! My order is to hang thirty and by God I'll do it.' The legless man was carried out and hanged with the others.

Of all the San Patricios captured by the Americans, only Riley was given clemency by General Winfield Scott, on the dubious grounds that he had only been giving the Mexicans token assistance while he helped captured American servicemen to escape. In the event, Riley received fifty lashes and was branded on the cheek with a 'D' for deserter – in fact the branding took place twice as the first time the 'D' was upside down. Riley survived to marry a Mexican heiress and lived to a ripe old age.

335 'STONEWALL' NORWOOD

Cowardice on the part of American cavalry officers in the 'Wild West' is, not surprisingly, an area that has received little attention. Nevertheless, several examples have been recorded.

During a skirmish with the Indians in 1881 a certain Captain Norwood of 'L' company, 2nd Cavalry, known among his fellow-soldiers as a coward, ordered his men to 'build a wall of stones around him'.

336 A SHORT STAY

The British Expeditionary Force retreated from Mons, in Belgium, in August 1914, closely pursued by the German First Army of General von Kluck.

During the British retreat from Belgium in August 1914 the soldiers reported their bitterest experience was in tramping over a strip of cloth in a small Belgian town bearing the words, 'Welcome to our saviours the British.'

337 A PREMONITION

During the Russian campaign of 1812 many French senior officers – generals and marshals – lost their lives or suffered severe injury. In 1812 Eugénie, wife of Marshal Oudinot, had a premonition of such a disaster.

I was expecting a bust of my husband which a fairly talented artist in Berlin had modelled at the end of our stay in that city. One morning the arrival of an enormous case from Germany was announced. I dragged my mother with me and eagerly hurried on the opening. Trembling with excitement I saw the covering removed then the first, the second and finally the last wrapping paper.

What was my shock on seeing that one of the shoulders of the cherished plaster was mutilated and about to break away from the body! Ominous thoughts seized my imagination. This foreboding was to be realized only too well since a few days later the Marshal had his shoulder smashed by grapeshot.

Source: G. Stiegler, *Marshal Oudinot, Duke of Reggio* (1894)

338 A NARROW ESCAPE

Jacques La Force, a young Huguenot, faced death in the St Bartholomew's Day Massacre but lived to become one of France's foremost soldiers.

In the chaos that followed the killing of the Huguenots in Paris in 1572, many took the opportunity to settle old scores. One of the most vicious killers was Annibal de Coconnas, favourite of the Duke of Alençon, who killed the Huguenot leader La Force and his eldest son. The younger son, Jacques La Force, who was only twelve, escaped by feigning death, lying amongst the dead bodies throughout the day. As evening came he heard a man sighing nearby, saying 'Oh God will punish this.' It was the marker of the tennis court. The child stood up and asked the man's help in reaching his sister's husband, Larchant, the captain of the guard, but the man refused and took him to his own house. What the boy did not know was that Larchant was no friend of his and had helped to kill his father. In the old man's house Jacques was hidden in the straw of his bed. The next day he disguised Jacques as a beggar and took him to the Arsenal where Marshal Biron had him hidden. But the story got around and Larchant, in whom the boy had trusted, came hurrying and demanded in the name of Catherine de' Medici to know the whereabouts of the young boy, his brother-in-law, in order to protect him. Biron refused to hand the boy over and helped him escape the next day, complete with a false passport, and after a difficult journey he reached safety with his uncle. Jacques survived to become the famous Marshal La Force, the Huguenot general, and lived to be nearly one hundred years old.

339 A SMALL VOICE

During the siege of the Lucknow Residence in the 1857 Indian Mutiny the rebel bombardment was relentless and caused many casualties among the defenders.

One shot collapsed a verandah, burying Deputy Commissioner William Capper under the rubble. Captain Anderson and Corporal William Oxenham ran to the scene only to conclude that they were too late – no one could have survived such a crush – Capper must be dead. Suddenly a small voice was heard – it was Capper calling, 'I'm alive! Get me out! Give me air, for God's sake.'

One of the spectators was pessimistic, 'It's impossible to save him,' he announced. But Capper was insistent. 'It is possible – if you try!' he said.

Everyone now put their back into shifting the rubble. But as they struggled they were in constant danger from the Sepoys outside, who now had a clear target and kept up an incessant barrage of shots.

Forty-five minutes passed and parts of Capper's body was free, but not his head or his legs. Another fifteen minutes passed and Oxenham, working relentlessly against time, had cleared Capper's legs and finally pulled him clear. As he sat up the dazed Capper managed to gasp to his helpers, 'See, I told you, it is possible – if you try!'

340 THE SCOURGE OF GOD

The battle of Châlons-sur-Marne in 451 resulted in a defeat for Attila, the 'Scourge of God', at the hands of the Romans and their German allies under Aetius and Theodoric. Sir Edward Creasey here describes the Hunnish leader's reaction to the check he received in the first day's fighting. In fact, Attila was not to die for another two years, traditionally of a nose bleed on his wedding night.

Expecting an assault of the morrow, Attila stationed his best archers in front of the cars and waggons, which were drawn up as a fortification along his lines, and made every preparation for a desperate resistance. But the 'Scourge of God' resolved that no man should boast the honour of having either captured or slain him; and he caused to be raised in the centre of his encampment a huge pyramid of the wooden saddles of his cavalry: round it he heaped the spoils and the wealth that he had won; on it he stationed his wives who had accompanied him in the campaign; and on the summit he placed himself, ready to perish in the flames, and baulk the victorious foe of their choicest booty, should they succeed in storming his defences.

Source: Sir Edward Creasey, *The Fifteen Decisive Battles of the World* (1851)

341 A FORTUNATE ESCAPE

After the battle of Hattin in 1187 and the fall of Jerusalem to the Muslims under Saladin, only the coastal city of Tyre remained in Christian hands. The arrival of Conrad of Montferrat breathed new life into the Christian forces and paved the way for the Third Crusade. However, his appearance in the Holy Land at all was by mere chance, as the Arab writer, Ibn al-Athir, tells us.

It happened that a Frank, from Outremer, called the Marquis – God damn him! – set out by sea with great wealth on a pilgrimage and trading mission, unaware of the disaster that had befallen the Franks. When he entered the harbour at Acre his suspicions were aroused by the absence of the manifestations of joy, ringing of bells and so on, that usually met the arrival in port of a Frankish vessel, and also by the style of dress of the people there. He dropped anchor, uncertain what might have happened. The wind had fallen. Al Malik al-Afdal, for his part, sent his men out in a small boat to see who it was and what he wanted. When the boat came alongside the Marquis, not recognizing it as one of their own, asked what had been happening, and the men on board told him of the Frankish defeat, the fall of Acre and other cities, and informed him at the same time that Tyre and Ascalon and certain other towns were still in Frankish hands, giving him the full details. Since the lack of wind prevented his moving, the Marquis sent the messenger back with a request for permission to enter the city in safety with his merchandise and money. This was granted, but he sent the messenger back again and again each time with new requests, to gain time until the wind should rise and he could use it to escape. In the course of these comings and goings the wind began to blow again and he at once set sail for Tyre. Al Malik al-Afdal sent a galley after him in pursuit but it failed to catch him and he reached Tyre, where a great number of Franks was gathered. For when Saladin took each town, Acre, Beirut and the others, he had allowed the populations to leave freely, and they had all come to Tyre. So the place was thronged but it lacked a leader to unite it and a commander to lead it in battle. The people were not warriors, and were talking of making a treaty with Saladin and offering to surrender the town to him when the Marquis arrived and dissuaded them from such an act and gave them new hope by promising to defend the city himself. He distributed the money he had with him on condition that the city and its territory belonged to him and no one else. When they agreed he made them swear to it, and after that took up residence there and governed the city. He was a devil incarnate in his ability to govern and defend a town, and a man of extraordinary courage.

Source: Ibn al-Athir, *The Perfect History* (Trans. Tornberg 1853–64)

342 LORD NELSON CHANGES TACK

A meeting between Lord Nelson and the Duke of Wellington – in their prime – would have been a splendid occasion. Unfortunately it never happened. Nelson's only encounter with Wellington was when the future duke was a little-known – though highly successful - 'Sepoy-general'.

I found also waiting to see the Secretary of State a gentleman who from his likeness to his pictures and the loss of an arm I immediately recognized as Lord Nelson. He could not know who I was, but he entered at once into conversation with me, if I can call it conversation, for it was almost all on his side and all about himself and in, really, a style so vain and so silly as to surprise and almost disgust me.

I suppose something that I happened to say may have made him guess that I was *somebody*, and he went out of the room for a moment, I have no doubt to ask the office keeper who I was, for when he came back he was altogether a different man, both in manner and matter. All that I had thought a charlatan style had vanished and he talked of the state of this country and of the aspect and probabilities of affairs on the continent with a good sense and a knowledge of subjects both at home and abroad, that surprised me equally and more agreeably than the first part of our interview had done; in fact he talked like an officer and a statesman.

Now if the Secretary of State had been punctual and had admitted Lord Nelson in the first quarter of an hour I should have had the same impression of a light and trivial character that other people have had but luckily I saw enough to be satisfied that he was really a very superior man; but certainly a more sudden and complete metamorphosis I never saw.

Source: J.W. Croker, *Correspondence and Diaries of J.W. Croker* (Ed. L. Jennings 1884)

343 AS THE FATES DECREE

In 274 BC King Pyrrhus of Epirus met his end at the siege of Argos.

Wherefore Pyrrhus seeing his people thus troubled and harried to and fro, took his crown from his head which he wore upon his helmet, that made him known to his men afar off, and gave it unto one of his familiars that was next unto him: and trusting then to the goodness of his horse, flew upon his enemies that followed him. It fortuned that one hurt him with a pike, but the wound was neither dangerous nor great: wherefore Pyrrhus set upon him that had hurt him, who was an Argian born, a man of mean condition, and a poor old woman's son, whose mother at that present time was gotten up to the top of the tiles of a house, as all other women of the city were, to see the fight. And she perceiving that it was her son whom Pyrrhus came upon, was so afrighted to see him in that danger, that she took a tile, and with both her hands cast it upon Pyrrhus. The tile falling off from his head by reason of his headpiece, lighted full in the nape of his neck, and broke his neck bone asunder: wherewith he was suddenly so benumbed that he lost his sight with the blow, the reins of his bridle fell out of his hand, and himself fell from his horse to the ground by Licymmias' tomb, before any man knew what he was, at the least the common people.

Source: Plutarch, *Life of Pyrrhus* (1st century; trans. Sir Thomas North 1579)

344 A LIFE-SAVING DISGUISE

The attack on Rorke's Drift, during the Zulu War of 1879, is one of the epic stories in British military history. Eleven Victoria Crosses were won in that single engagement. Four thousand Zulus attacked the small British garrison defending the mission station of Swedish missionary Dr Witt. Many of the garrison were sick and ill in the hospital, where Private John Waters was an orderly.

They came about twenty yards and then opened fire on the hospital. Some of them came in and set fire to it. While I was there I took refuge in a cupboard, and Private Beckett, an invalid, came with me. As they were going out I killed many of them and as I could not stay there long, the place being so suffocating, I put on a black cloak which I had found in the cupboard, and which must have belonged to Mr Witt, and ran out in the long grass and lay down. The Zulus must have thought I was one of their dead comrades,

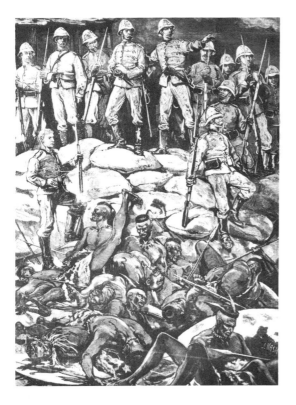

'The Gallant Defence of Rorke's Drift by Lieutenants Chard and Bromhead and One Hundred and Thirty-Seven Men.' Private John Waters had a lucky escape during the fighting (see number 344). When he saw the sight, next morning, of his 'comrades on the top of the mealie-sacks', he knew the battle was over and he was safe. It was less good news for the Zulus: within two months they had been decisively defeated at Kambula, and effectively ceased to exist as a nation.

as they were all round about me, and some trod on me. Beckett had gone out half an hour before me, and he poor fellow, was assegaied right through his stomach, and went into laager next morning. Dr Reynolds did all he could to save him, but did not succeed. I got up at daybreak, having expected every minute my life would be taken, and then saw my comrades on the top of the mealie-sacks, and I said, 'Thank God, I have got my life.'

Source: Private John Waters, *The Cambrian* 13 June 1879

345 THE LEAP OF A LIFETIME

After the failure of the Duke of Monmouth's revolt against James II in 1685 and the disastrous battle of Sedgemoor, many of the Duke's supporters were rounded up by local militiamen. One rebel, John Swain of Shapwick in Somerset, made the most of his local knowledge to effect his escape.

John Swain had returned to his home in Shapwick after the battle of Sedgemoor, but he had been arrested by the local militia and was marched towards Bridgwater to stand trial before Judge Jeffreys. Knowing what his chances would be if he ever reached his destination, Swain decided to escape. As he marched along the Bridgwater road, with his wife and children walking glumly behind, he passed Loxley Wood. He stopped and asked his captors – simple men one must assume – if he could demonstrate to his children his skills as a long jumper, so that they would have something to remember him by. His guards agreed, and as they stood back to watch Swain suddenly made three giant leaps from one stone to another across the nearby river and disappeared into the woods. The stones remain to mark Swain's athletic skills, and suggest a triple jump of some 41 feet!

346 DRAGOONED

The retreat to Corunna in 1808–9 during the Peninsular War is one of the epic stories of the British Army. Only the most vigorous leadership by Sir John Moore and his fellow generals kept the British soldiers ahead of the pursuing French and disaster. In this incident – unusually humorous for so grim a campaign – we see Lord Paget trying to maintain morale at an officer's expense.

Our stay at Cambarros was but short, for scarcely had the men lain down to repose, which was much wanted in consequence of the manner in which they had passed the previous night, when some of our cavalry came galloping in, reporting that the enemy was advancing in force. We were immediately ordered to get under arms, and hurried to form outside the town on that part facing Bembibre. While we were forming a dragoon rode up, and an officer who being ill was in one of the light carts which attended the reserve, cried out, 'Dragoon, what news?' 'News, sir? The only news I have for you is that unless you step out like soldiers, and don't wait to pick your steps like bucks in Bond Street of a sunday with the shoes and silk stockings, dammit! you'll all be taken prisoners.' 'Pray, who the devil are you?' came from the cart. 'I am Lord Paget,' said the dragoon; 'and pray, sir, may I ask who you are?' 'I am Captain D——, of the 28th Regiment, my lord.' 'Come out of that cart directly,' said his lordship; 'March with your men, sir, and keep up their spirits by showing them a good example.' The captain scrambled out of the cart rear, face foremost, and from slipping along the side of the cart and off the wheels, and from the sudden jerks which he made to regain his equilibrium, displayed all the ridiculous motions of a galvanised frog. Although he had previously suffered a good deal from both fatigue and illness, yet the circumstance altogether caused the effect desired by his lordship, for the whole regiment were highly diverted by the scene until we arrived at Bembibre, and it caused many a hearty laugh during the remainder of the retreat.

Source: Robert Blakeney, *A Boy in the Peninsular War* (1899)

347 CROSS ROADS

Death was always in the minds of the soldiers in the First World War.

I rode slowly along the marching battalions. I heard the regular sound of an engine and saw puffs of smoke shooting up from a house on the road. A steamsaw was cutting rhythmically through wood, working at high pressure with a tearing sound. Seeing the yard in front of the house piled high with wooden crosses and thinking to spare the men, I hurried in to have them removed. The Belgians engaged in the work threw up their hands in despair and pointed through the window to the back of the house and an even bigger pile. Nothing could be done. I watched the men as they passed by. Some smiled, others passed a joke, some wouldn't look. But I knew that they all saw and understood.

Source: Paul Maze, *A Frenchman in Khaki* (1934)

348 THE KING IS DEAD

It was a common ruse in the Middle Ages for kings to disguise themselves in battle, and, in order to confuse the enemy, a number of soldiers would be decked out in the king's apparel. Apparently the same process was used in biblical times. At the battle of Ramoth-Gilead, King Ahab of Israel persuaded Jehoshaphat to wear his kingly garb. However, fate was not kind to Ahab.

And the king of Israel said unto Jehoshophat, I will disguise myself and enter into the battle; but put thou on thy robes. And the king of Israel disguised himself, and went into the battle.

But the king of Syria, commanded his thirty and two captains that had rule over his chariots, saying Fight neither with small nor great, save only with the king of Israel.

And it came to pass, when the captains of the chariots saw Jehoshophat that they said, surely it is the king of Israel. And they turned aside to fight against him: and Jehoshophat cried out.

And it came to pass, when the captains of the chariots perceived that it was not the king of Israel, that they turned back from pursuing him.

And a certain man drew a bow at a venture, and smote the king of Israel between the joints of the harness: wherefore he said unto the driver of his chariot, Turn thine hand, and carry me out of the host, for I am wounded.

And the battle increased that day: and the king was stayed up in his chariot against the Syrians, and died at even: and the blood ran out of the wound into the midst of the chariot.

And there went a proclamation throughout the host about the going down of the sun, saying, Every man to his city, and every man to his own country!

Source: I Kings, 22:30-36

349 THE END OF THE LINE

The defeat of France in 1940 was a shattering blow to French morale. Many blamed the government for complacency and for not equipping French troops with modern weapons of war. Paul Reynard, who recounts the following, was briefly prime minister before the German occupation, and was imprisoned by the Germans until 1945.

I received a postcard at my address, found on the body of an officer of Corap's army, who had just committed suicide in Le Mans station. He wrote, 'I am killing myself Mr President to let you know that all my men were brave, but one cannot send men to fight tanks with rifles.'

Source: Paul Reynaud, *In the Thick of the Fight* (1955)

350 **TREASURE TROVE**

During the Indian Mutiny in 1857 British officers joined their men in looting Delhi after it had been captured in a bloodbath.

A young British lieutenant, impoverished and supporting a widowed mother, received an extraordinary reward from his loyal troopers in the 93rd. During their looting in Delhi they came upon a diamond-studded, golden tazza (wine-cup) which they decided to give to the young man to help him purchase a captaincy. They could hardly have imagined that they were handling one of the most valuable Indian treasures in existence, which fetched £80,000 in London and made the lieutenant one of the richest men in the country.

351 **NO SECOND STRING**

At the decisive naval battle of Svold Island in 1000, King Olav Tryggveson of Norway was defeated and killed by an alliance of rebel Norwegians and other Scandinavian powers.

During the battle Olaf sent into the rigging a young archer named Einar Tamberskelver, the best bowman in Norway, reputedly so strong that he could fire a blunt arrow through a cow's hide, and told him to kill the rebel Jarl Eric of Norway. Einar fired several arrows but Eric's guards took them on their shields. Einar had a rival, a Finnish archer aboard the rebel ship, who was so skilled that many thought his arrows were guided by sorcery. Jarl Eric ordered the Finn to silence Einar and bring him toppling down from his lofty perch. But the Finn, to show his marksmanship, was content to split Einar's bowstring, which broke and the bow sprang back with a loud cracking sound. 'What is that sound?' asked King Olaf, and Einar replied, 'It is the sound of the sceptre of Norway falling from your grasp.'

SOMEONE HAD BLUNDERED

352 **THE BATTLE OF THE BEAMS**

In November 1940 a German bomber, carrying a complete X-Gerät (part of the German beam bombing system), ran short of fuel over the south coast of England and landed on the beach near Bridport in Dorset.

It was a gift from heaven – a uniquely valuable opportunity for British Intelligence. But a malign fate was at work. A local army unit, concerned with the defence of the Dorset coast, took over the defence of the plane. They could not have known the value of this particular plane but they were determined that no one should be allowed to meddle with it. While an officer phoned for further orders, two soldiers were placed on guard, and were given clear orders: no one, and that meant no one, was allowed to go near it – not even if an Admiral should turn up.

Unfortunately for everyone concerned, the Germans had landed on the sand at low tide and as the sea began to come in it became obvious that the plane would soon be under water. Sailors from a nearby base came to offer the two soldiers some help to drag the plane up the beach, but the guards warned them off and grimly stuck to their orders. The level of the water rose and still their officer did not return. Eventually, the plane was submerged in water, flooding the cockpit with sand and pebbles, and destroying the light alloy components of the beam system. By the time the intelligence service technicians arrived the opportunity was lost and the delicate equipment spoiled by sand. The loss of this equipment delayed the British attempts to combat the German beam system and may have contributed to the failure to block the disastrous raid on Coventry eight days later.

353 A GLARING ERROR

During World War I several Russian generals displayed a marked lack of common sense. General Kuropatkin, whose performance in the war against Japan in 1904–5 should have barred him from holding command again, was just one of them. In an effort to break the stalemate imposed by the trench system he thought he had found a solution.

Planning a night attack on the German lines General Kuropatkin set up batteries of searchlights in order to dazzle the German defenders. Having blinded the enemy he now sent his men 'over the top', only for them to be shot down in thousands. Kuropatkin's common sense did not tell him that they would be silhouetted against the lights and therefore easy targets. The Russians lost 8000 men in a single night.

354 THE LOST ARMY

Following the abortive siege of Burgos in 1812, during the Peninsular War, the British army came as close as at any time to disintegrating. Wellington lost contact with some units of the army and retreat threatened to turn into rout.

In the retreat from Burgos Wellington's army became a disorderly rabble, short of food and closely pressed by the pursuing French. In the ensuing chaos 3000 British stragglers were captured and Lord Paget, commander of the First Division, was snapped up by French skirmishers. Three of his generals decided to disobey Wellington's orders and follow a shorter route that the commander had specifically forbidden them to take. As a result, they led their troops into a dead end, finding their way blocked by a river in flood. Such insubordination could have resulted in the loss of two divisions to the French, and undone all of Wellington's good work in Spain. When asked what the Iron Duke had said when he met the three errant generals, Lord Fitzroy Somerset replied, 'What did he say? Oh, my God, it was far too serious to say anything.' When Wellington met the officer in charge of the baggage he asked the wretched man what he was doing, and received the reply: 'I've lost my baggage.' Without stopping for a moment Wellington rode on, saying: 'I can't be surprised . . . for I cannot find my army.'

'The enemy will never suspect we're here.' A German lithograph of 1832 satirizing the incompetence of the French army of the Rhine in the early days of the French Revolutionary Wars (see number 356).

355 THAT SINKING FEELING

The fate of the dual-drive tanks launched offshore on D-Day, 1944, was disastrous. Equipped to float with impermeable canvas skirts these tanks were to propel themselves to the beach with an ad hoc propeller and then resume normal operation. That at least was the theory.

On D-Day, 32 of the dual-drive tanks were launched off the coast of Normandy, their skirts deployed; but in the high seas – doubtless because of fear of encountering enemy fire – they were set down too far from land. Twenty-seven sank with their complete crews, a tribute to stubborn hope, for tank after tank was launched one after another to sink like a stone, observed by everyone on the launching ship.

356 ORDERS, PLEASE

The French generals in the early stages of the French Revolutionary Wars were frequently inexperienced and promoted beyond their ability. Many had been mere privates or NCOs in the armies of the Ancien Régime.

On 13 October 1793 the French Army of the Rhine was demoralized and its generals lost their heads. Dubois on the right retired needlessly. Another general wanted a Commissariat officer to tell him what to do and, finding him unwilling to advise, called on him in the name of the law to do so, until the unfortunate officer rode off at a gallop. Yet another general, finding that an Austrian column had crossed the Rhine in his rear, instead of informing the commander-in-chief, wrote to the Jacobin club of Strasbourg to ask whether he ought to retreat.

357 HEAVENLY FIRE

The lack of weapons training of troops in the early months of the American Civil War was only too apparent when they were called into action at the first battle of Bull Run in 1861.

A Virginia regiment, at the battle of Bull Run in 1861, fired their first volley at an angle of 45 degrees. As one of their officers observed, 'I was fully assured that their bullets would not hit the Yankees unless they were nearer Heaven than they were generally located by our people.'

358 MANOEUVRES

Military manoeuvres were often fun for the men but provided nothing but headaches for the commanding officers, as this incident from Ireland in the late Victorian period shows.

We had many fine field days on the Curragh and one of them I shall never forget. There were five regiments of cavalry engaged, double that number of infantry, and about forty field guns. At the further end of the Curragh, towards Rathbride, ran an isolated ridge occupied by a skeleton enemy, and the plan of attack included the forcing of this position by the infantry which was carried out in gallant style whilst the cavalry in two bodies hovered on either flank, the left being composed of Lancers and the right of Hussars and Dragoons.

Beyond the ridge the country fell into the level again across which the beaten foe would have to retreat and to make a nice finish to the day's operations it was arranged that a couple of squadrons from each body of cavalry should charge in pursuit. In order to accomplish this they had to skirt the ends of the ridge and then incline to right and left until they met in the centre of the plain beyond, when they were to form in one line and charge.

My troop was amongst those selected for the right cavalry division and as the signal to go was given away we dashed, slashing and cutting the pursuing practice in fine style; and after rounding the end of the ridge made for the point of juncture in the plain beyond. But now ensued an altogether unexpected development for, as the two small bodies of cavalry approached each other, either through the excitement of the men, and their horses, or through the impetus of their gallop, instead of wheeling so as to come into line they followed a diagonal direction until they rode 'bash' into one another, almost front to front at the point of contact. The Lancers lowered the points of their lances to avoid spitting our men and some catching in the ground jerked the riders out of their saddles, whilst all of us came into violent collision. For a moment, it seemed like a regular battlefield, many of the horses being bowled over and others with empty saddles dashing madly about. As far as I myself was concerned the feeling I had when I saw a smash inevitable was 'Look out for Phil Garlie' (a well-known military 'mind yourself' expression) and warding off a thrust from a gallant Lancer, he received the benefit of a whack from my sword and the next moment I came full tilt against one of his comrades, and we both rolled on the turf.

This untoward business occurred through the men being allowed to go too fast, and getting out of hand, and was the fault of the officers. Such a finale to a field day in time of peace has, I fancy, been rarely seen. The general and all the infantry, who had crested the ridge, were looking at us, as well as thousands of spectators, and the former came galloping down with his staff, and when he arrived within shouting distance of our officers it was about the only time in my life that I felt no ambition to be a captain. On taking note of the casualties it was found that about half a dozen of our men were injured by lance thrusts and about the same number of Lancers from sword digs, whilst several of the horses had their shoulders put out from the effects of concussion . . .

Source: Sergeant-Major E. Mole, *A King's Hussar* (collected and condensed by Herbert Compton, 1893)

359 A LOT OF HOT AIR

The Spanish–American War of 1898 was fought both at sea and on land, and demonstrated the military incapacity of both sides. The American campaign in Cuba was particularly chaotic. During the attack on San Juan Hill the American troops had the assistance of a hot-air balloon, which was supposed to spot enemy positions and assist the artillery, but in the jungle it merely acted as a beacon to give away the positions of the American troops.

As 8000 men struggled along the congested jungle road they took with them an inflatable hot-air balloon, from which Lieutenant-Colonel Derby made observations. In case the Spanish defenders had any doubts as to where the American troops might be, the balloon served as a marker to bring down a rain of fire on the helpless masses below. Colonel Wood was unimpressed by Derby's 'aerial reconnaissance' and thought the balloon 'one of the most ill-judged and idiotic acts' he had ever seen. Had Shafter carried out reconnaissance of the region west of El Pozo the balloon would not have been necessary. However, no one, from divisional commander to private soldier, had had a chance to examine the ground leading to the Spanish position or to assess the numbers of the enemy or the strength of their defences.

The congestion on the jungle path was severe. From El Pozo Hill whence Shafter was trying to follow the advance, it appeared that 'the whole command was . . . swallowed up under a sea of green above which there arose only the delicate stems of the scattered palms and the majestic and swaying bulk of the balloon, accurately delineating the advance.' The Spaniards responded by raking the area around the balloon with shrapnel. No one in the American ranks could return the fire or even see where it was coming from.

Source: Geoffrey Regan, *Someone Had Blundered* (1987)

360 MOBILE WARFARE

The Suez Crisis of 1956 found Britain ill-prepared to react militarily. Britain's forces had been run down since the Second World War and Sir Anthony Eden's strong policy against President Nasser's nationalization of the Suez Canal could not be backed up at short notice by a rapid military response. Just how inefficient Britain's military machine had become is illustrated by the fate of the armoured brigades.

When news arrived that they were bound for Egypt the first task was to make the tanks operational. Some vehicles were decrepit and many needed spare parts. The store depots, however, were manned by civilians who took weekends off and so delays were common. The major task, though, was to transport the tanks from Tidworth to Southampton. The shortage of tank transporters presented the planners with a headache, but with true British improvisation they thought of Pickfords, and the removal firm was called in to help. Safety and security, but not speed marked the next four weeks. With Pickfords' men governed by union regulations, each of the massive transporters took a week over a journey the army thought should take three days, and behind each group of vehicles there trailed a number of spares in case of breakdown, as required by transport regulations. It eventually took four weeks to load the 93 tanks at Southampton.

361 TILTING AT WINDMILLS

The great armada against England planned for 1588 involved the whole Spanish state in an administrative and logistical exercise of some magnitude. During the summer of 1587 the Spanish novelist Cervantes was one of hundreds of officials employed in raising supplies throughout the country. Operating in Andalusia, Cervantes soon experienced the inefficiencies of the system that was to send an ill-equipped fleet the following year to combat the ships of Drake and Hawkins.

Cervantes set out with authority from the office of the Purveyor General to collect grain and provisions throughout the province of Andalusia. To support him he carried credentials listing his wide powers of search and procurement. But the ordinary Spanish citizen was more difficult to convince. When Cervantes arrived in Écija, a tall and gangling figure not unlike his own Don Quixote, he found himself plunged into the fantasy world of his own story. No one would take him seriously as a government official. The ordinary people of the town were unwilling to receive him due to a fiesta. If he wished to return in three weeks perhaps they would help him then, but perhaps not. When he insisted on meeting the town council, he was told that owing to the poor harvest and the failure by the government to recompense the town for the last purveyance, his mission was doomed to failure. Like his good knight, Cervantes lowered his visor and prepared to battle the giants of the town council, but he was soon toppled on his backside when they accused him of exceeding his powers and trying to steal the wheat. Cervantes turned to the Church for help, but a local Dominican priest said that he had violated divine law and then threatened to excommunicate him. Cervantes was in despair – but not for long.

The matter was referred to his masters back in Seville and then to the Royal Council in Madrid. Legal wrangles took until June 1588 to settle the problem of the town of Écija. By the summer of 1588 Cervantes was back in the saddle, supervising the production of the best available flour for ships' biscuit, minutely reporting on every stage of the work to his superiors, and turning down nearly eighty per cent of the wheat for failing to meet the exacting standards of the fleet. By August milling of the remaining grain had begun.

The problem was that time may have stood still for Cervantes and the people of Écija, but no one seems to have pointed out to them that the Armada had already sailed. The Duke of Medina Sidonia's ships, which should have been supplied with this flour, had already been defeated and were struggling home round the rough coasts of Scotland and Ireland. The wheels of Spanish bureaucracy had moved so slowly that the Armada had been forced to set sail without fresh flour and with much of the previous year's supply rotting in their holds. Nevertheless, Cervantes completed his mission and produced a voluminous report, which was filed somewhere and no doubt provided food for the mice.

362 KNOW YOUR ENEMY

Before the Allied troops were sent to Gallipoli they were encouraged to believe that the Turk was a poor fighter who would be only too happy to look for a chance to surrender. This dangerous underestimation of the capabilities of the Turks as defensive fighters was to result in heavy Allied casualties in 1915.

While the British and Australian troops in Egypt were being prepared for the expedition to the Dardanelles, they were presented with an official army leaflet that gave them the following useful information: 'Turkish soldiers as a rule manifest their desire to surrender by holding their rifle butt upwards and by waving clothes or rags of any colour. An actual white flag should be regarded with the utmost suspicion as a Turkish soldier is unlikely to possess anything of that colour.'

363 THE MAGINOT COMPLEX

In 1940 the French had so much confidence in the ability of the Maginot Line to resist German attacks that little attention was given to some of the traditional – if boring – aspects of military discipline that made recruits into good soldiers. The French Army had surrendered its great traditions in the face of a series of concrete shelters. British general Allan Brooke was particularly shocked when he visited some French frontline units. Nor were the generals any better.

I can still see those troops now. Seldom have I seen anything more slovenly and badly turned out. Men unshaven, horses ungroomed, clothes and saddlery that did not fit, vehicles dirty and complete lack of pride in themselves or their units. What shook me most, however, was the look in the men's faces, disgruntled and insubordinate looks, and although ordered to give 'Eyes left' hardly a man bothered to do so. After the ceremony was over Corap invited me to visit some of his defences in the Fort de St Michel. There we found a half-constructed and very poor anti-tank ditch with no defences to cover it. By way of conversation I said that I supposed he would cover this ditch with the fire from anti-tank pill-boxes. This question received the reply, *'Ah, bah! On va les faire plus tard – allons, on va déjeuner!'*

Source: Arthur Bryant, *The Turn of the Tide* (1957)

ANIMALS AT WAR

364 DANGER IN THE REEDS

In 1654 a British expedition to capture Jamaica from the Spaniards under the joint command of Admiral Penn and General Venables suffered an ignominious defeat.

As the boats carrying the British soldiers and marines approached the shore near the mouth of the Rio Hayna, there was a clearly audible rustling sound coming from within the dry reeds and undergrowth that fringed the beach. The men disembarked and cautiously moved towards the sound only for the rustling to increase and become more widespread. Fearing that the reeds contained a well-armed enemy force ready to fire a devastating volley into them, the British soldiers turned and fled back across the sand to the boats and put out to sea, refusing to return in spite of the entreaties and orders of their officers.

Later investigation revealed that the enemy who had put the British to flight were nothing more than hundreds of land crabs, which had been moving about among the reeds in alarm, producing the enormous rustling effect that had been heard.

365 AN OLD WARRIOR

Frederick the Great never forgot the debt he owed to the grey horse that had carried him to safety from the field of Mollwitz in 1741.

The horse, ever afterwards known as the 'Mollwitz Grey', was immediately put into retirement and looked after well for the rest of its life. Its field was near the parade ground in Potsdam and when a review was being held, and the regiments marched with their colours and the bands played, the magnificent horse all on its own marched with them across its field, proudly lifting its feet as if it carried Frederick himself into battle. It would continue parading itself around the field until the flags and drums had passed, whereupon it returned quietly to its grazing.

366 A PRIZE OF WAR

At the battle of Soor in 1745 Frederick the Great's baggage train was captured by Austrian Hussars commanded by General Nádasti.

The Austrians made off with all his money, horses, silverware and clothes. Even his favourite flutes were gone. But the greatest loss of all was Frederick's pet whippet Biche, which it was presumed had been murdered by the Hussars. The battle brought an end to the fighting, and when peace negotiations began it was revealed that Biche had survived her terrible experience and was a prisoner of the Austrians, in the safe keeping of General Nádasti's wife, who wanted to keep her. But Frederick insisted there could be no end to the war unless the whippet was returned. Frederick's friend, General Rothenburg, collected the dog and slipped her quietly into the king's bedroom, whereupon she leapt up on a table with her front paws about his neck and began licking him. Tears of joy sprang from Frederick's eyes.

367 BUSTLE

During the siege of Lucknow in 1857 it was vital that the defenders maintained absolute vigilance for fear of being overrun should they relax.

One British soldier, Private Metcalfe, found the Reverend Harris's little dog named Bustle very useful. Bustle would accompany Metcalfe on his watch and if he should become drowsy the dog bit his trousers and shook them vigorously until he awoke. Both Bustle and Private Metcalfe survived the siege. Metcalfe stayed in India for two more years before returning to Aldershot as a sergeant. While on duty one day, he saw a little dog running towards him. It was Bustle, who had recognized Metcalfe immediately.

368 THE BOER CAVALRY

During the evacuation of Ladysmith in 1899 by Sir George White disaster struck a British column commanded by Lieutenant-Colonel Frank Carleton.

The column was led by the Irish Fusiliers, with the Gloucesters bringing up the rear. Between the two regiments were 100 pack mules, fully loaded with ammunition and stores. Climbing a steep hillside road the mules suddenly panicked, rushing headlong down the path, scattering men and equipment as they came. Soon every mule was involved and the Gloucesters, at the bottom of the slope, heard cries of 'Boer cavalry!' The Gloucesters panicked, fixed bayonets, and began firing at the oncoming mass of four-footed creatures. The mules crashed through the regiment, sending over a hundred of them running all the way back to Ladysmith, convinced the Boers were on their heels.

369 RHINOCEROS

During the war in Africa in 1914–18 the participants frequently found that they faced enemies who, though impartial in the human struggle going on around them, were prepared to defend their territory to the best of their ability.

On one occasion a British patrol was routed by three rhinoceroses, and on another by a troop of enraged baboons. In one three-sided contest, a rhinoceros first drove a British patrol away, then turned on the Germans who had been firing at them, and lastly routed a group of Masai tribesmen who had merely been observing the battle.

370 BOBBIE

On 27 July 1880 a British force under Brigadier-General George Burrows was virtually wiped out at Maiwand by a vastly superior force of Afghans under Ayub Khan.

As the battle drew to a close a small mongrel dog named Bobbie, the property of one of the dead British soldiers, Sergeant Kelly of the 66th Foot, escaped through Afghan lines and found his way back to regimental headquarters at Kandahar. Bobbie's wounds were

King Pyrrhus of Epirus on a war elephant. Alexander the Great first came upon elephants in battle during his Asian campaigns, and his successors adopted their use to some effect. Pyrrhus himself (Alexander's cousin) used elephants as a shock tactic against the Romans. The Greeks used Indian elephants – usually with an Indian driver – but the Carthaginians managed to train African elephants, and Hannibal took 50 across the Alps. Initially these struck terror into the Romans – particularly their horses – but soon they learnt to cope with charging elephants simply by opening ranks to let them pass through. The tendency of elephants to run amok on the battlefield meant they were a rather unreliable weapon, as likely to trample friend as foe.

patched up at the fort, and when the rest of the regiment returned to England Bobbie went with them to be presented with the Afghan Medal by Queen Victoria herself. Unfortunately, Bobbie did not survive his master for very long, being run over and killed by a hansom cab. Nevertheless, the little dog had made such an impression on the men of the 66th that he was stuffed and placed in a glass cabinet, complete with medal and ribbon, and can still be seen at the regimental museum in Reading.

371 RUPERT'S FAMILIAR

During the English Civil War, 1642–6, the Royalist cavalry was commanded by the dashing Prince Rupert of the Rhine, nephew to King Charles I.

One of the most famous military dogs was Prince Rupert's dog Boy, a kind of white poodle, which accompanied the prince to all his battles. The Roundheads believed the dog had diabolical skills, could make himself invisible, and knew many tongues: 'He is weapon-proof himself, and probably hath made his master so too.' In fact poor Boy was not weapon-proof: he was killed at the battle of Marston Moor in 1644 after he had strayed onto the battlefield.

372 THE PEACOCK

With starvation becoming increasingly likely at the Lucknow Residency in 1857, during the siege by mutinous sepoys, Captain Robert Anderson faced an unusual dilemma.

On one occasion a peacock landed on the parapet just above Captain Anderson's head and stood there preening its feathers. Everyone wanted to catch the bird and kill it for food, but Anderson refused to do so on the grounds that to destroy such beauty was a callous and uncivilized action.

373 THE ANIMAL LOVERS

Fraternization during the Peninsular War was very common, though it was generally confined to the private soldiers of the warring parties.

In 1813 a French lady from the town of Bayonne was curious to get a first sight of the fearsome British redcoats. Unfortunately, she let her pet poodle jump out of her arms and the little dog ran in confusion towards the British lines. Despite every attempt by French soldiers to summon it back by whistling, it reached the enemy position and crouched by a British officer, Captain Cooke. The lady was distraught at the loss of her prized pet, but her fears were groundless as the gallant captain ordered one of his men to take the little dog back. She was overjoyed at the dog's escape and rewarded the redcoat with a goblet of wine, which he drank with some relish, touched his cap and returned, smoking a pipe and piled high with tobacco given to him by the thankful French soldiers.

374 THE FLYING COLUMN

In the deserts of the Middle East the Macedonian soldiers of Alexander the Great sometimes needed unusual guides to help them find their way.

Furthermore, when the marks were hidden from the guides to show them the way, and that they wandered up and down, they could not tell where: there came crows unto them that did guide them flying before them: flying fast when they saw them follow them, and stayed for them when they were behind. But Callisthenes writeth a greater wonder than this, that in the night time, with the very noise of the crows, they brought them again into the right way which had lost their way. Thus Alexander in the end having passed through this wilderness came unto the temple he sought for.

Source: Plutarch, *Life of Alexander* (1st century; trans. Sir Thomas North 1579)

375 LA BETE HUMAINE

Injuries to horses always evinced a particularly strong reaction from the men who worked with them. At the battle of Waterloo in 1815 Captain Mercer observed a tragic incident.

Bolton's people had not long been engaged when we saw the men of the gun next to us unharness one of the horses and chase it away, wounded, I supposed; yet the beast stood unmoved with firmness, going from one carriage to the other, whence I noticed that he was always eagerly driven away. At last two or three gunners drove him before them to a considerable distance, and then returned to their guns. I took little notice of this at the time, and was surprised by an exclamation of horror from some of my people in the rear. A sickening sensation came over me, mixed with a deep feeling of pity, when within a few paces of me stood the poor horse in question, side by side with the leaders of one of our ammunition wagons, against which he pressed his panting sides, as though eager to identify himself as of their society – the driver with horror depicted on every feature, endeavouring by words and gestures, (for the kindhearted lad could not strike) to drive from him so hideous a spectacle. A cannon shot had completely carried away the lower part of the animal's head, immediately below the eyes. Still he lived and seemed fully conscious of all around, whilst his full clear eye seemed to implore us not to chase him from his companions. I ordered the farrier to put him out of misery, which, in a few minutes, he reported having accomplished, by running his sabre into the animal's heart.

Source: Cavalié Mercer, *Journal of the Waterloo Campaign* (1877)

376 THE REGIMENTAL DOG

Sergeant Bourgoyne observed an unusual reversal of the normal adage that a dog is man's best friend during the French retreat from Moscow in 1812.

I recognized a man ahead of me who was walking as if weighed down by what he was carrying on his knapsack and shoulders. I hurried to catch him up and saw that the burden was a dog, and that the man was an old sergeant of our regiment, called Daubenton. I told him I was surprised to see him carrying such a weight when he had trouble enough to drag himself along. I asked him if the dog was to eat – if so, I would prefer the horse myself.

'No,' he answered, 'I would rather eat Cossack. Don't you recognize Mouton? His paws are frozen, and now he can't walk any longer.'

'Now I recognize him,' I said, 'but what can you do with him?'

As we walked, Mouton, whose back I patted with my bandaged right hand, raised his head and seemed to recognize me. Daubenton told me that from seven in the morning the Russians had occupied the suburbs where we had been lodging the night before and that all that remained of the Guard had left it at six, and that it was certain that more than 12,000 men of the army, officers and soldiers, who were no longer able to march, had fallen into the hands of the enemy. He had only just avoided the same fate himself through devotion to this dog. The day the French had arrived at Vilna – at twenty-eight degrees – the poor dog had had his paws frozen. This morning, seeing that Mouton could not walk, he had made up his mind to leave him; but poor Mouton seemed to understand that he was to be deserted and began to howl in such a way that in the end he decided to let him follow. But hardly had he set off along the street when he saw the unfortunate Mouton fall on his nose; so he fastened him across his shoulders and rejoined Marshal Ney, who with a handful of men formed the rearguard.

[At this point Bourgoyne and Daubenton – and Mouton – are attacked by a group of Cossacks.]

Daubenton was lucky enough to see the Cossack in time, and get ready for him, but not as well as he would have liked, for Mouton, barking like a good dog, hampered his movements. Meanwhile, although nearly dying of cold, I felt rather better, and arranged my right hand to make use of my weapon the best I could, having hardly any strength left.

The Cossack wheeled continually round Daubenton, a little way off, fearing a musket shot. But seeing that neither of us attempted to fire, and assuming that we had no powder, he attacked Daubenton and hit him a blow with his sword, which the latter parried with the barrel of his musket. Instantly the man crossed to the right and gave him a second blow upon the left shoulder, which struck Mouton on the head. The poor dog howled enough to break one's heart. Although wounded and with frozen paws, he leapt off his master's back to run after the rider; but being fastened to the straps of the knapsack, he pulled Daubenton down, and I thought it was all over with him. He could not get up because Mouton was dragging him sideways, howling and barking after the Cossack. Daubenton, although half dead with cold and hunger, his face thin, pale, and blackened by the campfires, still seemed full of energy; but he looked comical as that devil of a dog, barking all the time dragged him sideways. His eyes were shining, his mouth foaming with rage, at being at the mercy of a man who, in any other circumstances, would not have dared stand up to him.

The Cossack whom my old comrade was fighting had just passed to the left when Daubenton shouted out to me: 'Don't be frightened! Stay still! I'll finish him off.' Scarcely had he said these words, when he fired . . . The Cossack was struck under the right arm by a ball which passed out again on the left side. Uttering a savage cry, he moved convulsively and dropped his sword as he fell from his horse.

Source: Sergeant Bourgoyne, *Memoirs* (19th century)

377 BUCEPHALUS

Alexander the Great's horse, Bucephalus, is possibly the most famous horse in history. So many legends surround him that it is difficult to separate fact from fiction. Alexander certainly had the horse from his childhood and took him on his great campaigns into Asia. When the old horse died Alexander even named a city after him. Plutarch gives an account of Alexander's first meeting with Bucephalus.

At that time Philoneicus the Thessalian had brought Bucephalus the horse to sell him unto king Philip [Alexander's father, Philip II of Macedon], asking thirteen talents; they went into the field to ride him. The horse was found so rough and churlish that the riders said he would never do service, for he would let no man get up on his back, nor abide any of the gentlemen's voices about king Philip, but would jerk out at them. Thereupon Philip being afraid, commanded them to carry him away as a wild beast, and altogether unprofitable: the which they had done, had not Alexander that stood by, said; O Gods, what a horse do they turn away for lack of skill and heart to handle him! Philip heard what he said, but held his peace. Alexander oft repeating his words, seeming to be sorry that they should send back the horse again. Why, said Philip, doest thou control them that have more experience than thou, and that know better than thou how to handle a horse? Alexander answered, And yet me thinks I could handle him better than all they have done. But if thou canst not, no more than they, replied Philip: what wilt thou forfeit for thy folly? I am content (quoth Alexander) to jeopard the price of the horse. Every man laughed to hear his answer: and the wager was laid between them. Then ran Alexander to the horse, and took him by the bridle, and turned him towards the sun. It seemed that he had marked (as I suppose) how mad the horse was to see his own shadow, which was ever before him in his eye, as he stirred to and fro. Then Alexander speaking gently to the horse, and clapping him on the back with his hand, till he had left his fury and snorting, softly let fall his cloak from him, and lightly leaping on his back, got up without any danger and holding the reins of the bridle hard, without striking or stirring the horse, made him to be gentle enough. Then when he saw that the fury of the horse was past, and that he began to gallop, he put him to his full career, and laid on spurs and voice agood. Philip at the first with fear beholding his son's agility lest he should take some hurt, said never a word: but when he saw him readily turn the horse at the end of his career, in a bravery for that he had done all the lookers on gave a shout for joy. The father on the other side (as they say) fell a weeping for joy. And when Alexander was lighted from the horse, he said unto him kissing his head: O son, thou must needs have a realm that is meet for thee, for Macedon will not hold thee. Furthermore, considering that of nature he was not to be won by extremity, and that by gentle means and persuasion he could make him do what he would: he ever sought rather to persuade than command him in any thing he had to do.

Source: Plutarch, *Life of Alexander* (1st century; trans. Sir Thomas North 1579)

The Capitoline geese – sacred to Juno – save Rome from the Gauls in 390 BC; this at least is the famous legend recounted by Livy (see number 378). The Gauls – a Celtic people from northern Italy – had besieged and sacked the city, leaving only the Capitoline Hill in Roman hands. After seven months the besiegers were bought off and went home. It was the last time Rome's walls were to be breached for eight centuries.

378 THE CAPITOLINE GEESE

This is one of the Roman stories all children used to know. In 390 BC the Romans, besieged on the Capitoline Hill by the Gauls, are saved by a most unexpected ally.

The Gauls had noticed the tracks of a man, where the messenger from Veii had got through, or perhaps had observed for themselves that the cliff near the shrine of Parmentis afforded an easy ascent. So on a starlit night they first sent forward an unarmed man to try the way; then handing up their weapons when there was a steep place, and supporting themselves by their fellows or affording support in their turn, they pulled one another up, as the ground required, and reached the summit in such silence that not only the sentries but even the dogs – creatures easily troubled by noises in the night – were not aroused. But they could not elude the vigilance of the geese, which, being sacred to Juno, had, notwithstanding the dearth of provisions, not been killed. That was the salvation of them all; for the geese with their gabbling and clapping of their wings, woke Marcus Manlius – Consul of three years before and a distinguished soldier – who, catching up his weapons and at the same time calling the rest to arms, strode past his bewildered comrades to a Gaul who had already got a foothold on the crest and dislodged him with a blow from the boss of his shield. As he slipped and fell, he overturned those who were next to him, and the others in alarm let go their weapons and grasping the rocks to which they had been clinging, were slain by Manlius. And by now the rest had come together and were assailing the invaders with javelins and stones, and presently the whole company lost their footing and were flung down headlong to destruction.

Source: Livy, *The History of Rome* (1st century BC; trans. Church and Broadrill 1890)

379 SURVIVORS

The fate of the equine survivors from the battle of Waterloo in 1815 was of concern to the famous surgeon Sir Astley Cooper.

After the battle of Waterloo, all the wounded horses of the Household Brigade of cavalry were sold by auction. Sir Astley attended the sale, and bought twelve, which he considered so severely hurt as to require the greatest care and attention in order to effect a cure. Having had them conveyed, under the care of six grooms, to his park in the country, the great surgeon followed, and with the assistance of his servants, commenced extracting bullets and grape-shot from the bodies and limbs of the suffering animals. In a very short time after the operations had been performed, Sir Astley let them loose in the park; and one morning, to his great delight, he saw the noble animals form in line, charge and then retreat, and afterwards gallop about, appearing greatly contented with the lot that had befallen them. These manoeuvres were repeated generally every morning, to his great satisfaction and amusement.

Source: Captain Gronow, *Last Recollections* (1934)

380 MONKEY BUSINESS

The battle of Lepanto in 1571 was the greatest naval battle of the Galley Age. In the confused fighting between ships locked together many strange incidents were noted.

During the struggle between the Spanish flagship and the Turkish admiral, Don John's pet marmoset joined in the fighting. Noticing a live grenade land on his master's decks, he scampered across and dropped it overboard – some accounts even suggesting that he threw it back onto Ali's flagship the *Sultana*.

381 AN ELEPHANT REMEMBERS

During the siege of Argos, which was to cost King Pyrrhus of Epirus his life, an extraordinary incident took place which demonstrated an elephant's love for its keeper.

Another of the elephants that were entered before into the city, called Nicon (as much as to say, conquering), seeking his governor that was stricken down to the ground from his back with terrible blows: ran upon them that came back upon him, overthrowing friends and foes alike, till at length having found the body of his master slain, he lifted him up from the ground with his trunk, and carrying him upon his two tusks, returned back with great fury, treading all under foot he found in his way.

Source: Plutarch, *Life of Pyrrhus* (1st century; trans. Sir Thomas North 1579)

COURAGE

382 ALVARADO'S LEAP

During the Spanish withdrawal from the Aztec capital of Tenochtitlán in 1520 they suffered heavy casualties, so much so that the title 'Noche Triste' was given to that event. Cortes' lieutenant, Alvarado, commanding the rearguard of the Spanish column, won renown on that occasion for his athleticism, as William H. Prescott describes.

The cavaliers found Alvarado unhorsed, and defending himself with a poor handful of followers, against an overwhelming tide of the enemy. His good steed which had borne him through many a hard fight, had fallen under him. He was himself wounded in several places, and was striving in vain to rally his scattered column, which was driven to the verge of the canal by the fury of the enemy, then in possession of the whole rear of the causeway, where they were reinforced every hour by fresh combatants from the city. The artillery in the earlier part of the engagement had not been idle, and its iron shower, sweeping along the dike, had mowed down the assailants by hundreds. But nothing could resist their impetuosity. The front ranks, pushed on by those behind, were at length forced up to the pieces and, pouring over them like a torrent, overthrew men and guns in one general ruin. The resolute charge of the Spanish cavaliers, who had now arrived, created a temporary check and gave time for their countrymen to make a feeble rally. But they were speedily borne down by the returning flood. Cortes and his companions were compelled to plunge again into the lake – though all did not escape. Alvarado stood on the brink for a moment, hesitating what to do. Unhorsed as he was, to throw himself into the water, in the face of the hostile canoes that now swarmed around the opening, afforded but a desperate chance of safety. He had but a second for thought. He was a man of powerful frame and despair gave him unnatural energy. Setting his long lance firmly on the wreck which strewed the bottom of the lake, he sprung forward with all his might and cleared the wide gap at a leap! Aztecs and Tlascalans gazed in stupid amazement, exclaiming, as they beheld the incredible feat, 'This is truly the Tonatiuh – the child of the sun!' The breadth of the opening is not given. But it was so great that the valorous Captain Diaz, who well remembered the place, says the leap was impossible to any man.

Source: William H. Prescott, *History of the Conquest of Mexico* (1843)

383 'OLD CROP' LAID TO REST

During the French invasion of Syria in 1799 the British admiral Sir Sidney Smith successfully repulsed their attack on Acre. The fighting between the French and their Turkish opponents was particularly severe and the normal conventions of war were observed only in their breach. That the British did not stoop to this level is clear from the quaint story of Daniel Bryan.

An uncommon instance of intrepidity and good nature occurred at the memorable siege of Acre, the particulars of which are thus given in the Naval Chronicle:- Daniel Bryan was an old seaman, and captain of the fore-top, who had been turned over from the *Blanche* into Sir Sidney Smith's ship, *Le Tigre*. During the siege of Acre this hardy veteran made repeated applications to be employed on shore; but, being an elderly man and rather deaf, his request was not acceded to. At the first storming of the breach by the French, among a multitude of slain, fell one of the generals of that nation. The Turks, in triumph, struck off the head of this unfortunate officer, and after inhumanly mangling the body with their sabres, left it naked, a prey to the dogs. Precluded from the rights of sepulture, it in a few days became putrescent – a shocking spectacle – a dreadful memento of the horrors of war, the fragility of human nature, and the vanity of all sublunary ambitions, hopes and expectations. Thus exposed, when any of the sailors who had been on shore or had returned to the ship, enquiries were instantly made respecting the state of the deceased general. Dan frequently asked his messmates why they had not buried him; but the only reply that he received was, 'Go and do it yourself.' Dan swore he would, observing, that he had himself been taken prisoner by the French who always gave their enemies a decent burial, not like the Turks, leaving them to rot above board. In the morning, having obtained leave to go and see the town, he dressed himself as though for an excursion of pleasure, and went ashore with the surgeon in the jolly-boat. About an hour or two after, while the surgeon was dressing the wounded

Turks in the hospital, in came honest Dan, who, in his rough good-natured manner, exclaimed, 'I have been burying the general, sir, and now I'm come to see the sick!' Not particularly attending to the tar's salute, but fearful of his catching the plague, the surgeon immediately ordered him out. Returning on board, the coxswain inquired of the surgeon if he had seen old Dan. 'Yes, he's been burying the French general.' It was then that Dan's words in the hospital first occurred. The boat's crew, who witnessed the generous action, an action truly worthy of a British sailor in whose character are ever blended the nobler and the milder virtues, thus related its circumstances:-

The old man procured a pickaxe, a shovel, and a rope, and insisted on being let down, out of a port hole, close to the breach. Some of his more juvenile companions offered to attend him; 'No!' he replied, 'You are too young to be shot yet; as for me, I am old and deaf, and my loss would be no great matter.' Persisting in his adventure, in the midst of the firing, Dan was slung and lowered down, with his implements of action on his shoulder. His first difficulty, not a very trivial one, was to drive away the dogs. The French now levelled their pieces, they were on the instant of firing at the hero! It was an interesting moment; but an officer, perceiving the friendly intentions of the sailor, was seen to throw himself across the file. Instantaneously the din of arms, the military thunder ceased; a dead, a solemn silence prevailed, and the worthy fellow consigned the corpse to its parent earth. He covered it with mould and stones, placing a large stone at its head, and another at its feet. But Dan's task was not yet completed. The unostentatious grave was formed, but no inscription recorded the fate or character of its possessor. Dan, with the peculiar air of a British sailor, took a piece of chalk from his pocket, and attempted to write:- 'Here you lie, old crop!' He was then, with his pickaxe and shovel, hoisted into the town, and the hostile firing immediately recommenced.

A few days afterwards, Sir Sidney, having been informed of the circumstance, ordered Dan to be called into the cabin. 'Well, Dan, I hear you have buried the French general?' 'Yes, your honour.' 'Had you anybody with you?' 'Yes, your honour.' 'Why, Mr —— says you had not.' 'But I had, your honour.' 'Ah, who had you?' 'God Almighty, sir.' 'A very good assistant, indeed; give old Dan a glass of grog.' 'Thank your honour!' Dan drank his grog, and left the cabin highly gratified.

He was in 1805 a pensioner in the Royal Hospital at Greenwich.

Source: *Naval and Military Anecdotes* (1824)

384 TROJAN PEAT

During the Dutch revolt against Spain in 1590 the Dutch leader, Count Maurice of Nassau, captured the strategically important city of Breda with a variation on the idea of the Trojan Horse.

Learning that boats carrying peat were admitted to the castle at Breda without being searched, Maurice sought one of his father's own servants who operated a peat boat and persuaded him to carry only three loads of peat instead of the nine he usually delivered to the garrison. Secreted under the layers of peat were some eighty picked soldiers under the command of a Captain Héraugières. On 21 February the boat entered the castle and remained overnight without arousing suspicion. After midnight the surface layers of peat were pulled aside and out crept the Dutch soldiers. They seized the castle at a rush and signalled to Maurice's main forces, which advanced to capture the city in a brilliant *coup de main*.

385 **SULLY THE MAGNIFICENT**

At the battle of Ivry in 1590 the Huguenot Duke of Rosny, later to be even more famous as Henry IV's great minister Sully, describes how he was injured.

At the first onset, my horse was wounded by a musket-shot, which passed through his nostrils and struck his shoulder, and soon after a thrust of a spear carried away a large piece of the skin of his belly, and part of the thick of my leg; I received another wound in my hand; a pistol-shot gave me a third, more considerable, the ball entered my hip and came out near my groin; while I was in this condition, I was relieved by the kindness of my equerry, who brought me another horse, upon which I mounted, though with great difficulty. At a second charge, this horse was likewise slain, and in the same moment I received a pistol-shot in the thigh and a cut with a sword on the head. I fell to the earth, and with my senses lost all the remaining part of the action, which from the advantage the Count of Egmont had already gained, boded no good to us. All I know is, that a long time after, recovering my senses, I saw neither enemies nor any of my domestics near me, whom a terror and the disorder had dispersed – another presage which appeared to me no less unfavourable. I retired without a headpiece, and almost without armour, for mine had been battered to pieces. In this condition I saw a trooper of the enemy's running towards me, with an intention to take away my life. By good fortune I found myself near a pear-tree, to which I crept, and with that little motion I was still able to exert, made such good use of the branches, which were extremely low, that I evaded all my adversary's attempts and kept him at a distance, till being weary of turning round the tree, he at last quitted me. Feuquières had not the like good fortune; he was killed that moment before my eyes. Just then La Rocheforet (who has since become one of my attendants) passing by, I asked him for a little nag which he was leading, and paid him for it upon the spot thirty crowns; for it was always my opinion that on such occasions it is proper to carry a little money about one.

Thus mounted, I was going to learn news of the battle, when I saw seven of the enemy approach, one of whom carried the white standard belonging to the Duke of Mayenne. I thought it impossible to escape this new danger; and upon their crying out, 'Qui Vive?' I told my name as being ready to surrender myself a prisoner; but how was I astonished when, instead of attacking me, I found four of these persons entreating me to receive them for prisoners, and to save their lives; and while they ranged themselves about me, appear rejoiced at this meeting! I granted their request; and it seemed so surprising to me, that four men, unhurt and well armed, should surrender themselves to a single man, disarmed, covered with his own blood, mounted upon a little paltry nag, and scarce able to support himself, that I was tempted to take all I saw for an illusion. But I was soon convinced of the truth of it. My prisoners (since they would be so) made themselves known to be Messieurs de Chataigneraie, de Signone, de Chanteloup, and d'Aufreville.

They told me that the Duke of Mayenne had lost the battle; that the king was that instant in pursuit of the vanquished, which had obliged them to surrender . . .

Source: Duc de Sully, *Memoirs* (17th century)

386 COLONEL WALTER LORING

At the first battle of Ypres in 1914 the commanding officer of the Second Warwicks, Colonel Walter Loring, inspired his men with a display of aplomb that has hardly been equalled.

Accustomed to leading his men mounted on a white horse, Colonel Loring made no concessions to the Germans. Leading his men on the Menin Road his foot was smashed by a bullet. Ordered to the rear by the medical officer he told the man to 'Go to hell' and asked his servant to bring his carpet slippers. Equipped with these he remounted his charger, only to suffer a fall as the great white horse was shot under him. He then mounted a bay and rode on a short distance before this too was shot. Hobbling with a stick he continued to lead his men up the road and, urging them onwards, he passed into legend. He died that day, but how exactly is not recorded.

387 AN IRISHMAN IN A PADDY

The British defended their positions around Ypres in October 1914 with astonishing determination.

When a trench held by a few Connaught Rangers was rushed by Germans, Private Grogan was not prepared to follow his sergeant's orders to abandon his post: 'No, not if the King himself ordered me.' Grogan then appeared to go berserk, and with a roar rushed up the trench to where seven Germans were positioned. He killed all of them, returning a few minutes later with a cut forehead, four teeth missing, and a bayonet dripping blood. 'Where the hell have you been?' inquired his sergeant, 'There were Germans in this trench a few minutes ago.' To which Grogan merely grinned, saying, 'So there were, Sergeant dear, but they were not liking it so they went.'

388 A DUEL

The siege of Leningrad of 1941–44 saw a revival of the trench warfare of World War I, and also witnessed a duel between German and Russian snipers reminiscent of many a famous contest on the Western Front.

The Russian sniper, Lieutenant Gorbatenko, first detected his German opponent when he noticed a bush stirring on the edge of the German trench. He fired instinctively only to see, a few seconds later, a spade raised above the enemy trench and waved about, signifying a palpable miss. Gorbatenko was intrigued and stayed still for a long time, but nothing further stirred on the German side. Gorbatenko was in a well-camouflaged position but he wanted to get a closer view. As he shifted his head a shot was fired and a bullet whistled past his ear, singeing his hair. Gorbatenko hastily found a spade and waved it at the German, showing that he had survived the shot. Now it became a 'cat and mouse' contest, with each changing position and trying to trap his opponent into making a fatal mistake. For several hours the contest went on, with each signalling misses with their spades. At last Gorbatenko trapped his man. The German fired, but this time Gorbatenko did not wave his spade but played 'dead'. For a while the German stayed still until, eager to be certain, he peered over the edge of the trench. It was to be his last mistake; Gorbatenko shot him through the head.

Source: A. Fedayev, *Leningrad in the Days of the Blockade* (1946)

389 DEFENCE CUTS

The Gurkhas were much feared by the Germans during the North African campaign of World War II. The favourite weapon of the Gurkhas was the kukri (a large knife) and it frequently fell to them to carry out raids on enemy posts.

One Gurkha situation report carried the following information:
'Enemy losses: ten killed, ours nil. Ammunition expenditure nil.'

390 NICHOLSON'S PATHAN

During the Indian Mutiny in 1857 John Nicholson's 'Movable Column' was something of a law unto itself. Nicholson was particularly unconventional.

Nicholson's personal attendant was a huge Pathan, black-whiskered and moustachioed; this man never left his side, he slept across the door of Nicholson's tent, so that none could come in save over his body. When Nicholson dined at mess this Pathan stood behind his chair with a cocked revolver in one hand, and allowed none to pass a dish to his master save himself. The story of this man's devotion was, that years before, in one of the many frontier skirmishes, this man's father saved Nicholson's life by throwing himself between Nicholson and a descending sword which must have killed him, and furthermore, in another of these skirmishes, this man was taken prisoner and carried off, and John Nicholson, single-handed, gave chase, and cutting his way through, bore him away in safety across his saddle bow. It may be mentioned here that Nicholson had the reputation of being one of the best swordsmen in India, and his sword had the credit of being the best sword in India. It was presented to him by the Sikh nation.

Source: Ensign R.G. Wilberforce, *An Unrecorded Chapter of the Indian Mutiny* (1894)

391 JUMPING TO CONCLUSIONS

During the Ashanti Campaign of 1874, Colonel Evelyn Wood almost punished a man unjustly.

The Native soldiers for choice carried everything on their heads, blankets, ammunition, rifles and cooking pots, thus when a shot was fired in the bush or a man moved unexpectedly everything came down with a crash and as we had several false alarms I was obliged to provide against this trouble. This I did by issuing two cross belts for each black soldier. For two successive mornings I noticed that one man in the Elmina company was still carrying loads on his head. I fined him a day's pay and when I saw him disobeying orders the third day I had him made a prisoner. He still refused to carry his kit except on his head so I sent for the doctor and said to the Elmina, 'When the men have eaten I shall flog you.' While I was having a cup of cocoa a deputation came to the tree under which I was sitting to beg their comrade off saying, 'You have put us in front on every occasion when you or your white officers went out, whether they belonged to our company or not, we have always escorted them and we beg you will not flog this man.' I explained that he must obey orders. They still gave me no indication of why the man had refused to obey orders but when I saw him and asked for a reason he replied simply, 'The belts hurt me.' And on my further questioning him he opened the front of his shirt and showed a deep hole in his body which he had received from a slug in action at Ordasu and into which, without troubling a doctor, he had stuffed a lump of grass. I rejoiced in my persistence in questioning the man which was the means of saving me from doing a great injustice.

Source: Sir Evelyn Wood, *From Midshipman to Field Marshal* (1906)

392 SETTING THE STANDARD

During Julius Caesar's first invasion of Britain in 55 BC the Roman soldiers hung back in their boats, frightened by the depth of the sea and horrified by the barbaric antics of the Britons waiting on the shore to fight them. Caesar tells what happened next.

And then, while our troops hung back, chiefly on account of the depth of the sea, the eagle-bearer of the Tenth Legion, after a prayer to heaven to bless the legion by his act, cried, 'Jump down, soldiers, unless you wish to betray your eagle to the enemy. It shall

The eagle-bearer of the Tenth Legion leads the way in Caesar's first invasion of Britain (see number 392). Loss of a legion's standard was a dire disgrace, so where the eagle-bearer led the legionaries were honour-bound to follow. When three legions were annihilated by German tribesmen in the Teutoburger Wald in AD 9 (see number 90), the loss of their standards was felt as a burning shame to all Romans for years, and the numbers of the lost legions were never used again.

be told that I at any rate did my duty to my country and my general.' When he had said this with a loud voice, he cast himself from his ship and began to bear the eagle against the enemy. Then our troops exhorted one another not to allow so dire a disgrace, and leapt down from the ship with one accord. When the troops on the nearest ships saw them, they likewise followed in, and drew near to the enemy.

Source: Julius Caesar, *Commentaries* (1st century BC)

393 BLUE JACKETS

There were few European survivors from the battle of Isandwhlana in 1879, and of those who did escape most were wearing blue jackets – the Zulus had apparently been told to concentrate on killing the red soldiers. One of the men who owed his life to his blue coat was Horace Smith-Dorrien, later a corps commander in the British Expeditionary Force of 1914.

I jumped off and led my horse down. There was a poor fellow of the mounted infantry struck through the arm, who said as I passed, that if I could bind up his arm and stop the bleeding he would be all right. I accordingly took out my handkerchief and tied up his arm. Just as I had done it, Major Smith of the Artillery came down by me wounded, saying, 'For God's sake get on, man, the Zulus are on top of us.' I had done all I could for the wounded man and so turned to jump on my horse. Just as I was doing so the horse went with a bound to the bottom of the precipice, being struck with an assegai. I gave up all hope as the Zulus were all round me, finishing off the wounded, the man I had helped and Major Smith among the number. However, with strong hope that everybody clings to that some accident would turn up, I rushed off on foot and plunged into the river, which was little better than a roaring torrent. I was being carried down the stream at a tremendous pace, when a loose horse came by me and I got hold of his tale and he landed me safely on the other bank; but I was too tired to stick to him and get on his back. I got up again and rushed on and was several times knocked over by our mounted niggers who would not get out of my way, then up a tremendous hill with my wet clothes and boots full of water. About twenty Zulus got over the water and followed us up the hill, but I am thankful to say they had not their firearms. Crossing the river, however, the Zulus on the opposite side kept firing at us as we went up the hill and killed several of the niggers around me. I was the only white man to be seen until I came to one who had been kicked by his horse and could not mount. I put him on his horse and lent him my knife. He said he would catch me a horse. Directly he was up he went clean away. A few Zulus followed us for about three miles across the river, but they had no guns and I had a revolver, which I kept letting them know. Also the mounted niggers stopped a little and kept firing at them. They did not come in close, and finally stopped altogether.

Well, to cut it short, I struggled into Helpmakaar, about twenty miles off, at nightfall, to find a few men who had escaped.

Source: Lieutenant H.L. Smith-Dorrien, *Memories of Forty-Eight Years' Service* (1925)

394 A LITTLE GIRL AND A DOG

At the battle of Fredericksburg in 1862 it was sometimes difficult to persuade the civilian population of the town to either evacuate their homes or take shelter. Robert Stiles noted the following incident.

Buck Denman . . . a Mississippi bear hunter and a superb specimen of manhood, was colour sergeant of the Twenty First . . . He was as rough as a bear in manner but withal a noble, tender-hearted fellow and a splendid soldier.

The enemy finding the way now clear were coming up the street full company front with flags flying and bands playing while the great shells from the [Federal siege guns] were bursting over their heads and dashing their hurtling fragments after our retreating skirmishers.

Buck was behind the corner of a house taking sight for a last shot. Just as his fingers trembled on the trigger a little three-year-old fair haired baby girl toddled out of an alley accompanied by a Newfoundland dog and gave chase to a big shell that was rolling lazily along the pavement, she clapping her little hands and the dog snapping and barking furiously at the shell.

Buck's hand dropped from the trigger. He dashed it across his eyes to dispel the mist and make sure he hadn't passed over the river and wasn't seeing his own baby girl in a vision. No – there is a baby amid the hell of shot and shell and here come the enemy. A moment and he has grounded his gun, dashed out into the storm, swept his great right arm round the baby, gained cover again and baby clasped to his breast and musket trailed in his left hand is trotting after the boys up to Marye's Heights.

Source: Adjutant Robert Stiles, *Four Years Under Marse Robert* (1910)

395 THE MIGHTY MINSTREL

Sir Edward Creasey describes the opening of the battle of Hastings in 1066 in which Duke William's minstrel, Taillefer, asked permission to strike the first blow against the English.

Then Taillefer, who sang right well, rode mounted on a swift horse, before the Duke, singing of Charlemagne and of Roland, of Oliver and the Peers who died at Roncesvalles. And when they drew nigh to the English, 'A boon, sire!' cried Taillefer; 'I have long served you, and you owe me for such long service. Today, so please you, you shall repay it. I ask as my guerdon, and beseech you for it earnestly, that you will allow me to strike the first blow in the battle!' And the Duke answered, 'I grant it.' Then Taillefer put his horse to a gallop, charging before all the rest, and struck an Englishman dead, driving his lance below the breast into his body, and stretching him upon the ground. Then he drew his sword and struck another, crying out, 'Come on, come on! What do ye, sirs? Lay on, lay on!' At the second blow he struck, the English pushed forward, and surrounded and slew him. Forthwith arose the noise and cry of war, and on either side the people put themselves in motion.

Source: Sir Edward Creasey, *The Fifteen Decisive Battles of the World* (1851)

396 DEATH OF SERPENT-WOMAN

At the battle of Otumba in 1520 Cortes inflicted a decisive defeat on the Aztecs. His personal contribution to the battle in killing Serpent-Woman, the Aztec commander-in-chief, can hardly be exaggerated. Prescott, recounting the incident in the 19th century, betrays the Eurocentrism of his period.

At this critical moment, Cortes, whose restless eye had been roving round the field in quest of any object that might offer him the means of arresting the coming ruin, rising in his stirrups descried at a distance, in the middle of the throng, the chief who from his dress and military cortege he knew must be the commander of the barbarian forces. He was covered with a rich surcoat of featherwork; and a panache of beautiful plumes, gorgeously set in gold and precious stones, floated above his head. Rising above this, and attached to his back, between the shoulders, was a short staff bearing a golden net for a banner – the singular customary symbol of authority for an Aztec commander. The cacique, whose name was Cihuaca, was borne on a litter, and a body of young warriors, whose gay and ornamented dresses showed them to be the flower of the Indian nobles, stood round as a guard of his person and the sacred emblem.

The eagle eye of Cortes no sooner fell on this personage than it lighted up with triumph. Turning quickly round to the cavaliers at his side, among whom were Sandoval, Olid, Alvarado and Avila, he pointed out the chief, exclaiming, 'There is our mark! Follow and support me!' Then crying his warcry, and striking his iron heel into his weary steed, he plunged headlong into the thickest of the press. His enemies fell back, taken by surprise and daunted by the ferocity of the attack. Those who did not were pierced through with his lance or borne down by the weight of his charger. The cavaliers followed close in the rear. On they swept with the fury of a thunderbolt, cleaving the solid ranks asunder, strewing their path with the dying and the dead, and bounding over every obstacle in their way. In a few minutes they were in the presence of the Indian commander, and Cortes, overturning his supporters, sprang forward with the strength of a lion and striking him through with his lance, hurled him to the ground. A young cavalier, Juan de Salamanca, who had kept close by his general's side, quickly dismounted and despatched the fallen chief. Then, tearing away his banner, he presented it to Cortes as a trophy to which he had the best claim. It was all the work of a moment. The guard, overpowered by the suddenness of the onset, made little resistance, but, flying, communicated their own panic to their comrades. The tidings of the loss soon spread over the field. The Indians, filled with consternation, now thought only of escape. In their blind terror, their numbers augmented their confusion. They trampled on one another, fancying it was the enemy in their rear.

Source: William H. Prescott, *History of the Conquest of Mexico* (1843)

397 A DEATH SENTENCE

In the later stages of the French Wars of Religion the French king, Henry IV, was fighting the united strength of the Catholic League and Spain. He employed many mercenary troops – English and German – in his ranks.

This officer, for whose valour and abilities he [Henry IV] had a great respect, came to him (pressed by the mutinous spirit of his men) the day before the battle of Ivry, to urge

184

the payment of part of their arrears. Henry, irritated in the midst of his anxieties and arrangements previous to a battle where the enemy's numbers were fully double the army he commanded, hastily asked him 'Was that a time to come for pay, when he ought to be asking for his orders to prepare for battle?' Schomberg withdrew overwhelmed with vexation and distress at this unmerited treatment, for his only object had been, to secure the obedience of his unmanageable troops, until the battle should have taken place. Next day he appeared at the head of his Germans with a countenance of deep depression, which Henry observed, and immediately recollecting what had passed the previous evening, rode up to him with kindness and friendship in his looks, and said loud enough to be heard by all around, 'Monsieur Schomberg, I have offended you. This day may perhaps, be the last of my life; God forbid that I should fall, under the impression that I had insulted the honour of a gentleman, without any offer for the reparation of such an injury! I am convinced both of your valour and your merit. I entreat you to pardon me.' – 'It is true,' answered the Colonel, 'that your Majesty wounded me lately, but today you kill me; for your conduct at this instant will force me to sacrifice my life in your service.' Before the end of the combat this brave man was slain, fighting by the side of the king.

Source: Lord de Ros, *The Young Officer's Companion* (1868)

398 **TOUGH NUT**

The retreat from Kabul in 1842 was one of the great disasters of the Victorian Age. Only one European survived the march through the Khyber Pass in mid-winter, and he here recounts how he escaped.

The confusion now was terrible; all discipline was at an end. I started leading poor Marshall's horse, who was unable to guide it; and Blair, Bott, and another wounded officer, all of the 5th Lt. Cy., were on a camel close to me. We had not gone far in the dark before I found myself surrounded, and at this moment my khidmutgar rushed up to me, saying he was wounded, had lost his pony, and begged me to take him up. I had not time to do so before I was pulled off my horse and knocked down by a blow on the head from an Afghan knife, which must have killed me had I not had a portion of Blackwood's Magazine in my forage cap. As it was, a piece of bone about the size of a wafer was cut from my skull, and I was nearly stunned, but managed to rise on my knees, and seeing that a second blow was coming, I met it with the edge of my sword, and I suppose cut off some of my assailant's fingers, as the knife fell to the ground; he bolted one way, and I the other, minus my horse, cap, and one of my shoes, – the khidmutgar was dead; those who had been with me I never saw again.

Source: Surgeon William Brydon, quoted in Lady Sale, *The First Afghan War* (Ed. P. McCrory 1969)

399 **TO SOOTHE THE SAVAGE BREAST**

During the siege of Leningrad 1941–44 great efforts were made to maintain civilian morale. In

David uses Goliath's own sword to cut off his head after killing him 'with a sling and with a stone' (see number 400). With their champion dead, the Philistines lost heart and were easily defeated. David's continuing successes against the Philistines – 'Saul hath slain his thousands, and David his ten thousands' – aroused the jealousy of King Saul. Hearing of Saul's plot to kill him, David fled the court, taking Goliath's sword with him.

spite of every effort by the Germans, the spirit of the people remained unbroken.

In November 1941 a live concert of Beethoven's 9th Symphony was broadcast from Leningrad to London. The first two movements were completed without interruption, but at the beginning of the great adagio movement the sirens began to wail. Bombs started to explode all round the concert hall, and the sound of anti-aircraft fire was clearly audible. Undismayed by the violence outside, the musicians continued to play the symphony to the end, and listeners in London were wished a 'peaceful good night' by the Russian announcer at the conclusion of the concert.

400 DAVID AND GOLIATH

The story of David and Goliath contains a truth that all great commanders have recognized in war time: do not underestimate the enemy, however small and insignificant they may seem.

And Saul and the men of Israel were gathered together, and pitched by the valley of Elah, and set the battle in array against the Philistines.
And the Philistines stood on a mountain on one side, and Israel stood on a mountain on the other side; and there was a valley between them.
And there went out a champion out of the camp of the Philistines, named Goliath, of Gath, whose height was six cubits and a span.

And he had an helmet of brass upon his head, and he was armed with a coat of mail; and the weight of the coat was five thousand shekels of brass.

And he had greaves of brass upon his legs, and a target of brass between his shoulders.

And the staff of his spear was like a weaver's beam; and his spear's head weighed six hundred shekels of iron; and one bearing a shield went before him.

And he stood and cried unto the armies of Israel and said unto them, why are ye come out to set your battle in array? am I not a Philistine, and ye servants to Saul? choose you a man for you and let him come down to me.

If he be able to fight with me, and to kill me, then will we be your servants but if I prevail against him and kill him then shall ye be our servants, and serve us.

And the Philistine said, I defy the armies of Israel this day; give me a man, that we may fight together . . .

And David girded his sword upon his armour, and he assayed to go; for he had not proved it. And David said unto Saul, I cannot go with these; for I have not proved them. And David put them off him.

And he took his staff in his hand, and chose him five smooth stones out of the brook, and put them in a shepherd's bag which he had, even in a scrip; and his sling was in his hand; and he drew near to the Philistine.

And the Philistine came on and drew near unto David; and the man that bare the shield went before him.

And when the Philistine looked about, and saw David, he disdained him: for he was but a youth, and ruddy, and of a fair countenance.

And the Philistine said unto David, Am I a dog, that thou comest to me with staves? And the Philistine cursed David by his gods.

And the Philistine said to David, Come to me, and I will give thy flesh unto the fowls of the air and to the beasts of the field.

Then said David unto the Philistine, Thou comest to me with a sword, and with a spear, and with a shield: but I come to thee in the name of the Lord of hosts, the God of the armies of Israel, whom thou hast defied.

This day will the Lord deliver thee into mine hand; and I will smite thee and take thine head from thee; and I will give the carcases of the host of the Philistines this day unto the fowls of the air and to the wild beasts of the earth; that all the earth may know that there is a God in Israel.

And all this assembly shall know that the Lord saveth not with sword and spear: for the battle is the Lord's, and he will give you into our hands.

And it came to pass, when the Philistine arose, and came and drew nigh to meet David, that David hasted, and ran towards the army to meet the Philistine.

And David put his hand in his bag and took thence a stone, and slang it, and smote the Philistine in his forehead, that the stone sunk into his forehead and he fell upon his face to the earth.

So David prevailed over the Philistine with a sling and with a stone . . .

Source: I Samuel, 17:2-10, 39–50

401 **CUT AND THRUST**

John Nicholson's Pathan Guards were an elite force. They were witnessed in action against rebel cavalry by Ensign Wilberforce outside Delhi in 1857.

It is the creed of these men that to be individually in action without accounting for someone is a matter of shame. In pursuance of this doctrine, we saw two of the body-guard, out on our right, apparently challenge two of the Bengal Cavalry to single combat; anyway, the challenge was accepted, and the four rode at each other, the Pathans on their ponies, their tulwars waving in circles round their heads, their loose garments flowing. The Bengalees sat erect on their big horses, their swords held ready to deliver the 'point', a stroke no regular cavalryman comprehends, and he does not in his sword exercise learn to parry the thrust. For a moment all eyes were on the four combatants: the thrust was delivered, but instead of piercing the bodies of the Pathans, it passed over them, for they threw themselves back on their ponies, their heads on the crupper, their feet by the ponies' ears, and in that position swept off the heads of the Bengal cavalrymen. Instantly the ponies wheeled round, the men straightened themselves in their saddles, and they passed away from our vision.

Source: Ensign R.G. Wilberforce, *An Unrecorded Chapter of the Indian Mutiny* (1894)

402 **THE DEATH OF SAUL**

On Mount Gilboa Saul and the army of the Israelites faced total destruction at the hands of the Philistines.

And the battle went sore against Saul, and the archers hit him; and he was sore wounded of the archers.
Then said Saul unto his armour-bearer, Draw thy sword, and thrust me through therewith: lest these uncircumcised come and thrust me through, and abuse me. But his armour-bearer would not; for he was sore afraid. Therefore Saul took a sword, and fell upon it.
And when his armour-bearer saw that Saul was dead, he fell likewise upon his sword, and died with him.
So Saul died, and his three sons, and his armour-bearer, and all his men, that same day together.

Source: I Samuel, 31:3–6

403 **HAIL, CAESAR**

The civil war between Julius Caesar and Pompey was decided by the decisive battle of Pharsalus in 48 BC.

There was in Caesar's army a volunteer of the name of Crastinus, who the year before had been First Centurion of the Tenth Legion, a man of preeminent bravery. He, when the signal was given, says 'Follow me, my old comrades, and display such exertions on behalf of your general as you have determined to do; this is our last battle, and when it shall be won he will receive his dignity, and we our liberty.' At the same time he looked back to Caesar and said, 'General, I will act in such a manner today, that you will feel grateful to me, living or dead.'

Source: Julius Caesar, *Commentaries: The Civil War* (1st century BC)

404 THE OPEN ROAD

In December 1941 the Japanese invaded Malaya and drove through the peninsula to the great British base at Singapore, considered impregnable by its builders – but only to attacks from the seaward side. The British garrison – over 100,000 strong – eventually surrendered to the Japanese on 15 February 1942.

Thompson Road was now a veritable death trap, for transport from the north, west and east was converging on this main Singapore artery, and movement on the choked highway was slow and tedious. Enemy artillery was shelling many targets, snipers were harassing the drivers and every now and then the enemy planes unloosed their loads of horror. The screams of the wounded and dying, the roar of burning trucks and cars, the deafening explosions of shells and bombs and the sickening whine and thud of small arms bullets were something to instil fear into the stoutest heart.

On a little side road, nearly in the centre of the carnage, was a Tommy private, with a Vickers, mounted for ack-ack, pouring fire from a red hot barrel at every plane that passed. Right in the centre of the road he stayed and carried on, no camouflage and no fear, and his answer to all and sundry was, 'The bloody ——s will never think of looking for me in the open, and I want to see a bloody plane brought down.'

Source: Ian Morrison, *Malayan Postcript* (1942)

405 HOLOCAUST

In 1187, after his victory over the Crusaders at Hattin, Sultan Saladin besieged the holy city of Jerusalem. Remembering the terrible massacre of Muslims that had taken place when the city fell to the Christians in 1099 (see number 205), Saladin was prepared to take the city by 'fire and sword'. Jerusalem was but sparsely garrisoned with professional soldiers and its governor, Balian of Ibelin, asked the great Muslim leader to spare the inhabitants a massacre. When Saladin pointed out his commitment to avenging the earlier massacre, Balian used one final threat to change his mind.

O Sultan, know that we soldiers in this city are in the midst of God knows how many people, who are slackening the fight in the hope of thy grace, believing that thou wilt grant it them as thou hast granted it to the other cities – for they abhor death and desire life. But for ourselves, when we see that death must needs be, by God we will slaughter our sons and our women, we will burn our wealth and our possessions, and leave you neither sequin nor silver to loot, nor a man or a woman to enslave; and when we have finished that, we will demolish the Rock and the Mosque al-Aqsa, and the other holy places, we will slay the Muslim slaves who are in our hands – there are 5000 such – and slaughter every beast and mount we have; and then we will sally out in a body to you,

The defence of Hougoumont at the battle of Waterloo witnessed many courageous acts, but none braver than that of Sergeant James Graham (see number 406).

and we will fight you for our lives: not a man of us will fall before he has slain his likes; thus shall we die gloriously or conquer like gentlemen.

Saladin was impressed by such heroism – or frightened by such fanaticism – and allowed the Christians to leave Jerusalem on the most generous terms.

Source: Ibn al-Athir, quoted in Geoffrey Regan, *Saladin and the Fall of Jerusalem* (1987)

406 **THE PRIZE**

In 1818 an English clergyman decided to confer a small annuity on a British soldier who had shown great courage in the recent battle of Waterloo. The Duke of Wellington was asked to choose a worthy recipient for the award and handed on the difficult task to Sir John Byng. Byng decided to make his choice from the 2nd Brigade of Guards, which had distinguished itself in the defence of Hougoumont.

There were many gallant candidates, but the election fell on Sergeant James Graham, of the light company of the Coldstream. This brave man had signalised himself, throughout the day, in the defence of that important post, and especially in the critical struggle that took place at the period when the French, who had gained the wood, the orchard, and detached garden, succeeded in bursting open a gate of the courtyard of the chateau itself and rushed in large masses, confident of carrying all before them. A hand-to-hand fight, of the most desperate character, was kept up between them and the Guards for a few minutes; but at last the British bayonets prevailed. Nearly all the Frenchmen who had forced their way in were killed on the spot; and, as the few survivors ran back, five of the Guards, Colonel Macdonnell, Captain Wyndham, Ensign Gooch, Ensign Hervey and Sergeant Graham, by sheer strength, closed the gate again, in spite of the efforts of the French from without, and effectually barricaded it against further assaults. Over and through the loopholed wall of the courtyard, the English garrison now kept up a deadly fire of musketry, which was fiercely answered by the French, who swarmed round the curtilage like ravening wolves. Shells too from their batteries, were falling fast into the besieged place, one of which set part of the mansion and some of the outbuildings on fire. Graham, who was at this time standing near Colonel Macdonnell at the wall, and who had shown the most perfect steadiness and courage, now asked permission of his commanding officer to retire for a moment. Macdonnell replied, 'By all means, Graham; but I wonder you should ask leave now.' Graham answered, 'I would not, sir, only my brother is wounded and he is in that outbuilding there, which has just caught fire.' Laying down his musket, Graham ran to the blazing spot, lifted up his brother, and laid him in a ditch. Then he was back at his post, and was plying his musket against the French again before his absence was noticed, except by his colonel.

Source: Sir Edward Creasey, *The Fifteen Decisive Battles of the World* (1851)

407 TWO HEARTS

The American wars against the Indians in the late 18th century were marked by extreme savagery. At the battle of Fallen Timbers in 1794 American captain Asa Hartshorn was separated from his men and surrounded by Indians.

After he was left by his troops he defended himself with his spontoon (a form of halberd) against the enemy until they despaired of being able to tomahawk him while alive. One of them fired an arrow into his chest, which killed him instantly. The Indians were filled with admiration for the brave officer who had fallen, and put two hearts made out of leather into an incision they made in his breast, as testimony that he had courage enough for two men.

408 THE SULTAN THWARTED

By 1453 the city of Constantinople had been the bastion of Christianity against Muslim invaders for 800 years. The Turks had tried many times to take the city but had been held off by the courage of its defenders. But Sultan Mehmed II was not prepared to be thwarted this time – even if help was sent from the West.

As early as the beginning of April, five great ships equipped for merchandise and war, would have sailed from the harbour of Chios, had not the wind blown obstinately from the north. One of these ships bore the Imperial flag; the remaining four belonged to the Genoese; and they were laden with wheat and barley, with wine, oil and vegetables, and above all, with soldiers and mariners, for the service of the capital. After a tedious delay a gentle breeze, and on the second day, a strong gale from the south, carried them through the Hellespont and the Propontis; but the city was already invested by sea and land, and the Turkish fleet at the entrance of the Bosphorus was stretched from shore to shore, in the form of a crescent, to intercept, or at least to repel, these bold auxiliaries.

The reader who had presented to his mind the geographical picture of Constantinople will conceive and admire the greatness of the spectacle. The five Christian ships continued to advance with joyful shouts, and a full press both of sails and oars, against an hostile fleet of three hundred vessels; and the rampart, the camp, the coasts of Europe and Asia, were lined with innumerable spectators, who anxiously awaited the event [outcome] of this momentous succour. At the first view that account could not appear doubtful; the superiority of the Muslims was beyond all measure or account, and, in a calm, their numbers and valour must inevitably have prevailed. But their hasty and imperfect navy had been created, not by the genius of the people, but by the will of the sultan: in the height of their prosperity the Turks have acknowledged that, if God had given them the earth he had left the sea to the infidels; and a series of defeats, a rapid progress of decay, has established the truth of their modest confession. Except eighteen galleys of some force, the rest of their fleet consisted of open boats, rudely constructed and awkwardly managed, crowded with troops, and destitute of cannon; and since courage arises in a great measure from the consciousness of strength, the bravest of the Janissaries might tremble on a new element. In the Christian squadron five stout and lofty ships were guided by skilful pilots, and manned with the veterans of Italy and Greece, long practised in the arts and perils of the sea. Their weight was directed to sink or scatter the weak obstacles that impeded their passage; their artillery swept the waters; their liquid fire was poured on the heads of the adversaries, who, with a design of boarding, presumed to approach them; and the winds and waves are always on the side of the ablest navigators. In this conflict the Imperial vessel, which had been almost overpowered was rescued by the Genoese; but the Turks in a distant and a closer attack, were twice repulsed with considerable loss. Mahomet [Sultan Mehmed] himself sat on horseback on the beach, to encourage their valour by his voice and presence, by the promise of reward, and by fear more potent than the fear of the enemy. The passions of his soul, and even the gestures of his body, seemed to imitate the actions of the combatants; and, as if he had been lord of nature he spurred his horse with a fearless and impotent effort into the sea. His loud reproaches, and the clamours of the camp, urged the Ottomans to a third attack, more fatal and bloody than the two former; and I must repeat, though I cannot credit, the evidence of Phranza, who affirms from their own mouth, that they lost above twelve thousand men in the slaughter of the day. They fled in disorder to the shores of Europe and Asia, while the Christian squadron triumphant and unhurt steered along the Bosphorus and securely anchored within the chain of the harbour. In the confidence of victory they boasted that the whole Turkish power must have yielded to their arms; but the admiral, or captain bashaw, found some consolation for a painful wound in his eye, by representing that accident as the cause of his defeat. Balta Ogli was a renegade of the race of the Bulgarian princes: his military character was tainted with the unpopular vice of avarice; and under the despotism of the prince or people, misfortune is a sufficient evidence of guilt. His rank and services were annihilated by the displeasure of Mahomet. In the royal presence the captain bashaw was extended on the ground by four slaves, and received one hundred strokes with a golden rod: his death had been pronounced, and he adored the clemency of the Sultan, who was satisfied with the milder punishment of confiscation and exile.

Source: Edward Gibbon, *History of the Decline and Fall of the Roman Empire* (1776–88)

409 DROPS OF RAIN

During the disastrous battle of The Little Big Horn in 1876, some of the 7th Cavalry, retreating with Captain Winfield Scott Edgerly, showed great heroism. One man in particular, Private Saunders, displayed considerable sang froid under fire.

In the heat of the battle Captain Edgerly noticed that Private Saunders had a broad grin on his face although he was sitting in a perfect shower of bullets. He didn't have time to question him then but the next day after the firing ceased he asked him what he was laughing at at such a time. Saunders replied, 'I was laughing to see what poor shots those Indians were. They were shooting too low and their bullets were spattering dust like drops of rain.' Edgerly admitted that he had never seen a cooler man under fire than Private Saunders.

410 WATCHFUL

Sentry duty in the forts of the American West was usually a routine activity, but when Indians planned a night attack it was necessary for sentries to show the kind of coolness illustrated here by Private 'Humpy' Brown.

At 8.20 Private H. Harbers went to the farthest end of his beat to change position with the adjoining guard. When Harbers got to number three post, 'Humpy' Brown did not report and so Harbers hurried to rouse the corporal of the guard. When the guard came an officer hunted in the haystack and found Brown with two arrows in his neck. He asked him why he had not called out and Brown said, 'I did not want to give away my position until the Indian showed himself. Then I was going to get him.'

411 SINGLE-HANDED

Medieval sea battles were notably bloody as there was no escape from the battlefield and it was impossible to take many prisoners. In a great battle against the Spanish in 1350, fought off Winchelsea, the English vessel Salle du Roi *was in danger of being captured by a much larger Spanish ship.*

These Spaniards would have led the *Salle du Roi* away at their ease; but then a servant of the ship's captain, Lord Robert of Namur, who was called Hankin, did there a great feat of arms; for with his sword naked in his hand he sprang and leapt into the Spanish ship, and came to the mast and cut the rope that held the sail, so that the ship slackened and had no force; and with this, by a great feat of his body, he cut four principal ropes that governed the mast and the sail in so much as the said sail fell down upon the ship, and stayed the ship quite, that she could go no further. Then Sir Robert of Namur and his men, when they saw this advantage, they advanced, and leapt into the Spanish ship with a good will, with their swords naked in their hands, and sought out and attacked whom they found in her; so that they were all slain and put overboard, and the ship was won.

Source: Froissart, *Chronicles* (Trans. T. Johnes 1853)

CHIVALRY

412 GOTHIC ART

During the Gothic Wars in Italy in the 6th century the Byzantine army under the command of the eunuch Narses faced the Goths under their king, Totila, at Taginae in 552. Totila, expecting reinforcements, was in no hurry to begin the battle and used the opportunity to impress his enemies with his skills . . .

Totila rode out alone into the area between the two armies . . . to show the enemy what kind of man he was. He was wearing ornate armour completely decorated with gold: from his helm and his lance there floated beautiful purple plumes, appropriate for a king. Riding on a magnificent horse, he handled his weapons expertly on the open ground. First he had his steed make the most graceful turns and leaps. Then at a gallop he cast his lance high into the air, and as it fell spinning, he caught it in the middle. He tossed it in skilful alternation, from one hand to the other, thereby showing his agility; he jumped down from his horse to the rear and to the front, as well as on both sides, and leapt up again like one who had practised the skills of the riding ring ever since his youth. He spent the whole morning doing this.

Narses, over 80 at the time, was unimpressed. He won the battle, and Totila, for all his accomplishments, was killed and his army destroyed.

Source: Procopius, *The Gothic Wars* (6th century; trans. H.B. Downing 1914)

413 A WEDDING RECEPTION

The Crusader kingdom of Jerusalem was able to survive for so long largely owing to the strength of its castles. These mighty structures – like Kerak in this example – proved too strong for the Muslim armies of Saladin. From Kerak, Reynald of Chatillon carried out raids on Muslim caravans and even raided the Arabian coast near Mecca, with the plan to carry off the Prophet's body. Saladin vowed to slay Reynald, but on this occasion he was unsuccessful due to the intervention of King Baldwin IV.

In 1183, at the great castle of Kerak, the marriage took place between the eleven-year-old Princess Isabella, and Humphrey of Toron, aged seventeen. The young princess's guardian, Reynald of Chatillon, was determined to celebrate the marriage with all the pomp at his disposal. For weeks guests arrived from all over the Crusader kingdom and with them came entertainers, dancers, jugglers and musicians. Suddenly the festivities were interrupted by the news that the Muslim leader Saladin was approaching Kerak with a large army.

Immediately farmers and shepherds from the surrounding countryside fled into the castle grounds, bringing their flocks with them for safety. Saladin arrived shortly afterwards and began his siege, using nine great mangonels to try to break down the defences. While rocks crashed against the walls outside, the wedding ceremonies continued in the castle, with people singing and dancing and feasting as if nothing could threaten the happy occasion. The Lady Stephanie, mother of the bridegroom, actually prepared dishes from the bridal feast and sent out selected dainties to Saladin. The Sultan, ever receptive to such acts of chivalry and kindness, asked in return in which tower the young pair were to be housed, giving orders that it should not be bombarded by his siege engines. But otherwise he did not relax his efforts to take the castle and slay his enemy, the lord of Kerak.

Meanwhile, messengers had reached Jerusalem, begging the king for help. Baldwin summoned the royal army, which he placed under the command of Count Raymond of Tripoli; Baldwin himself, although suffering from advanced leprosy, insisted on accompanying the army in his litter. As they approached Kerak, Saladin, frustrated by his inability to breach the strong walls, lifted the siege and moved back towards Damascus. King Baldwin was carried in triumph into the castle and the wedding guests were free to go home.

414 THE BLOOD OF A HERO

During the Seven Years War the Prussians under Frederick the Great were fighting the Austrians, whose army was commanded by Marshal Daun.

In 1760 Marshal Daun's Austrians swept the Prussians under General Fouqué from a ridge near Landshut. Fouqué and his cavalry were surrounded by hussars and the general, bleeding from several wounds, was only saved by the intervention of Colonel Voit of the Löwenstein dragoons. Seeing the Prussian general bleeding, Voit brought up his parade horse and begged Fouqué to mount. He refused, saying, 'The blood would soil your fine saddle.' But Voit replied, 'It will become far more precious when it is stained with the blood of a hero.'

415 BYZANTINE CHIVALRY

The Byzantines never understood the importance the Germans and Franks attached to notions of chivalry. To them the interests of the state dictated policy and they had no time for personal or even national honour where it conflicted with the security of the emperor or the state.

In 813 the Bulgar Khan Krum besieged Constantinople. The Byzantine Emperor, Leo V, unable to drive away his enemy, agreed to talk terms. He invited Krum to come to the seashore near the Blachernae Gate of the city and there he would meet him, both men to be accompanied by just three unarmed attendants. But Leo had no intention of playing fair, and the night before he had filled nearby houses with soldiers who would kill Krum on a given signal. The next day Krum arrived by horse and awaited Leo's boat. When the emperor arrived with his attendants one of them removed his helmet, which was the signal for the soldiers to attack. Unfortunately, however, unknown to the Byzantines, uncovering one's head in the presence of the khan was a sign of severe disrespect. Krum took instant offence, mounted his horse and rode away, just as the Byzantine soldiers lying in ambush rushed out from hiding. To compound the fiasco Byzantines watching from the city walls began to bellow 'The Cross has triumphed', which only alerted Krum to his peril and he made good his escape amidst a hail of arrows.

Napoleon before the Sphinx. During Napoleon's Egyptian campaign, many French soldiers were to pay homage to the wonders of the ancient world (see number 417).

416 THE QUALITY OF MERCY

Acting is a fraternity that has often transcended national barriers or minor matters like war.

During the later years of the Napoleonic Wars a young naval officer, the nephew of the great French actor, Tlama, was captured by the British. Hearing of this, the famous English tragedian Charles Kemble helped to secure his release. In return Tlama personally pressed Napoleon to reciprocate, and a young British doctor named Blount was sent back to England.

417 AWESTRUCK

The French army of Napoleon, which invaded Egypt in 1798, took with them scientists and archaeologists, who unearthed some of Egypt's grandest monuments, viewed for the first time by Europeans. The effect, even on the common soldier, was astounding.

During Napoleon's Egyptian campaign in 1798, General Denon took part of the army down the Nile as far as Karnak. On the morning of 27 January, as the sun rose over the river, the magnificent ruined temples of Karnak and Luxor were revealed as if in a dream to the battle-hardened French troops. Spontaneously the men broke out into applause and then the whole battalion, without orders, stood at attention and presented arms in homage to the ancient Egyptians who had built these wonders.

418 THE MORNING AFTER THE NIGHT BEFORE

As men of the world, French officers were able to understand the small weaknesses that were common to gentlemen throughout Europe at the time of Napoleon.

During the Peninsular War, a banquet was held to honour General Beresford's award of the Knighthood of the Bath. Having dined well and doubtless toasted the brave Beresford the appropriate number of times, certain senior officers became hopelessly lost on their way back to camp and found themselves behind French lines. The French, showing a gentlemanly understanding of their enemy's predicament, returned them safely to their camp at first light.

419 HONOUR ENOUGH

Sir Thomas Fairfax, one of the Parliamentary commanders in the English Civil War, was not a man to court popularity or value the world's opinion if it involved violating his own high principles.

At the battle of Naseby in 1645 Fairfax risked his life with a casual disregard for his own danger. Late in the battle he personally engaged and killed a Royalist ensign and took a regimental colour. Afterwards a soldier claimed that it had been he who had taken the colour. When those who had seen Sir Thomas take the flag accused the man of lying, Fairfax quietened them by saying, 'I have honour enough, let him take that honour to himself.'

420 A FAMILY REUNION

In the English Civil War the fate of women and children, in England at least, was generally a kind one. Rival commanders, like Fairfax and Newcastle, understood the niceties of civilized behaviour and practised them.

In the autumn of 1643 the fortunes of the Fairfaxes, the Parliamentary leaders in the north, had reached a low ebb under the attacks of the Earl of Newcastle. On one occasion Sir Thomas Fairfax found himself trapped by the besieging Royalists in Bradford, with both his wife and his baby daughter. Deciding to break out and ride for safety in Hull, he mounted his wife Anne behind one of his officers, while a nursemaid carried the little girl Moll. At dawn Fairfax tried to force his way through a regiment of 300 Royalist cavalry, but in the mêlée that ensued only he, twelve troopers and the nursemaid managed to escape, with the rest of his band, along with his wife, being taken prisoner. Fairfax had no time for heroics and rode on with his companions for forty hours, fighting his way through a score of enemy-held villages and towns. Before crossing the River Humber on the final stage of the journey, Fairfax had decided to leave the nursemaid and his daughter in a house at Thealby, wondering if he would see either his wife or little Moll again. Fortune smiled on him. The following day a boat crossed the River Humber and returned with his daughter and her hardy protector, while a few days later a carriage, escorted by Royalist cavalry, rode into Hull under a flag of truce. Inside was Anne Fairfax, returned to her husband by the chivalrous Earl of Newcastle.

421 CRACKSHOT CELLINI

During the sack of Rome in 1527 by Imperial forces under the Duke of Bourbon, the renowned Roman goldsmith and sculptor Benvenuto Cellini took refuge with Pope Clement VII in the Castle Sant'Angelo. An inveterate boaster, he claims in his autobiography to have been a remarkable shot with all kinds of cannon and tells of how on one occasion he carried out one homicide in the presence of the Pope.

I now gave my whole attention to firing my guns, by which means I did signal execution, so that I had in a high degree acquired the favour and good graces of His Holiness. There passed not a day that I did not kill some of the army without the castle.

One day amongst others the pope happened to walk upon the round rampart, when he saw in the public walks a Spanish colonel, whom he knew by certain tokens; and understanding that he had formerly been in his service, he said something concerning him, all the while observing him attentively. I who was above at the battery, and knew nothing of the matter, but saw a man who was employed in getting the trenches repaired, and who stood with a spear in his hand, dressed in rose-colour, began to deliberate how I should lay him flat. I took my swivel, which was almost equal to a demi-culverin, turned it round, and charging it with a good quantity of fine and coarse powder mixed, aiming it at him very carefully, giving it a good elevation, because he was at so great a distance that it could not be expected such pieces should carry so far. I fired off the gun, and hit the man exactly in the middle. He had arrogantly placed his sword before him in a sort of Spanish bravado; but the ball of my piece struck against his sword, and the man was seen severed into two pieces. The pope, who did not dream of any such thing, was highly delighted and surprised at what he saw, as well because he thought it impossible that such a piece could carry so far, as that he could not conceive how the man could be cut into two pieces. Upon this he sent for me, and made an enquiry into the whole affair. I told him the art I had used to fire in that manner; but as for the man's being split into two pieces, neither he nor I was able to account for it. So, falling upon my knees, I entreated His Holiness to absolve me from the guilt of homicide, as likewise from other crimes which I had committed in that castle in the service of the Church. The pope, lifting up his hands, and making the sign of the cross over me, said that he blessed me, and gave me his absolution for all the homicides I had ever committed or ever should commit, in the service of the Apostolic Church.

Source: Benvenuto Cellini, *Memoirs* (1558–62)

422 HONOURING THE DEAD

During the 'Phoney War' civilian attitudes in Britain towards the enemy had not reached the intensity they would after the Blitz.

When in April 1940 a Heinkel bomber crashed in Clacton-on-Sea, causing great damage on the ground and killing among others its crew of four Germans, the war was so new that as the German dead were borne to the local cemetery with full military honours (supplied by the RAF), women sobbed for them: 'The gallant foe were laid to rest amidst numerous floral tributes, their coffins being covered with wreaths of lilies, irises and other Spring flowers.' Some of these wreaths bore the words 'From all ranks of the Royal Air Force' and 'With heartfelt sympathy from a Mother.'

423 NO HARD FEELINGS

In 1859 France under the Emperor Napoleon III went to war with Austria on behalf of Piedmont's claim to Austrian-held Lombardy. The war ended prematurely because of Napoleon's horror at the carnage.

After the battle of Solferino in 1859 an Austrian artillery officer recalled how he had been knocked senseless by a Zouave's rifle butt. When he recovered his senses he found himself being propped up by the same Zouave who was holding a wine-filled water bottle to his lips, saying soothingly, 'Have a drop, Captain. It'll put you on your feet again.'

424 THE HIGHEST CASTE

The British Army in India always experienced difficulties with India's caste system.

In 1907 a young British officer died at Jodhpur and at the funeral only three Christian officers could be found to carry the coffin. When a fourth could not be found Sir Pertab Singh, regent of the state of Jodhpur, volunteered to stand in, even though warned by Brahmin priests that he would lose caste by touching a Christian coffin. Sir Pertab resolutely refused to undergo purification on the grounds that there was just one caste, in his opinion, the highest of all: that of a soldier.

425 A VISIT FROM LORD RAGLAN

During the Crimean War British troops were under the command of the amiable but incompetent Lord Raglan.

Whatever the deficiencies of Lord Raglan as a military commander he was a lovable human being. On one occasion he heard that the wife of a corporal had given birth to a baby girl in a hole scooped out of the frozen earth. He immediately sent his personal physician to inspect the baby and sent hot food from his kitchen. The next day he made a personal visit on a day so cold that it was said that ink froze as men tried to write their letters home. It was snowing heavily as he reached the little dog-tent where the family were staying, and he crawled into the tent on all-fours to talk to her and admire the new baby. He gave her warm clothes and food and the next day he sent her a rubber sleeping-bag lined with flannel, which he had been sent by a wellwisher in England.

426 HOME TO MOTHER

During the American Civil War, both armies included many youngsters, often aged twelve or less. They were not always as fortunate in the treatment they received as this tiny drummer boy captured by the Confederates. A private in the Seventeenth Virginia regiment recorded the event.

While returning from escorting a lot of prisoners to the rear, I met a large party of prisoners hurrying by, while a short distance behind them a little drummer boy was trying to keep up. He was bareheaded, wet, and muddy, but still retained his drum.

'Hello, my little Yank; where are you going?' I said.

'Oh, I'm a prisoner and am going to Richmond,' he replied.

'Look here,' I said, 'you are too little to be a prisoner; so pitch that drum into that fence-corner, throw off your coat, get behind those bushes and go home as fast as you can.'

'Mister, don't you want me for a prisoner?'

'No.'

'Can I go where I please?'

'Yes.'

'Then you bet I'm going home to my mother!'

Saying this as he threw his drum one way and his coat another (and became, in appearance, a civilian), he disappeared behind a fence and some bushes; and I sincerely hope he reached home and mother.

Source: Private James Hodham

427 A KING'S WORD

Richard I, the 'Lionheart', was a legendary warrior and Crusader but a poor king of England.

Richard Coeur de Lion, in besieging the castle of Chalus, in 1199, was shot in the shoulder by an arrow; and an awkward surgeon in endeavouring to extract the shaft mangled the wound in such a manner that it turned gangrenous. The castle being taken, and the king, perceiving he should not live, ordered Bertram de Gourdon who had shot the arrow to be brought into his presence.

'What harm did I ever do thee,' asked the king, 'that thou should'st kill me?'

Bertram replied with great magnanimity and courage. 'You killed with your own hand my father and two of my brothers and you likewise designed to have killed me. You may take your revenge. I should cheerfully suffer all the torments that can be inflicted were I sure of having delivered the world of a tyrant who filled it with blood and carnage.'

This bold and spirited answer struck Richard with remorse. He ordered the prisoner to be presented with one hundred marks and set free; but after Richard's death one of his courtiers ordered Bertram to be flayed alive in revenge.

Source: *Naval and Military Anecdotes* (1824)

428 THE FLOWER OF CHIVALRY

Sir Philip Sidney was the Elizabethan ideal of 'Renaissance Man' – scholar, poet, statesman, warrior. During the Earl of Leicester's campaign in the Low Countries in 1586, Sidney was present at the battle of Zutphen, where, seeing that the Earl of Leicester had ridden without thigh armour, Philip thought it cowardly to wear his own. After charging the Spanish lines

Francis I (standing) surrenders his sword in the chivalric manner after his defeat at Pavia (1525). In fact, Francis had great difficulty in surrendering. After his horse had fallen, he was surrounded by Spanish pikemen, all eager to kill him. It was Francis's enemy, Charles of Lannoy, viceroy of Naples, who came to his rescue, hacking his way through his own men to reach the French king. Lannoy used his own body to shield Francis until they reached a willow hedge. When the viceroy's Neapolitan guardsmen arrived they had to kill four pursuing Spaniards until Francis could emerge safely, 'three parts naked and covered in blood'.

three times he was hit by a bullet in the thigh and died later at Arnhem. His friend and biographer, Fulke Greville, left this immortal picture of Sidney's death – although it has recently been suggested that Sidney's dying words were invented by Greville himself.

In this sad progress, passing along by the rest of the army where his uncle, the general, was and being thirsty with excess of bleeding he called for drink which was presently brought him, he saw a poor soldier carried along . . . ghastly casting up his eyes at the bottle; which Sir Philip perceiving took it from his head before he drank and delivered it to the poor man with these words, 'Thy necessity is yet greater than mine.'

Source: Fulke Greville, *Life of the Renowned Sir Philip Sidney* (1652)

429 THE WORD OF A ROMAN

During the struggle for control of southern Italy between King Pyrrhus of Epirus and the Romans, Pyrrhus met and came to admire the consul Caius Fabricius. In 278 BC Fabricius sent a messenger to Pyrrhus, bearing a letter.

As Fabricius was in his camp, there came a man to him that brought him a letter from King Pyrrhus's physician, written with his own hands: in which the physician offered to poison his master, so ending the wars without further danger. Fabricius detesting the wickedness of the physician, and having made Q. Aemilius, his colleague and fellow-consul, also to abhor the same: wrote a letter unto Pyrrhus and bade him take heed, for there were those that meant to poison him. The contents of his letter were these: Caius Fabricius and Quintus Aemilius, Consuls of Rome, unto King Pyrrhus, greeting. You have, O king, made unfortunate choice, both of your friends and of your enemies, as shall appear unto you by reading of this letter, which one of yours has written unto us: for you make wars with just and honest men, and do yourself trust altogether the wicked and unfaithful. Hereof therefore we have thought good to advertise you, not in respect to pleasure you, but for fear lest the misfortune of your death might make us unjustly to be accused: imagining that by treachery of treason, we have sought to end this war, as though by valiantness we could not otherwise achieve it. Pyrrhus, having read this letter, and proved the contents thereof true, executed the physician as he had deserved: and to requite the advertisements of the Consuls, he sent Fabricius and the Romans their prisoners, without paying of ransom . . .

Source: Plutarch, *Life of Pyrrhus* (1st century; trans. Sir Thomas North 1579)

430 WELLESLEY BAHADUR

While in India Sir Arthur Wellesley – later the Duke of Wellington – won the admiration of all the native troops who served under him.

At the battle of Assaye a havildar of native cavalry captured a great Maharatta standard and brought it to present to him. Wellesley showed impeccable propriety and promoted the man on the spot, using the man's own language to do so. Many years later, when Wellesley was world famous as the 'Iron Duke', the Indian soldier attended a grand dinner to commemorate the victory at Assaye and admitted that his field promotion had been the greatest moment of his life. When reference was made to his old commander as the Duke of Wellington, the Indian replied that he recognized no other title for him but 'Wellesley Bahadur' – Wellesley the Invincible.

431 SOUTHERN CHIVALRY

General Robert E. Lee was so gentlemanly a commander that he became a legend in both North and South.

I was at the battle of Gettysburg myself, and an incident occurred there which largely changed my views of the Southern people. I had been the most bitter anti-Southman and fought and cursed the Confederates desperately. I could see nothing good in any of them. The last day of the fight I was badly wounded. A ball shattered my left leg. I lay on the ground not far from Cemetery Ridge, and as General Lee ordered his retreat, he and his officers rode near me. As they came along I recognized him, and, though faint from exposure and loss of blood, I raised up my hands, looked Lee in the face and shouted as loud as I could, 'Hurrah for the Union!'

The General heard me, looked, stopped his horse, dismounted, and came towards me. I confess that I at first thought he meant to kill me. But as he came up he looked down at me with such a sad expression upon his face that all fear left me, and I wondered what he was about. He extended his hand to me, and grasping mine firmly and looking right into my eyes, said, 'My son, I hope you will soon be well.'

If I live a thousand years I shall never forget the expression on General Lee's face. There he was, defeated, retiring from a field that had cost him and his cause almost their last hope, and yet he stopped to say words like those to a wounded soldier of the opposition who had taunted him as he passed by! As soon as the General had left me I cried myself to sleep there upon the bloody ground!

Source: Quoted in A.L. Long and Marcus J. Wright, *Memoirs of Robert E. Lee* (1887)

432 WINNING HIS SPURS

During the battle of Crécy in 1346 Edward III's 16-year-old son, the Prince of Wales, commanded one of the English divisions. Those French knights who survived the famous arrow storm came to hand-to-hand fighting with the prince's men-at-arms, and at one stage it seemed possible that the prince's men might be defeated. But the king had confidence not only in his son but in the professional commanders whom he had placed alongside him to cover for such an emergency.

The first division, seeing the danger they were in, sent a knight off in great haste to the king of England, who was posted upon an eminence near a windmill. On the knight's arrival, he said, 'Sir, the Earl of Warwick, the Lord Stafford, the Lord Reginald Cobham, and the others who are about your son, are vigorously attacked by the French and they entreat that you will come to their assistance with your battalion, for if numbers should increase against them, they fear he will have too much to do.' The king replied, 'Is my son dead, unhorsed, or so badly wounded that he cannot support himself?' 'Nothing of the sort, thank God,' rejoined the knight, 'But he is in so hot an engagement that he has great need of your help.' The king answered, 'Now, Sir Thomas, return to those that sent you, and tell them from me not to send again for me this day, nor expect that I shall come, let what will happen, as long as my son has life; and say that I command them to let the boy win his spurs, for I am determined, if it please God, that all the glory of this day shall be given to him, and to those into whose care I have entrusted him.' The knight returned to his lords and related the king's answer, which mightily encouraged them, and made them repent they had ever sent such a message.

In fact, the king did send the Bishop of Durham with 30 knights to strengthen the prince's division. The prince is said to have won his sobriquet 'The Black Prince' from the colour of the armour he wore that day.

Source: Froissart, *Chronicles* (Trans. T. Johnes 1853)

433 THE OTHER SIDE OF THE RIVER

Edward III, after his successes at Crécy and elsewhere, set up the greatest of all orders of English chivalry – the Garter. He was fortunate in being able to surround himself with a galaxy of brilliant 'Garter knights' of whom Sir John Chandos was perhaps the finest. The death of Chandos, in a tragically futile skirmish, was a loss to the English cause that could not be replaced.

At Chauvigny, Sir John Chandos with Lord Thomas Percy entered an hotel and ordered a fire to be lighted. Sir Thomas, however, soon left, accompanied by about thirty lances, impatient to meet with some adventure; but Sir John was out of spirit, having failed in his intended attack on St Salvin, and sat in the kitchen of the hotel warming himself at the fire, and occasionally conversing with his people. He had continued some time in this position, when a man entered the hotel saying, 'My lord, I bring news.' 'What is it?' asked Sir John. 'My lord, the French have taken the field, I set out from St Salvin with them.' Sir John then asked who they were and what road they had taken. To which the messenger replied, 'that they were Sir Louis de St Julien and Carnet le Breton, with their companies, and that they had taken the road to Poitiers.' 'Well,' replied Sir John, 'it is indifferent to me, I have no inclination to exert myself today.'

However, after remaining silent for a short time, he resolved to collect his men and return to Poitiers. The French were a good league before them on the same road when Sir John and his party started, and their intention was to cross the river at the bridge of Lussac; but Lord Thomas Percy and his company were on the other side of the river and gained the bridge before them. Both parties on coming to the bridge dismounted and prepared for a struggle. At this moment, Sir John Chandos and about forty lances came up; but as the bridge was very high in the middle, Lord Thomas and the English on the other side knew nothing of their arrival. Sir John, in an ill humour, immediately began to revile the French, and while so doing a Breton drew his sword and struck an English squire to the ground. Upon seeing which Sir John cried out, 'Dismount! dismount!' and in a moment all his company were on foot ready to begin battle; he himself was dressed in a large robe which fell to his feet, blazened with his arms on white sarcenet. There had been a hoar frost in the morning which made the ground slippery and as he was marching he entangled his legs with his robe and stumbled; just at the same moment a French squire made a thrust at him with his lance, which took him under the eye, and from the force of the blow entered his brain. Sir John fell, twice turned over in the greatest agony, and spoke no more. The English, when they saw their commander in so piteous a state, fought like madmen; one of them singled out the squire who had given the blow to Sir John, ran him through both his thighs as he was flying, and then withdrew his lance; the squire continued his flight, but his wounds were mortal and he died at Poitiers; notwithstanding the English fought so desperately, they were overpowered by the French and Bretons, and the greater part made prisoners. Had Lord Thomas Percy and his men been aware of what was going on, the result might have been different; but finding the French did not attempt to cross the bridge to attack them, they continued their march to Poitiers quite unconscious of what was being done on the other side of the river. When the French had retired, poor Sir John Chandos was gently disarmed by his own servant, laid upon shields, and carried to Mortemer. The barons and knights of Poitou bitterly lamented over him. 'Oh Sir John Chandos, flower of knighthood, cursed be the forging of that lance that wounded thee!' The gallant knight survived but a day. God have mercy upon his soul. His loss was severely felt by the prince and princess, in short by the English generally, who loved him for the many excellent qualities which he possessed.

Source: Froissart, *Chronicles* (Trans. T. Johnes 1853)

RUSES AND REVERSES

434 A 16TH-CENTURY INDUSTRIAL DISPUTE

During the Italian Wars of the first part of the 16th century many mercenary soldiers from Switzerland and Germany fought in French or Imperial armies. The German landsknechts were notoriously difficult to control and often went on strike if their pay was not forthcoming. This incident concerns the French chevalier Bayard, the most esteemed soldier of the period.

During the French siege of Puente la Reyne in 1521 a detachment of German mercenaries was ordered to form a storming party to force an entry through the breach that had been made in the city walls. When the French officer, the famous chevalier Bayard, gave the order, he was astounded when the landsknechts replied that it was the custom that at assaults of breaches the troops received double pay for the month – and unless he was willing to pay up the Germans announced that they would not move. Furious at this ultimatum, Bayard felt he had no alternative but to agree to their demands as time was pressing, but he made it clear that they would only be paid after the fortress had been taken.

Even now the Germans made no haste and so Bayard turned to a company of French 'adventurers', and begged them to take on the task for the honour of France. Spurred on by his words the French soldiers stormed into the breach and the fortress fell. When the fighting had finished, three landsknecht captains came to Bayard and asked for their money as the fortress had been taken. 'But you didn't take it,' replied the angry knight,

The chevalier Bayard, the epitome of a chivalrous soldier, had a great deal of difficulty dealing with the mercenary ways of the German landsknechts serving under him (see number 434). Described as 'le chevalier sans peur et sans reproche' ('the knight without fear and without blame'), Bayard is said on one occasion to have held a bridge single-handedly against 200 Spaniards, while on another occasion, with only 1000 men, he held a town against an army of 35,000.

'and I shall report you to the Duke of Suffolk, your commander, as impudent cowards.' This only stirred up a hornet's nest, and the landsknechts began to threaten Bayard so that he was forced to call out a company of men-at-arms to protect himself.

That evening a very drunk landsknecht burst in to a dinner party of officers, shouting that he had come to kill Captain Bayard, the man who had promised money and didn't give it. Fortunately he was so drunk that Bayard's friends were able to befuddle him with more drink so that he forgot his purpose, and went off saying that Bayard was a fine fellow and that no one should harm a man who had such very good wine.

435 MILITARY CUTS AND HOW TO AVOID THEM

During the War of the Austrian Succession, 1740–8, the Habsburg armies had fared very badly against the troops of the Prussian king Frederick the Great. The Empress Maria Theresa looked for ways of improving the performance of her armies in battle but found that she was up against the Austrian military hierarchy, a very conservative body indeed.

One day in 1747 Maria Theresa was watching a regiment parading. While expressing her general approval she noted that their coats were too long, making them inconvenient for the men on the march, notably in rain or sun. She suggested that their coats be shortened on the Prussian model. The Austrian officers, some of whom had vested interests in the supply of uniforms, objected that the coats had to be long to keep the men warm at night. The Prussians, they pointed out, did not need long coats as they all slept in tents at night. The empress rejoined that her soldiers must have tents as well. The next day the officers submitted estimates of the cost of new coats and tents. They grossly exaggerated the expense of the tents, of the pack horses needed to carry them, of the men needed to look after the horses, so that the final bill was enormous and the empress had to give up the idea.

436 SURVEYING

Frederick the Great was by no means as reactionary as this example suggests. However, his successes in the Wars of the Austrian Succession and the Seven Years War convinced him that he knew more about the science of war than young whippersnappers of the kind we meet here. The War of the Bavarian Succession occurred in 1788, very late in Frederick's life.

During the War of the Bavarian Succession Frederick the Great asked one of his officers to go into the hills to determine the range for his artillery. The young officer, an exponent of the scientific method, worked out the range by triangulation and returned so swiftly that the king was suspicious.

Frederick: Have you actually been on the hills?

Officer: No, your Majesty, but . . .

Frederick: And you want me to believe that you know the range?

Officer: With your Majesty's permission, may I explain that through a simple geometric calculation . . .

Frederick: To hell with your calculations! Away with you!

437 DOUBLE-DEALING

During the Dutch revolt against the Spanish in 1588, English troops under Lord Willoughby were defending the town of Bergen-op-Zoom against the attacks of the Spaniards under the Duke of Parma. Willoughby feared that the Spaniards would cut the town's lifeline to Zeeland in the north by capturing the thinly held north fort and forcing him to surrender. While desperately seeking a way to thwart the attack on the fort, an answer came to him from an unexpected source.

An ensign in Captain Baskerville's company in the north fort, William Grimston, offered to act as a double agent and lead the Spaniards into a well-prepared ambush.

According to Grimston, an acquaintance, one Robert Redhead, held two Spanish prisoners of war, one of whom, Cosimo d'Alexandrini, occasionally 'used some English words wherein his perfect pronunciation gave great suspicion'. In Grimston's estimation d'Alexandrini was more than a mere soldier – he was a spy. To win the confidence of the two Spaniards Redhead agreed to pretend that he was a Catholic and a supporter of the English renegade, Sir William Stanley, who led a company in the Spanish army. D'Alexandrini now admitted that he was English and that if Redhead could find anyone to open the gates to the Spaniards he would be well rewarded. Redhead passed the news to Grimston and Willoughby, who now forged letters to the Spanish commander Parma assuring him that Grimston was a good Catholic who would willingly help deliver the fort to the army of the king of Spain.

Parma rose to the bait, promising Grimston 7000 gold crowns and a captaincy in Sir William Stanley's regiment, as well as 1200 crowns for Redhead. Grimston went ahead and planned the action for the night of 4 October only to find that Willoughby could not organize his troops at such short notice. The resourceful Grimston had to forge further letters for Parma explaining the delay and promising to admit the Spanish troops on 7 October instead. But again Willoughby insisted on a delay of a further three days. This time the Spanish grew suspicious and when eventually Grimston went out to meet them on 10 October they seized him and bound his hands, accusing him of treachery. Pushing him ahead of them at the point of a pike the Spanish troops moved through the darkness towards the north fort, while elsewhere Parma staged feint attacks on other parts of Bergen to keep the defenders occupied.

When Grimston reached the fort he called to an English sergeant to open the portcullis, which he did, and then he went forward followed by about 30 Spanish soldiers. Suddenly Grimston let out a cry for help and the waiting English troops sprung the trap, closing the portcullis and attacking the surprised Spaniards. In the confusion that followed Grimston made his escape, not without some difficulty. Although the 30 Spaniards inside were soon accounted for, the many troops outside now attacked the fort. For 90 minutes the issue was in doubt, until Parma called them back, though many were drowned by the rising tide. Nearly 800 Spaniards died that night and many gentlemen and captains were taken by the English. It was a great victory, celebrated by a church service the next morning and the public execution of the two Spanish spies in the afternoon. For his pains Grimston was made a captain, given a wealthy prisoner to ransom and sent home to England for safety. With winter close at hand Parma now abandoned his attempts to capture Bergen-op-Zoom.

Spanish soldiers plundering Antwerp in 1576. Eleven years later the burgers were to have their revenge, thanks to a disappointed Italian engineer (see number 438).

438 INFERNAL REVENGE

During the Dutch War of Independence in the late 16th century the Italian engineer Federico Giambelli offered his services to the king of Spain, Philip II. However, Philip rejected his military inventions as pointless gadgetry.

Furious at his rebuttal Giambelli sailed for the Netherlands saying that the Spaniards would soon be hearing from him again and they might not be very pleased when they did. Giambelli settled in Antwerp and offered his services to the rebels while the city was undergoing a Spanish siege. Giambelli stuffed two boats with over 7000 pounds of gunpowder each as well as every kind of stone, iron and wooden implement that came to hand to act as shrapnel. On 5 April 1585 the 'infernal machine', as it came to be called, was floated down on the tide towards the Spanish bridge of boats across the Scheldt, from which the siege was being conducted. Although one of the boats failed to reach the bridge the other exploded with unbelievable force, raining debris for fully a minute on the surrounding area. The bridge was smashed and 800 Spanish soldiers vaporized, while one Spanish commander was found wrapped around an anchor chain and another plastered against a bridge pile like so much putty. Giambelli had been as good as his word.

439 CHINESE BOXES

The siege of Turin in 1640 ranks as one of the most baffling military actions of all time, testing the ingenuity of besieged and besieger alike.

At the centre of a series of concentric siegelines was a hard core of French soldiers, holding out in the citadel of Turin. They were withstanding a siege by 12,000 Piedmontese troops led by Prince Thomas of Savoy, who held the outer walls of the city. These in turn were besieged by 10,000 French troops under Count Harcourt. To complete the encirclement the Marquis of Leganés with 18,000 Spanish troops were besieging Harcourt's Frenchmen. Each side tried to contact their compatriots by bypassing the intervening enemy lines. Leganés was particularly ingenious, filling mortar bombs with flour, musket balls, food and ammunition and sealing them in with clay. The Spaniards then carefully lobbed the bombs from their mortars, firing over Harcourt's lines and landing the much needed supplies within the city. It is reported that one bomb fired by Leganés contained a quantity of fat quails and a message from a lovelorn Spaniard to his mistress in Turin. It is not reported how the lady managed to reply.

440 SPARE THE ROD . . .

During the War of the Spanish Succession the successful partnership of Prince Eugène of Savoy and the Duke of Marlborough was briefly disturbed by their attitudes towards discipline.

In one instance Eugène condemned to death one of his soldiers who had been caught looting. The man was popular with his officers and they asked Marlborough to intercede with the Prince to save his life. However, when the Duke asked Eugène to pardon the man, the Prince replied, 'If your Grace has not executed more men than I have done for this offence, I will pardon the man.' Marlborough was convinced that the man was saved. However, when enquiries were made it was soon found that Eugène had executed far less men. He replied to the Duke, 'There, my lord, you see the benefit of example. You pardon many and therefore have to execute many; I never pardon one, therefore few dare to offend, and of course few need to suffer.'

441 ORBAN'S SUPERGUNS

During the 15th century the development of artillery made medieval castles and fortifications obsolete. The walls of Constantinople had withstood countless sieges for nearly a thousand years but their time had come.

A skilled Hungarian gun-maker named Orban had become so dissatisfied with service under Constantine IX Palaeologus, the last of the Byzantine emperors, that he offered his skills to the Turks. The Turkish sultan Mehmet II offered him a great reward if he could design an enormous cannon to breach the walls of Constantinople. Orban duly responded with a gun of staggering size. To test it out Orban fired a single shot at a Venetian galley, hit it amidships and cracked it open like an eggshell, sending it straight to the bottom. The Turks were delighted and ordered a second gun – twice as big. Orban obliged with 'Mahometta', a gun that fired a stone ball weighing half a ton.

'Mahometta' took up to 140 oxen to pull, 100 men to prepare and two hours to reload. When it fired, it was said, women miscarried – but so, unfortunately, did the gun. It cracked on the fifth day and was permanently out of action. Nevertheless, Orban's other guns soon wrecked the walls of Constantinople and repaid the emperor for his miserliness.

442 THE BASILISK

The Turkish obsession with big guns continued into the 16th century.

In 1516 a Turkish galley equipped with a huge gun, known as a basilisk, attacked a group of Portuguese vessels. Unfortunately the recoil from the mighty basilisk was so great that the galley turned turtle and sank with all hands.

443 COUNTING CHICKENS

During the summer of 1940 the Germans were so convinced that an invasion of Britain was imminent that they even tried to film the event – in advance.

In early September a film crew arrived in Antwerp and selected a nearby beach to represent the shores of southern England. For two days invasion barges drew into the shore and German soldiers leapt out and waded shorewards, while light tanks landed on the concrete esplanade under dummy fire. The reasons for the charade were explained to puzzled onlookers. As the real invasion would take place at night it would be impossible to film and as Operation Sea Lion would be the decisive event of the war it was something that Hitler did not want his people to miss. The film crew assured everyone that no cost had been spared to make the film as accurate as possible.

444 SOME MISTAKE

Operation Barbarossa took the Russians by surprise in June 1941.

No sooner had they crossed into Soviet territory than the Germans were picking up panicky signals from Russian front-line units to their command headquarters like this one.
    'We are being fired on. What shall we do?'
    'You must be insane. And why is your signal not in code?'

445 THE POWER OF SONG

In the 15th century the religious fervour of the Hussites in Bohemia made them fearsome opponents for the German crusaders.

During the German crusades against the Hussites in August 1431, the German commanders took up position at the top of a hill overlooking the road by which they expected to see their enemies approach. Seeing nothing of the enemy they were astounded to see some of their own wagons beginning to drive off in retreat. Only then, and with the Hussites still several miles away, did they begin to hear the sound of the enemy war-carts creaking and rattling, as well as the song of the Hussites, 'All ye war-

The religious zeal of the Hussites had a terrifying effect on their opponents (see number 445).

riors of God', sung by thousands of voices. At this the German army turned and fled in panic, without firing a shot.

446 SCYTHING THE SCYTHIANS

The Byzantine emperor Alexius I (1081–1118) was one of the greatest of the later rulers. He was particularly fortunate in having a remarkable daughter for his biographer. Here is her description of one of the emperor's ruses against the Scythians.

Seeing that Tzouroulus was a fortified town, situated on a fairly steep hill, and that the entire Scythian army was bivouacking down below in the plain, and that his forces were insufficient to allow him to attempt a pitched battle against their overwhelming numbers, he devised a most ingenious plan. He requisitioned the inhabitants' wagons and lifted off the bodies from the wheels and the axle trees and then suspended the latter for he had them hung out in order from the battlements on the outside of the walls and tied by ropes to the parapets. He no sooner thought of this than it was done. And within an hour there was a circle of wheels with their axle trees hanging up, a regular row of circles touching each other and fastened to one another by their axles. In the morning he armed himself and got the army ready and led out his soldiers from the gates and placed them in full view of the enemy. Now it happened that our troops were placed just on that side of the wall where the wheels were hanging and the opposing army was straight opposite them. Then Alexius stood in the middle of the army and explained to the soldiers that, when the trumpets sounded the attack, they were to dismount and march forward slowly against the foe and by using mostly their arrows and javelins to provoke the Scythians to the attack; and as soon as they saw them drawn on and urging on their horses to the attack, they were to turn hastily and in fleeing wheel off a little to the right and left and thus open to the enemy a clear path for coming close up to the walls. And he had given orders to the men on the walls that when they saw the ranks dividing, they were to cut the ropes with their swords and let the wheels and the axles fall headlong down from above. All this was carried out according to the emperor's orders. The Scythian horsemen raised their barbaric shout and hurled themselves in a body upon our lines who were marching slowly towards them, the emperor alone being on horseback. Then our men accordingly to Alexius' plan drew back step by step and, pretending to retreat, unexpectedly split into two parts as if opening a very wide entrance for the enemy into the town. Directly the Scythians had entered this mouth, as it were, of the two parts of our army, the wheels came whirring down. Each wheel rebounded at least a cubit's length from the wall and through their rims springing back from the wall they seemed to be ejected from catapults and came hurtling down into the midst of the Scythian cavalry with tremendous impetus. Partly owing to their descent in unison caused by their natural weight, and partly because they gained further momentum from the sloping nature of the ground, they fell upon the barbarians with terrific force and crushed them on every side, mowing down, as it were, the legs of the horses. And no matter whether the wheels hit the fore or the hind legs of the horses, in either case they forced the horses to sink down on the side they had received the blow and consequently to throw their riders. So the Scythians fell one after another in great numbers, and our men charged them from both sides; the battle pressed terribly on the Scythians from all sides, some were killed by the flying arrows, others wounded by spears, and most of the rest were forced into the river by the violent impact of the wheels and there drowned.

Source: Anna Comnena, *The Alexiad* (Trans. E. Dawes 1928)

447 TREATMENT FOR WIND

Colonel William Stiles, commanding a Georgia regiment in the American Civil War, found an interesting way of dealing with one of his men whose courage was open to doubt.

During a charge Stiles noticed the man dropping out and hiding behind a tree, whereupon he crept up on the shirker and struck him a resounding blow on the back with the flat of his sword, shouting, 'Up there, you coward.' The skulker, feeling that he had been struck by an enemy shot, clasped his hands and fell over backwards, crying 'Lord, receive my spirit.' Stiles promptly kicked him in the ribs to persuade him to get up, saying 'Get up, sir, the Lord wouldn't receive the spirit of such an infernal coward.' The man leapt to his feet rejoicing. 'Ain't I killed? The Lord be praised.' He then grabbed his musket and joined the attack, apparently cured of his cowardly ways.

448 **FIFE AND DRUM**

During the retreat from Belgium in August 1914 an incident took place at St Quentin that
demonstrated the extremes of military qualities present in the British army at that most trying
time. The town was crowded with British infantry, many of them stragglers from two regiments
of the 4th Division. Their morale was low and they were openly critical of their own leaders
who seemed to have got them into a terrible mess. With the Germans only a few miles behind
them many of the British had given up hope and were simply exhausted and sleeping in the
streets, while some of their officers had just made their escape on the last train to Paris out of
St Quentin.

It was at that moment that a cavalry officer, Major Tom Bridges, rode into St Quentin
and was horrified by what he saw of the disintegration of the British forces. Addressing
groups of men he tried to encourage them to form up and continue the retreat, but he
met with hostility and derision. He was told to keep his cavalry nose out of infantry business and that the regiments' colonels had already agreed to surrender to the Germans.
Bridges was horrified and went at once to see the mayor of St. Quentin to ask for transport to help move out the wounded. The mayor told Bridges that it was all too late and
that the British troops in the town had already agreed to surrender to the Germans.
Bridges simply would not believe this until the mayor produced a document signed by
two senior British officers agreeing to surrender, which he had sent to the Germans
under a white flag.

Bridges told the mayor that as a loyal Frenchman he had no right to surrender to the
Germans, but the man explained that he was acting on behalf of the citizens of the town.
He had asked the British officers to go and fight the Germans outside the town but they
had refused, saying that they had lost their artillery and could not fight. He then asked
the British to leave quickly and escape but again the officers had refused, saying the men
were too tired. Faced with such blank refusals, the mayor told Bridges that he had had
no alternative but to ask the British to surrender and this the officers had agreed to do.

Bridges took the surrender document, which was signed by Lieutenant-Colonel
Mainwaring of the Royal Dublin Fusiliers and Lieutenant-Colonel Ellington of the 1st
Battalion of the Royal Warwickshire Regiment and tucked it into his pocket. He then
began organizing transport of all kinds. But the main problem was how to rouse the soldiers and make them see that escape was possible. Bridges came up with a brilliant solution. Lacking a band, he decided to improvise. He went to a toyshop in St Quentin and
bought a toy drum and a penny whistle. Calling his company trumpeter he gave the man
the whistle and then joined in on the drum, marching round the square and banging the
drum to the tune of 'The British Grenadiers'. Soon the soldiers stood up and began to
take notice. Surely the man was mad, but their attitude towards him was already changing. He was providing the leadership that had been missing all day. Within minutes they
had begun to form up into a column and, with Bridges and the trumpeter at the head,
and with occasional mouth organs joining in, the footsore soldiers marched out of the
town. Into the distance they marched with the trumpeter now changing the tune to 'It's a

long way to Tipperary'. The retreat continued – Bridges had saved the day.

On 9 September Colonels Ellington and Mainwaring were tried by court martial and drummed out of the service. It is interesting to note that Mainwaring returned to France and joined the Foreign Legion under a pseudonym. He fought bravely, became a sergeant and was awarded the Croix de Guerre for his courage. Although badly wounded he survived the war and during the 1930s he was reinstated to his colonelcy by King George V on account of his war service.

449 A FLAME-THROWER

Thucydides describes the siege weapons used to capture Delium in 424 BC.

The Boeotians now marched against Delium and attacked the rampart, employing among other military devices an engine, with which they succeeded in taking the place; it was of the following description. They sawed in two and hollowed out a great beam, which they joined together again very exactly, like a flute, and suspended by chains a vessel at the end of the beam; the iron mouth of a bellows directed downwards into the vessel was attached to the beam, of which a great part itself was overlaid with iron. This machine they brought from a distance on carts to various points of the rampart where vine stems and wood had been most extensively used, and when it was quite near the wall they applied the bellows to their own end of the beam, and blew through it. The blast, prevented from escaping, passed into the vessel which contained burning coals and sulphur and pitch; these made a huge flame and set fire to the rampart so that no one could remain upon it. The garrison took flight and the fort was taken.

Source: Thucydides, *The History of the Peloponnesian War* (Trans. R. Crawley 1874)

450 THE WALLS OF JERICHO

The siege of Jericho by the Israelites under Joshua is so famous it really needs no introduction.

Now Jericho was straitly shut up because of the children of Israel: none went out and none came in.
And the Lord said unto Joshua, See, I have given into thine hand Jericho, and the king thereof, and the mighty men of valour.
And ye shall compass the city, all ye men of war, and go round about the city once. Thus shalt thou do six days. And seven priests shall bear before the ark seven trumpets of rams' horns: and the seventh day ye shall compass the city seven times, and the priests shall blow with the trumpets.
And it shall come to pass that when they make a long blast with the ram's horn, and when ye hear the sound of the trumpet, all the people shall shout with a great shout; and the wall of the city shall fall down flat, and the people shall ascend up every man straight before him . . .
So the people shouted when the priests blew with the trumpets; and it came to pass, when the people heard the sound of the trumpet, and the people shouted with a great shout, that the wall fell down flat, so that the people went up into the city every man straight before him, and they took the city.

Source: Joshua 6:1–5, 20

451 **RUMOURS**

Between 61 and 58 BC Julius Caesar campaigned against the Helvetii, a German tribe inhabiting what is now Switzerland and southern Germany. These people were an unknown quantity to the Romans, who were noticeably apprehensive after hearing of their fearsome reputation.

While he [Caesar] was halting for a few days close to the Vesontio to collect corn and other supplies, a violent panic seized the whole army, completely paralysing everyone's judgement and nerve. It arose from the inquisitiveness of our men and the chatter of the Gauls and the traders, who affirmed that the Germans were men of huge stature, incredible valour and practised skill in war; many a time they had themselves come across them, and had not been able even to look them in the face or meet the glare of their piercing eyes. The panic began with the tribunes, the auxiliary officers, and others who had left the capital to follow Caesar in the hope of winning his favour and had little experience in war. Some of them applied for leave of absence, alleging various urgent reasons for their departure, though a good many anxious to avoid the imputation of cowardice, stayed behind for very shame. They were unable, however, to assume an air of unconcern, and sometimes even to restrain their tears; shutting themselves up in their tents, they bemoaned their own fate or talked dolefully with their intimates of the peril that threatened the army. All over the camp men were making their wills. Gradually even legionaries, centurions and cavalry officers, who had long experience of campaigning, were unnerved by these alarmists. Those who did not want to be thought cowards said that it was not the enemy they were afraid of, but the narrow roads and the huge forests which separated them from Ariovistus, or the difficulty of bringing up grain.

Source: Julius Caesar, *Commentaries* (1st century BC)

452 **THE WORD OF A LOCRIAN**

Polyaenus, a Macedonian, compiled a collection of military ruses, of which this is one of the more despicable.

The Locrians swore to observe a treaty with the Sicilians so long as they trod the earth they then walked on, or carried their heads on their shoulders: the next day they threw away the heads of garlic which they had carried under their cloaks on their shoulders, and the earth they had strewn in their shoes, and began a general massacre of the Sicilians.

Source: Polyaenus, *Strategemata* (2nd century AD)

453 **A PIOUS STRATAGEM**

In medieval warfare the word of a knight was sacrosanct.

About the year 1344, two years before the battle of Crécy, Edward III had employed his cousin, the Earl of Derby, for the government and defence of the rich province of Guienne. The earl not only secured Guienne, but pushed his troops into the neighbouring provinces, and made several successful attacks on the French, capturing among other towns, the important city of Angoulême. The reason he was enabled to carry on these conquests with little opposition was the utter ruin and depression of the finances of King Philip; but that monarch, having at length recruited his army and obtained some supplies, sent his eldest son the Duke of Normandy with a large force against the earl who, unable to meet so formidable an enemy, was reduced to the defensive and obliged to remain a passive observer while the Duke of Normandy laid siege to Angoulême. This city was defended by Lord Norwich, an able and experienced officer with a good garrison; but after a brave resistance, finding the place no longer tenable against the overwhelming force of the French, he had recourse to a stratagem which certainly evinced a wonderful confidence in the chivalrous honour of the French prince. He presented himself one day on the walls of the town and by his herald demanded a conference with the duke, who shortly arrived and opened the business by saying to Lord Norwich that he concluded he had made up his mind to capitulate. 'Not at all,' replied the Governor; 'but as tomorrow is the Feast of the Virgin, to whom I know that you, sir, as well as myself, bear a great devotion, I desire a cessation of arms for that day.' This proposal the duke agreed to; but early the next morning the besiegers, to their surprise, beheld one of the gates suddenly thrown open and the whole garrison, with Lord Norwich at their head, deliberately marching out of the town with all their baggage. The French flew to arms, and were about to attack the head of the column, when they were met by a herald from Lord Norwich to the Duke of Normandy, sent to remind him of his engagement for a cessation of arms for the day, and to claim his right to march even through the French camp, without molestation.

To the great honour of the duke, who prided himself on keeping his word, he satisfied himself with exclaiming, 'I see this governor has outwitted me. Let us be content with gaining the town.' Nor would he permit the smallest hindrance to be opposed to the free passage and escape of the English garrison through the camp.

Source: Lord de Ros, *The Young Officer's Companion* (1868)

ENVOI

454 SALAAM

During May 1915 the Turkish commanders were convinced that the Australian and New Zealand troops at Anzac Cove could be driven into the sea. On 11 May the Turks launched an all-out attack on the Anzacs with catastrophic results. So terrible was the carnage that both sides agreed to a truce to bury the dead. Lieutenant Aubrey Herbert took responsibility for implementing the arrangements.

We were at the rendezvous on the beach (near Gaba Tepe) at 6.30 a.m. Heavy rain soaked us to the skin. At 7.30 a.m. we met the Turks, Miralai Izzedin, a pleasant, rather sharp little man: Arif the son of Achmet Pashe, who gave me a card, 'Sculpteur et Peintre' and 'Etudiant de Poésie' . . . We walked from the sea and passed immediately up the hill, through a field of tall corn filled with poppies, then another cornfield; then the fearful smell of death began as we came upon scattered bodies. We mounted over a plateau and down through gullies filled with thyme, where there lay about 4000 Turkish dead. It was indescribable. One was grateful for the rain and the grey sky. A Turkish Red Crescent man came and gave me some antiseptic wool with scent on it, and this they renewed frequently . . . The Turkish captain with me said, 'At this spectacle even the most gentle must feel savage, and the most savage must weep.' The dead fill acres of ground, mostly killed in the one big attack, but some recently. They fill the myrtle-grown gullies. One saw the results of machine-gun fire very clearly; entire companies annihilated – not wounded but killed, their heads doubled under them with the impetus of their rush and both hands clasping their bayonets . . . I talked to the Turks, one of whom pointed to the graves. 'That's politics,' he said, then he pointed to the dead bodies and said, 'That's diplomacy. God pity all of us poor soldiers' . . .

At 4 o'clock the Turks came to me for orders. I do not believe this could have happened anywhere else. I retired their troops and ours, walking along the line. At 4.07 p.m. I retired the white flag men, making them shake hands with our men. Then I came to the upper end. About a dozen Turks came out. I chaffed them, and said they would shoot me next day. They said, in a horrified chorus, 'God forbid!' The Albanians laughed and cheered, and said: 'We will never shoot you.' Then the Australians began coming up and said, 'Goodbye old chap, good luck!' And the Turks said, 'Smiling may you go and smiling come again.' Then I told them all to get into their trenches, and unthinkingly went up to the Turkish trench and got a deep salaam from it. I told them that neither side would fire for twenty-five minutes after they had got into the trenches. One Turk was seen out away on our left, but there was nothing to be done and I think he was all right. A couple of rifles had gone off about twenty minutes before the end, but Potts and I went hurriedly to and fro seeing it was all right. At last we dropped into our trenches, glad that the strain was over . . . I got some raw whisky for the infection in my throat, and iodine for where the barbed wire had torn my feet. There was a hush over the peninsula.

Source: Aubrey Herbert, *Mons, Anzac and Kut* (1919)

217